Visual Arts Library
Main B1997.S4 I963
Schapiro, Ja/Condorcet and the rise of l

3 2660 00006417 3

D1651233

WITHDRAWN
From School of Visual Arts
Library Collection

MARIE-JEAN-ANTOINE-NICOLAS CARITAT,
MARQUIS DE CONDORCET

CONDORCET

AND

THE RISE OF LIBERALISM

BY

J. Salwyn Schapiro

OCTAGON BOOKS

A DIVISION OF FARRAR, STRAUS AND GIROUX

New York   1978

Copyright 1934, by J. Salwyn Schapiro
©1962, by J. Salwyn Schapiro

Reprinted 1963
by special arrangement with Harcourt Brace Jovanovich, Inc.

Second Octagon printing 1978

OCTAGON BOOKS
A DIVISION OF FARRAR, STRAUS & GIROUX, INC.
19 Union Square West
New York, N.Y. 10003

LIBRARY OF CONGRESS CATALOG CARD NUMBER: 63-20895
ISBN: 0-374-97068

Manufactured by Braun-Brumfield, Inc.
Ann Arbor, Michigan
Printed in the United States of America

To

KATHRINE KERESTESY SCHAPIRO

Devoted Wife, Critic, and Guide

The Author Dedicates this Book

FOREWORD

IN depicting the spirit of a period in history the great figure is usually held up as its embodiment. In truth the great figure is too unique, too far above his age, to express its true hopes and desires. The secondary figure, if he is sufficiently original and comprehensively versatile, is a far better guide to the advanced thought of his day. The philosophe, Condorcet, a secondary figure in the intellectual movement of the eighteenth century, stands out as an almost perfect expression of the pioneer liberalism of the period. Every aspect of the philosophy of liberalism, and every phase of its political evolution, from moderate constitutional monarchy to democratic republicanism, from propertied suffrage to universal suffrage for both men and women, from laissez faire to social reform, all are clearly and comprehensively found in his writings. The other philosophes represented one or more phases of the liberal movement; only Condorcet, "the last of the encyclopedists and the most universal of all," represented all of them. His writings form an almost perfect synthesis of French liberal thought in the eighteenth century in all its strength and weakness: its love of abstract political and social ideas; its rigid rationalism; its hatred of the past and its hopes for the future; its passionate devotion to humanity; and its facile optimism. "He who knows Condorcet well has an almost complete idea of what one would call the state of mind during the period of about 1780" is the view of Brunetière, a hostile but competent critic of the philosophe.

CONTENTS

I. INTRODUCTION 3

II. THE SOCIAL AND ECONOMIC TRANSFORMATION OF FRANCE DURING THE EIGHTEENTH CENTURY 7

III. THE RISE OF THE PHILOSOPHES 23

IV. CONDORCET BEFORE THE FRENCH REVOLUTION 66

V. CONDORCET DURING THE FRENCH REVOLUTION 83

VI. POLITICAL LIBERALISM 110

VII. INTELLECTUAL AND SOCIAL LIBERALISM 136

VIII. ECONOMIC LIBERALISM 156

IX. RELIGIOUS LIBERALISM 178

X. FEMINISM 187

XI. POPULAR EDUCATION 196

XII. THE REDISCOVERY OF AMERICA 215

XIII. THE IDEA OF PROGRESS 234

XIV. CONDORCET AND LIBERALISM, AN EVALUATION 271

NOTES 279

INDEX 307

CHAPTER ONE

INTRODUCTION

LIBERALISM was the ideal that dominated the life and thought of the Western nations during the nineteenth century. No phase of their development, no aspect of their culture, political, social, economic, and intellectual, remained untouched by its influence. As an attitude of mind, liberalism was as old as Greek philosophy, but as a state polity and as a form of social organization it was first clearly and boldly outlined in the eighteenth century.

Liberalism was predicated on the idea of freedom, which found expression in the policies that it advocated and in the philosophy that it proclaimed. In the sphere of politics it meant self-government by means of representative parliaments, a political system in harmony with its doctrine of popular sovereignty. Whether the suffrage was restricted to the propertied classes, as in the early, bourgeois stage of liberalism, or was made universal and equal, as in the later, democratic stage, government under liberalism was based on the principle of responsibility to the people.

In regard to the relations between nations liberalism was committed to the doctrine of self-determination. It was primarily responsible for the "principle of nationality" which brought into existence a united Italy and a united Germany during the nineteenth century, and which finally succeeded in creating the Europe of today, in which there are almost as many independent nations as there are peoples.

In the sphere of economics liberalism meant the establishment of the "free market" by means of freedom of enterprise, or laissez faire. Economic liberalism gave free rein to the exploitation of natural resources and to the investment of capital by establishing the principle of "freedom of contract" which became the legal foundation of the competitive system in industry. A free market in industry demanded a system of free labor. Animated by humanitarian motives and compelled by the necessities of the new industrial order, liberalism abolished serfdom and slavery and created a body of free laborers who worked for wages. Freedom of contract was now the tie that bound employer and worker as it bound buyer and seller.

In the sphere of religion liberalism stood for freedom of conscience. During the early struggles between the embattled faiths it raised the banner of toleration for the weaker side. Later, after toleration had become an accepted policy, liberalism became identified with the principle of religious equality, and, most important of all, with the policy of secularizing the state through separation of church and state.

Popular education was another hallmark of liberalism. Because of its profound faith in progress through universal enlightenment, liberalism sought to educate the masses in order to create a body of free citizens. A national system of popular education was a necessary adjunct to the liberal state, which could function only through the active participation of the citizens.

Freedom of the individual has been the very soul of liberalism, which it could abandon only at the peril of its existence. The right to one's person, to one's property, and to one's opinion was regarded by liberalism as a right conferred by nature itself, which no government could abridge or deny. Without civil rights, guaranteeing these "natural rights," there could be no equality before the law. No matter how restricted was the power of parliament and how circumscribed was freedom of enterprise, a country could be described as being "liberal" if it faithfully upheld civil rights.

Liberalism is now being challenged. The "climate of opinion" in which it flourished so luxuriantly, during the nineteenth century, is vanishing, and a new "climate of opinion" is arising. Throughout the Western world liberalism has been either totally and violently repudiated, as in communist Russia and in fascist Italy and Germany, or is undergoing a transformation as in democratic England, France, and the United States.

To understand fully the significance and the historic rôle of liberalism it is necessary to study the eighteenth century, when it arose; and France, during that period, where it became a militant, intellectual movement. The French liberal thinkers of the eighteenth century, unlike the English liberal thinkers of the preceding century, waged open war against the then existing political and social order, known as the Old Régime. In the conflict which ensued the French liberals were compelled to clarify their tenets and to intensify their activities. And, as a consequence, French liberalism had a unity, a comprehensiveness, a clarity, and a boldness that made it the prime source of inspiration to liberals all over the world. For this reason the intellectual movement in eighteenth-century France, associated with the philosophes, is of supreme importance in the study of modern liberalism.

This movement did not arise in a vacuum. However bold and original were the speculations of the philosophes, and however brilliant their literary gifts, they would have remained merely a literary coterie had it not been for the fact that they voiced the demands of a new age. It is necessary to consider the political, social, and economic changes that were transforming feudal France into a modern nation. For it was in response to these changes that the intellectual movement arose.

CHAPTER TWO

THE SOCIAL AND ECONOMIC TRANSFORMATION OF FRANCE
DURING THE EIGHTEENTH CENTURY

DURING the eighteenth century, France was the scene of a silent struggle between the dying feudal order and the nascent capitalist order which was emerging. A new economic life, based on free enterprise, was developing alongside the restrictive system of guilds and corporations that still prevailed. Economic France, in the eighteenth century, was a child of the Commercial Revolution of the sixteenth and seventeenth centuries. And, as in the case of England, this great change was to be followed by a still greater one, the Industrial Revolution.[1]

The system of free enterprise, in France, began with the breaking away from guild restrictions by the establishment of "royal manufactures" during the reign of Louis XIV, and even earlier. "Royal manufactures" was a term generally applied to large factories that were established by capitalists through royal aid and encouragement. In the process of consolidating France into a national state the Bourbon monarchy had need of new sources of revenue, hence the royal encouragement of new industries. The "royal manufactures" were freed from the control of the guilds whose regulations would have hampered their activity. Some of the "royal manufactures" were owned by the state and managed by government officials, such as the famous Gobelin tapestry factory in Paris, the tapestry factory in Beauvais, and the porcelain factory in Sèvres. Their products were costly luxuries and were sold chiefly to the court and to the nobility.[2]

Another type of "royal manufactures" was privately owned and privately managed, but under a system of special privileges. To encourage the establishment of new industries the government granted loans and subsidies to the owners of new enterprises, pensions to the managers, rewards to inventors, and prizes to workmen. These new industries were given monopoly privileges in their districts. A famous instance of this type of "royal manufactures" was the great cloth works at Abbeville, established in 1665, by the Hollander van Robais. The government was so eager to advance industry that it granted special privileges, even to foreigners, in order to induce them to start new enterprises in France.[3]

Some of these enterprises were of huge size for those days, and employed large numbers of workers. The van Robais establishment employed over 1500 men.[4] The textile factory at Limoges employed 1800 workers; the cloth factories at Sedan over 10,000; and the hosiery factory at Orleans, 800.[5] Lyons was famous as the center of the world's silk industry, which employed thousands of workers, and supplied silk to the upper classes of all Europe.[6] Unlike the guild system of production the "royal manufactures" were organized along the lines of large scale production, a characteristic of modern industry, despite the fact that modern machinery was hardly used. Alongside the shop, with its master and few assistants, there were now large establishments in which there was a division of labor.

The development of *la grande industrie* in France during the eighteenth century created a situation favorable to the machine production of the Industrial Revolution. The common idea that the Industrial Revolution was introduced in France after the Napoleonic wars was disproved by the pioneer work of Charles Ballot.[7] Even before 1789 English machinery and English workers were brought into France, despite the prohibitions imposed by the English government.[8] As in England, the Industrial Revolution in France was intimately connected with the cotton industry. Early in the century the manufacture of cotton goods was prohibited by law, as it was feared that cotton would compete with the older textiles, wool and linen, and even with silk.[9] But the popularity of cotton was so great that the law became a dead letter, and was repealed in 1759. During the second half of the eighteenth century the new English machinery for cotton manufacturing, Kay's flying shuttle and Hargreaves' spinning jenny, found their way into France. An Irishman, named John Holker, was active in establishing cotton factories in Rouen, which used the new machinery. In 1784 Arkwright's spinning machine, the water frame, was set up at Amiens. The metallurgical industries, too, were being developed. Iron foundries were built, and coke, instead of charcoal, was used in casting. Coal was beginning to be used as a source of power. Concessions were granted by the government to various capitalists to develop the coal and iron mines. The famous Creusot iron works was founded by the Wendel family at the end of the eighteenth century. The Compagnie d'Anzin, in 1789, employed 4000 men in the mining of coal.[10] The use of machinery in manufacturing perhaps explains why the French Encyclopaedia gave so much space to the mechanical arts. "The tendency of large scale industry in the direction of scientific methods, however imperfect these methods were, was clearly seen in the last stage of the Old Régime." [11]

Despite the encouragement given by the government, the Industrial Revolution, in France, did not develop as rapidly as it did in England. The use of the steam engine, a sure indication of industrial development, was not as widespread in France as it was in England during the eighteenth century.[12] In part the slowness of France's industrial development may be explained as being due to the lack of a class of cheap, industrial laborers, entirely divorced from their land. The Enclosure Acts, in England, had created a mass of landless laborers who were absorbed by the factories, whereas, in France, the mass of peasants remained tied to the soil by the feudal system.

With the advance of industry came naturally a great advance in trade, both domestic and foreign. The magnificent system of roads and canals, built by the government, greatly promoted internal trade, despite the then existing provincial tariffs. Foreign trade was chiefly with Spain, with the Spanish colonies, and with England. It is impossible to give exact figures on foreign trade because of the widespread smuggling that went on during the eighteenth century. It is estimated that between 1715 and 1787 the legal foreign trade of France increased more than four times, and was second only to that of England.[13]

THE MORIBUND GUILDS AND CORPORATIONS

The introduction of large scale industry and free enterprise and the growth of overseas trade undermined the restrictive system of commerce and industry under the Old Régime. The actual condition of the *régime corporatif,* or the system of monopolistic guilds and corporations, revealed that disintegrating influences were present in the system of labor as in the system of industry. To all appearances the guilds and corporations maintained intact, as in former days, their rights and privileges. Toward the close of the eighteenth century, their regulations became even more strict than formerly; and their membership, even more restricted.[14] They hunted down vigorously anyone, outside of their ranks, who presumed to manufacture those articles over which they had an exclusive monopoly. By exacting high entrance fees and by demanding prolonged and costly examinations, they virtually closed their doors to the majority of the journeymen. These requirements were, however, relaxed in favor of the sons and sons-in-law of the members, and the guilds became, in fact, castes.[15]

It was plain that the guilds no longer corresponded to the industrial needs of the day. Due to the Commercial Revolution, commerce had outrun industry, and the master merchants had become more important than the master craftsmen. The rise of the "royal manufactures" and of machine industry had created a situation in which the guild was "in complete antagonism with the world in which it was compelled to live; it had to adapt itself or die." [16] But it could not adapt itself to the new system of free enterprise because of its strict regulation of prices and methods of manufacture.

These age-old monopolies began to crumble, due to disintegration from within and to attacks from without. A system of bootleg manufacturing and trading began, which was overtly encouraged by the government. Journeymen, despairing of ever becoming masters, set up shops in their homes; and the guilds, fearful of competition, organized raids against these bootleg shops.[17] In the country districts, where the power of the guilds was weak, a domestic system of manufacture arose, based upon free labor. A government decree of 1762 gave permission to rural inhabitants, who were not members of a guild, to manufacture cloth.[18] As in England, the domestic system which was arising in France applied chiefly to cotton goods; the workers were supplied by capitalists with raw materials which they converted into finished products. These workers in the domestic system were the forerunners of the industrial laboring class that was to appear in the new economic order of free enterprise.[19]

Another attack upon the guilds was launched by the government. The national state, as it was being consolidated by the absolute monarch, had an ever-increasing need of money to maintain a national army and a national civil service. In the wealthy guilds the kings of France saw a source of revenue which they could easily tap. They instituted a system of *lettres de Maîtrise,* or guild memberships, which were sold to anyone; those, who bought them, became members of the guild and were exempt from examinations and from the heavy initiation fees. By this method the government obtained funds that formerly went to the guilds. Often the guilds themselves bought these *lettres* in order to prevent their membership from being diluted by outsiders. In 1767 *lettres des Maîtrise* were sold in considerable numbers by the king, and the guilds, especially, were forbidden to buy them.[20] The government had another way of mulcting these corporations, by creating new offices in the guilds and selling them, often to the guilds themselves. Toward the end of the eighteenth century these corporations, formerly so powerful and wealthy, were in a parlous state. Their treasuries were depleted by government exactions and by lawsuits. Their monopoly was seriously threatened by outside competition. Their membership was diluted by the sale of the *lettres des Maîtrise*. "It may be said that at the end of the eighteenth century the guild system . . . was reduced to bankruptcy." [21]

The blows, directed against the guilds, were approved by the public generally. They were regarded with universal hatred as reactionary survivors of the feudal order in industry. Their abolition was demanded by enlightened public opinion, especially by the Physiocrats, whose fundamental principle was based on the idea of complete freedom of labor and of trade. In 1776 Turgot, the famous Minister of Finance, issued an edict decreeing the abolition of the guilds. After Turgot's fall they were partially restored, and they continued to exist in a confused, sickly state.

Another staggering blow was dealt the guilds by the reciprocity treaty of 1786 between France and England. According to this treaty France reduced her duties on English woolens, cottons, and hardware; in return, England reduced her duties on French products, chiefly wines, brandies, and glassware.[22] This treaty brought a new factor into the guild situation by introducing foreign competition in some of their products, which still further undermined the monopoly of the guilds.

As the power of the guilds waned, that of free enterprise waxed. The free laborer, the free manufacturer, the free merchant, all took full advantage of the opportunities that were now open to free enterprise. When, in 1791, the French Revolution, definitely and finally, suppressed the guilds, these ancient bodies were already almost lifeless.

THE MORIBUND FEUDAL SYSTEM

What was the situation in regard to the feudal order? Much has been written about the aristocrats with their privileges and their pensions, and about the downtrodden peasants with their dues and services. An examination of the actual situation reveals the fact that the system of landholding under the Old Régime was, like the system of industry, a hollow shell. As in the case of the guilds and corporations, the feudal system was undergoing a process of decay, due to disintegration from within and to attacks from without.

The growth of peasant proprietorship, during the eighteenth century, was one of the factors undermining the old order. Ever since the appearance of de Tocqueville's work on the Old Régime in France, in which he maintained that peasant proprietorship had grown rapidly under the Old Régime, a view has been growing of the more favorable condition of the peasants during that period.[23] Serfdom had all but disappeared; it lingered on in a few places, Franche-Comté, Lorraine, and Berry. The free peasants were generally proprietors, but what was a "proprietor"? It is safe to say that proprietorship, as it exists today in France, had no counterpart under the Old Régime. Neither the peasant nor his lord then had property in land in the full and exclusive sense as it is understood today. Landholding in France still maintained a feudal character with its complicated system of rights, privileges, dues, and services.[24] A small number of fortunate peasants, the *franc-alleux*, held lands that were not subject to dues and services. About one-quarter of the peasantry held no land at all, and worked for wages as farm hands. All the rest held land subject to dues and services, which were fairly light for some, and very heavy for others. These were "proprietors," in the feudal sense, as their holdings were hereditary; they could will, sell, give, or rent them. A system, known as *métayage*, which is still common in France, was widespread under the Old Régime. It was a system of profit sharing: the lord supplied the land, the buildings, and the tools; and the *métayer* supplied the labor. Both shared about equally in the product. The free peasants were constantly increasing their holdings by buying more land; and it is estimated that, in 1789, they controlled about one-half of the land in France.[25]

To a still greater extent the feudal aristocrats were losing their lands as a result of the acquisition of estates by wealthy bourgeois. The nobles of the court were hardly representative of the nobility of France, the great majority of whom lived on their estates in the country, many of them in a condition of genteel poverty. Too proud to work, too disdainful of any occupation save that of the army and the church, often too poor to keep up their "castles," they maintained themselves at the expense of their peasants. By all sorts of methods, often dishonest, they tried to get more dues and services, which involved them in lawsuits. "Then comes a new race, the lawyers, astute bourgeois, who after having involved the squires in numerous lawsuits, buy up their estates for a song and through them become ennobled." [26]

Another factor in the undermining of the feudal order was the diluting of the old aristocracy by ennobling the bourgeois, a process that had been going on for several centuries. Many of the French nobles, who went to the guillotine during the Reign of Terror, were no more the descendants of the crusaders than were the English lords who so bitterly fought the Reform Bill of 1832. Partly in order to stabilize the monarchy against feudal disorder, as in the case of the Fronde during the middle of the seventeenth century, partly to fill his coffers, Louis XIV sold titles of nobility wholesale to wealthy, socially aspiring bourgeois. In 1696 more than five hundred titles of nobility were sold to bourgeois, "distinguished for merit, virtue and good qualities"; in 1702 two hundred were sold; and, in 1711, one hundred.[27] In his comedy *Bourgeois Gentilhomme* Molière ridiculed these new nobles who were still steeped in bourgeois habits and manners.

Another way by which a bourgeois could enter the ranks of the nobility was by purchasing a public office that carried with it a title of nobility. Offices were created and sold wholesale by the government, and *la venalité des offices* became an established method for raising money without going into debt. It is figured that, by 1789, there were as many as four thousand offices that conferred titles of nobility on those who held them.[28] The highest of the "nobility of function," as this class of ennobled was designated, were the members of the parlements, or judges of the higher courts. Only the richest of the bourgeois could aspire to the "nobility of the robe" as the judges were known, to distinguish them from the "nobility of the sword," or the members of the old feudal families. The "robe," like the "sword," was hereditary. At first there was a deep antagonism between the two aristocracies. The "sword" regarded the ennobled bourgeois with disdain as upstarts; and the "robe" despised the old nobles as loafers and hangers-on who often came to them to borrow money. By the end of the eighteenth century, however, they had become consolidated as a privileged aristocratic class. "They now mingled their ranks, allied their interests and families and associated their traditions and politics."[29] The process of assimilating the rich bourgeois with the nobility went still further in the breaking down of the social frontier which separated these two classes. Members of old noble families, rich in pride but poor in worldly goods, married the daughters of wealthy bourgeois

SOCIAL, ECONOMIC TRANSFORMATION

in order "to manure their lands" and "to reguild their 'scutcheons" with the dowries that their wives brought them.[30] Real power under the Old Régime was slipping from the hands of the privileged aristocracy into the hands of the wealthy bourgeois. More and more did the government tend to rely on the latter to fill its coffers and to finance its wars.

THE MORIBUND STATE

The swift collapse of the monarchy during the French Revolution was not alone due to the furious onslaught of the revolutionists. Like the Russian autocracy, in 1917, it was a rickety structure that needed but a vigorous push to send it crashing to the ground. The elements that had given strength to the French monarchy in the days of Louis XIV, a powerful landed aristocracy and a militant church, were now weak, discredited, hated, and despised. The vigorous and powerful element in the nation, the bourgeoisie, could not use, in its interests, a political system organized, as was the French monarchy, in the interest of a privileged, landed aristocracy. What is known as "enlightened despotism" was really an attempt to make the monarchy serve the interests of the enlightened and, progressive bourgeois by instituting reforms in the social and political order. This attempt did not get very far because it would have disrupted the system of privilege which was the very life of the dominant aristocratic class.

At the end of the eighteenth century the French monarchy might be said to have become almost functionless. It had succeeded in suppressing political feudalism and in establishing national unity by centralizing the government. Its historic mission was now over. The characters of Louis XV and Louis XVI, in a sense, symbolized the real political situation. The former was "a crown without a head."[31] He was lazy, sensual, corrupt, cynical, and without any interest in the problems of the state. To Louis XV the government of France was an unfailing means of supplying him with money, luxury, entertainment, and mistresses. Louis XVI was lazy, incompetent, good-natured, and dull. Only once, before 1789, did he show an active interest in the affairs of the state, and that was in the appointment of Turgot, but not for long. He soon dismissed that statesman whose reforms demanded a sustained, active interest on the part of the King. It is unnecessary to describe here the details of the Old Régime in France, which are familiar to every informed reader. Its corruption, its wastefulness, its tyranny, its intolerance, its narrowness, and its incompetence were but so many external signs of its internal disintegration.

THE MORIBUND CHURCH

As in the case of the feudal order and the state, the church, likewise, no longer represented the living forces of the nation. The bitter struggle between Catholics and Protestants had ended in the apparent triumph of the former through the revocation of the Edict of Nantes whereby the Huguenots were compelled to flee the country or to remain under heavy civil disabilities. Though repudiated, condemned, and outlawed, Protestantism, nevertheless, profoundly influenced Catholic France. Its ideals found lodgement within the triumphant church itself. Two movements gained rapid headway that were distinctively Protestant in spirit: (1) Gallicanism which aimed to establish in France a *national* Catholic church in opposition to the Ultramontanes who championed the supreme authority of the pope; and (2) Jansenism which preached the doctrine of conversion-by-the-will-of-God, a doctrine that was similar to that of predestination, preached by Calvinism.

Gallicanism arose in 1682, when Louis XIV compelled the French bishops to issue the Declaration of the Liberties of the Gallican Church, which asserted that the temporal sovereignty of the king was independent of the pope, and that the latter was subject in spiritual matters to the decisions of Ecumenical Councils. This document inspired the anti-papal policy of the French kings, who wished to imitate the kings in Protestant lands by extending the royal power over the church as well as over the nation.

In spirit, in practices, and, even in theology, Jansenism, so called from its founder, the Catholic Bishop Jansen, was Calvinism in Catholic dress. Before long it aroused the antagonism of the "minute men" of Catholicism, the Jesuits. Chiefly through their influence the pope, in 1713, issued the famous bull, *Unigenitus*, which condemned Jansenism as heretical. But the condemnation did not lead to the suppression of the Jansenists. Instead, it led to acrimonious quarrels between the Jesuits and the Jansenists, which lasted down to the Revolution. Jansenism was espoused by the wealthy bourgeois, especially by those who were members of the parlements. It was too dangerous to attempt to suppress this influential element, that controlled the courts, and that often defied the absolute monarch himself. Although couched in theological language, the social and political significance of Jansenism lay in that it was one of the forms of discontent of the bourgeois with the Old Régime.

The victories of the church over its enemies resulted, however, in weakening, not in strengthening, Catholicism. The bloody wars and massacres of the Protestant Revolution, the struggles between Ultramontanes and Gallicans, and the bitter quarrels between Jesuits and Jansenists, all had the effect of discrediting Christianity in general, and Catholicism in particular. It led straight to the rationalist movement which began timorously, in the seventeenth century, with the demand for religious toleration, and burst with fury, in the eighteenth century, in the aggressive war of the philosophes against revealed religion. "A plague on both your houses!" cried the philosophes to Catholics and Protestants, to Jesuits and Jansenists. The rationalist attack of the philosophes, which is described in the following chapter, openly and defiantly asserted the will to disbelieve in all revealed religion. It won widespread support among the educated of all classes, and created an "intellectual climate" in France in which the most violent attacks on Catholicism received the heartiest applause. These attacks met with special favor among the bourgeois who were hostile to the church, not so much because of its theology, but because its asceticism, its otherworldliness, and its spiritualism created an atmosphere inimical to the worldly, materialistic concerns of business enterprise. In the newly developing free economy of the eighteenth century the bourgeois saw the possibility of bettering their lot through the accumulation of wealth, and they naturally regarded the church as a stumbling block in their acquisitive career.

Moreover, the great wealth of the church roused bourgeois hostility. Its vast estates, which could not be alienated, were as effectively withdrawn from "circulation" as were the noble estates through the system of primogeniture, thereby restricting still more the accumulation of capital for investment. Moreover, church property did not pay the heavy land taxes; and the clergy did not pay the heavy income taxes under the Old Régime, privileges not enjoyed by the bourgeois.

To all appearances the position of the church seemed impregnable. Its doctrines were officially recognized and enforced by the state. Its vast wealth escaped taxation. Its clergy were in the privileged position of being the First Estate. Its influence was supreme in education, from the lowest to the highest grades. But its old authority was gone. Rarely did the church dare to persecute, and when it did so, as in the famous Calas and de la Barre cases, it roused against itself an avalanche of fury. Unbelief was so widespread that it hardly caused any comment; even atheism was openly avowed. "To be impious was to be in the fashion," writes Aulard, "and that fashion was followed by the nobility, especially by the Court nobles: a great lord who was pious, even a pious Bourbon, became an anomaly, and his piety aroused surprise." [32]

THE RISING BOURGEOISIE

Nothing was more deceptive than the imposing appearance of the Old Régime in France. The absolutism of the king, the privileges of the nobility and the clergy, and the vested interest of the guilds and corporations were so many veils that hid the true situation in France. The really powerful elements were the financiers, the wealthy merchants and manufacturers, the professionals, and the new landed proprietors. "In short the great social event of France during this century (eighteenth) was the rise of the bourgeoisie, and nothing was more justified than Sieyes' answer, on the very eve of the Revolution, to the question as to what the Third Estate was—'Everything.'" [33]

Under the Old Régime the bourgeois performed important, though subordinate, political functions. If they could not lead armies, or guide policies, or rule the church they could control the finances and administer the laws. Colbert, in the reign of Louis the XIV, John Law in the reign of Louis the XV, and Turgot and Necker in the reign of Louis XVI, who controlled the public finances of France, were all of bourgeois origin. The high officials in the national administration, the intendants and the magistrates, and the mass of the bureaucracy were almost entirely recruited from the bourgeoisie. "The events of 1789 did not establish its power; they merely revealed it." [34]

At the very top of the bourgeois class were the financiers, the Farmers General, who played a highly significant rôle under the Old Régime. They were feared, hated, and fawned upon, even more than were the great nobles of the court. Their chief source of wealth was the indirect taxes which were farmed out to them by the government. In return for fixed sums of money, which they gave to the king, they were given the privilege of collecting the indirect taxes, the most important of which was the infamous gabelle, or salt tax. They collected all that the traffic could bear, keeping as much as they could as their "commission." Everyone came to the financiers for loans: the king, the noble, the church, the guild master, the merchant, and the manufacturer. The king greatly depended upon the financiers for loans, as the extravagance, wastefulness, and corruption of the government made it impossible to balance the budget from taxes. But, as France was nearing 1789, the king found it increasingly difficult to raise loans, which led to a demand for the calling of the Estates General. When that body convened it was, as has been well said, a meeting of creditors called to liquidate the estate of a bankrupt government.

CHAPTER THREE

THE RISE OF THE PHILOSOPHES

IN eighteenth-century France conditions were highly favorable to the growth of a critical spirit. As described in the last chapter the Old Régime was disintegrating as a result of the impact of the new social forces that were emerging. The inability of the Old Régime to cope with the new political, social, and economic problems made its vices glaringly visible, and resulted in almost universal discontent. Most discontented of all were the bourgeois, the most vital force in the emerging new society. As it has so often happened in history the special interests of a rising class were joined to the noble aspiration of a new generation. "In each period there have been men who related their own wants to those of their neighbors, who were not satisfied with the filling of their own stomach, and were in search of a society where the hunger neither of the body, nor of the mind should go unsatisfied." [1]

To voice the aspirations of the new generation a new intellectual class arose, known by the general name of "philosophes." They were part of a general movement, now known as the Intellectual Revolution which, like the Renaissance in the fifteenth century, spread throughout western Europe.

In England it was associated with the names of Bolingbroke, Hume, Gibbon, Adam Smith, Godwin, and Bentham. In Germany the Aufklärung, as the intellectual movement was known, was associated with the names of Kant, Lessing, Herder, and Goethe. In Italy it was associated with the names of Vico and Beccaria. But its head and center was France, as Italy had been the head and center of the Renaissance. In France the Intellectual Revolution, known as the "Age of Reason," was associated with the philosophes, who succeeded in spreading its influence, not only in their own country, but throughout the world.

The philosophes declared war *à outrance* against the Old Régime, and their aims, if not their methods, were revolutionary. They sought to destroy the Old Régime, and to establish a new one in which humanity would be liberated from tyranny and superstition, in which all would be equal before the law, and in which all nations would be at peace, united in fraternal relations. Hitherto, solitary thinkers, Locke, Descartes, Bayle, Grotius, Spinoza, had challenged the ideas and institutions of their day, but their influence was hardly felt outside a narrow circle of scholars. In the eighteenth century the situation changed. Voltaire, Rousseau, Montesquieu, and Quesnay were not solitary thinkers but the spokesmen of a movement whose influence spread far and wide among powerful elements in every country in Europe.[2]

What is the explanation of the extraordinary influence of the philosophes? Is it to be sought in the scintillating wit of Voltaire? in the thrilling eloquence of Rousseau? in the learning and profundity of Montesquieu? in the originality of Quesnay? These personal qualities, powerful as they undoubtedly were, do not sufficiently explain the fact that, by the end of the eighteenth century, the philosophes were the masters of public opinion in France. The fundamental explanation is to be sought rather in the relation that the intellectual movement bore to the social and economic situation in France. The new society, which was emerging in the eighteenth century, found its progress hampered by the restrictions of the Old Régime. France was bristling with problems: political, social, economic, religious, which arose in the clash of interests between the old and the new orders. It was these problems, which the philosophes daily encountered on all sides, which stimulated them to think of creating a new society in which everyone would be free and happy. "It was not by chance," remarks de Tocqueville, "that the philosophers of the eighteenth century thus coincided in entertaining notions so opposed to those which still served as bases to the society of their time: these ideas had been naturally suggested to them by the aspect of the society which they had all before their eyes." [3]

The philosophes were not, as is commonly supposed, closet philosophers who sat and meditated on abstract principles. They were practical persons whose ideas grew out of the fertile soil of the new forces that were making themselves felt in eighteenth-century France, the free commerce, the free industry, the free labor, the free opinion. It was the fact that the abstract principles of the philosophes arose out of the problems of the day, and, therefore, harmonized with the concrete interests of the new forces in society that brought them great popular support. Everyone not a member of the privileged classes regarded the philosophes as his spokesmen. Especially, did they get the powerful support of the rising bourgeois, because the libertarian ideas, preached by the philosophes, would, if universally accepted, destroy the restrictions that hindered business enterprise and abolish the aristocratic privileges which burdened the bourgeois with so many taxes. "The essentially new thing about the bourgeois of the eighteenth century was that he began to give serious attention to books and to the writers of books and to the ideas which they promulgated." [4]

What augmented, still more, the influence of the philosophes, was that they were the representatives of a professional literary class. In the intellectual history of modern Europe few events were more significant than the appearance, in the eighteenth century, of the man-of-letters as a professional. Literature now became a means of earning a livelihood, like law, medicine, and the ministry. Hitherto, the writer did not write for a public but for a circle. His maintenance depended, therefore, not on his readers, but on a patron, a rich noble who gave him his patronage or a king who gave him a pension. And he catered to them just as, today, he caters to his readers. The philosophes, as professional men, were now a part of the middle class. As a merchant could rise to influence through his wealth so could an author now rise through his pen. A successful author was welcomed everywhere in France: at court, in the salons, and in the mansions of the most exclusive aristocracy.

What caused this significant transformation was the appearance of a reading public large enough to support financially the professional writer, and influential enough to give him a sense of power and independence. This reading public, compared with that of today, was very small. In eighteenth-century France there was no national system of public education, therefore, the majority of the people were illiterate.[5] Nevertheless, the reading public was influential to a remarkable degree, and its views came to be known as "public opinion." *L'opinion, c'est celle de la France lettrée ou riche.*[6]

How did this large reading public come into existence? One answer, and perhaps the most important one, was the almost universal use of the vernacular as a literary language. Writing a masterpiece in the mother tongue was as old as Dante's Divine Comedy. But the prestige of Latin as the language of culture maintained itself, though with increasing difficulty, until the eighteenth century, when it became the language of an esoteric culture, used by theologians in their disputes and by university students in their theses. The writers of the eighteenth century no longer wrote in Latin; they only quoted it. The broad sweep of European culture was now definitely in the vernacular. Latin was only in the eddies.

The new class of readers were, in the main, from the middle class. In the cities and towns of France there were numerous merchants, professionals, and craftsmen, all literate, who eagerly read the works of the philosophes, as the new intellectual class was popularly called. From these elements came what was called in the eighteenth century the *honnêtes gens*, intelligent, solid, prudent people who were sharply critical of the injustice and irrationality of the Old Régime. The influence of the philosophes was felt outside the exclusive circle of the salon. Newspapers appeared, though not regularly, which were sold in the streets by news vendors. France was inundated with cheap books and pamphlets which found many buyers. A visitor in Paris described the passion for reading in the following manner: "People read while riding in carriages, while walking, during intermissions in the theater, in the cafés, in the baths, in shops, on the doorsteps of their houses on Sunday: the lackeys read in the rear of the carriages and the coachmen in front: the soldiers read at their posts, and the porters at their stations."[7] Those in authority became aware of a new check on their power, public opinion, *le Roi On* who was a "king without visible attributes, pomp, or throne, but one at whose voice all tremble and obey." [8] There was now a public to which the philosophes could turn for support when they began their war against the Old Régime. According to Grimm the professional writers were "ambitious to be the organs and even the arbiters of public opinion. A more serious taste in literature spread, and the desire to teach was stronger than the desire to please. The dignity of the man-of-letters, a new and just characterization, quickly came into common usage." [9]

Nearly all of the philosophes were free lances, as there were few established journals to employ them. Diderot, before he became editor of the Encyclopaedia, was an excellent illustration of a free lance journalist who could turn his hand easily to writing on all sorts of topics, from sermons to imaginary travels. Even the publicity man made his appearance. "Enlightened despotism," to which are devoted solemn pages of history, was largely a publicity campaign undertaken by Voltaire and Diderot on behalf of their patrons, Catherine the Great of Russia and Frederick the Great of Prussia, a task for which they were handsomely paid. These shrewd monarchs realized that a new force had appeared in Europe, public opinion, which could be manipulated in their interests provided they employed those who dominated it, namely, the philosophes in France. Of the enlightened laws that the "benevolent" Catherine and Frederick gave to their subjects there is but little record.

The philosophes, like all powers, were divided into ranks with respect to their influence. In the first rank were Voltaire (1694-1778), Rousseau (1712-78), Diderot (1713-84), Montesquieu (1689-1755), and Turgot (1727-81). The influence of Voltaire and Rousseau was so great that they might

RISE OF PHILOSOPHES

well be described as the intellectual dictators of eighteenth-century Europe. Voltaire's influence was dominant during the first half of the century, the period of "reason" and *bon sens;* and Rousseau's, during the second half, the period of emotion and sensibility. Diderot, despite the fragmentary character of his writings, was sufficiently important to be put into the first rank because of his connection with the Encyclopaedia. He and his associates on the Encyclopaedia constituted a special group of philosophes, known as the "Encyclopaedists." Montesquieu, although he studiously kept aloof from the philosophes whom he secretly despised as clever pamphleteers, was, nevertheless, part of the movement. Turgot's great work as a reform statesman has put into the background his truly remarkable powers as an economist and social philosopher. He, like Montesquieu, studiously avoided the "sect," yet he, too, must be numbered among its leaders.

In the second rank belonged Condorcet (1743-94), the subject of this book, d'Alembert (1717-83), Helvétius (1715-71), d'Holbach (1723-89), Abbé Saint-Pierre (1658-1743), Abbé Raynal (1713-96), and Abbé Mably (1709-85). D'Alembert's chief importance lay in the field of mathematics. He was, however, intimately connected with the philosophe movement through his editorship of the Encyclopaedia and through his essays and letters. Helvétius wrote little, but what he wrote had an immense influence in his day. His book *On the Human Mind* laid the foundation of the materialist philosophy, and was the inspiration of English Utilitarianism. Baron d'Holbach was a German, living in France, who was completely identified with French intellectual life. He was a rigid and complete atheist, rejecting both revealed religion and deism. Like Helvétius, d'Holbach advocated a materialist philosophy on which he based a system of atheism. Abbé

Saint-Pierre was a prolific writer on social and political reforms which were motivated by a deep love of mankind. He was a pacifist, and his name has been associated with a famous plan for perpetual peace. Abbé Raynal leaped into fame with his book *Philosophic and Political History of the Two Indies* which had a great vogue in its day because of its bitter attack on religion, on slavery, and on European imperialism. Abbé Mably was a political and social reformer with a moralistic bent of mind. He was opposed to private property in land, and, for that reason, he has been classed by some as a socialist.

In the third rank there are many names, only few of which are at all known. The best known is Baron von Grimm (1723-1807) who, like d'Holbach, was a German Francophile. His *Correspondence* is a famous source for the intellectual history of France during the eighteenth century.[10] Marquis de Chastellux (1734-88) was a philosophic historian whose book, *On Public Felicity*, surveyed the progress of mankind. His test of progress was the happiness of the greatest number of individuals. Abbé Morellet (1727-1819) was a liberal theologian who wrote many of the ecclesiastical articles in the Encyclopaedia. Morelly (1769-?) was the one philosophe who might be described as a socialist. His *Code of Nature* contained a bitter attack on private property, and advocated a co-operative commonwealth.

The philosophes must be distinguished from the *gens de lettres*, or purely literary men; from the scholars, or specialists; and from the philosophers, or metaphysicians. Their real importance in intellectual history lies in the fact that they were the forerunners of, what is now called, the "intelligentsia," or revolutionary intellectuals. It was from the philosophes of eighteenth-century France that the revolutionary

RISE OF PHILOSOPHES 31

intellectuals learned to divorce principles from abstract philosophy, and to employ them as the motivating force in the revolutionary movements of the nineteenth and twentieth centuries.

For long a controversy has raged in France over the question whether or not the philosophes were responsible for the French Revolution. The theme of the reactionary writers of the Restoration, de Maistre, de Bonald, and Chateaubriand, was that France had been demoralized by a vicious and un-Christian philosophy which had its logical outcome in the bloodshed and terrorism of the Revolution. According to Chateaubriand the French Revolution "was accomplished before it occurred." Taine, who was neither an absolutist nor a Catholic, nevertheless, took the same point of view. France in 1789, he declared, was like a man of healthy appearance who swallowed a new kind of cordial and was seen "suddenly to fall to the ground, foam at the mouth, act deliriously and writhe in convulsions. . . . The philosophy of the eighteenth century contained poison, and of a kind as potent as it was peculiar." [11]

In opposition to these views a school of opinion arose that belittled the influence of the philosophes on the French Revolution. Aubertin [12] and Rocquain [13] asserted that the French Revolution was not the outcome of abstract ideas about natural rights, but of the struggle between the king and the parlements. Champion [14] made the strongest case against the influence of the philosophes through his study of the *cahiers*, the statements of grievances of the voters during the elections for the Estates-General in 1789. He showed that these documents paid little attention to abstract principles, and confined themselves to specific grievances, often local in character. This view was also that of Aulard, whose history of the French

Revolution is Jacobin in sympathy.[15] The publicist, Faguet, who had no love for the philosophes and no sympathy for the French Revolution, nevertheless, agreed with Aulard and Champion that it was the breakdown of the Old Régime, and not the intellectual movement, which brought about the Revolution. The uprising, he declared, contained "nothing idealistic, nothing philosophic, nothing religious, nothing sublime, nothing *in excelsis.*" [16]

On the other hand, this was not the view of another great historian of the French Revolution, Sorel. "The philosophes and the literary men," he declared, "were the great inspiration of the Revolution. To them is due its most generous ideals and its most evil innovations, its humane beginning, its ferocious character, its enthusiasm, and its fanaticism." [17] Roustan's book, *Les Philosophes et la société française au xviii*^{e} *siècle,* by presenting a new viewpoint, revived an acrimonious debate that was growing rather stale. Roustan asserted that the French Revolution was definitely the work of the philosophes, as the Old Régime had broken down before their influence was felt. There was as great discontent, he declared, in the middle of the eighteenth century as in 1789, and it was the philosophes who had directed this discontent into the channel of revolution.[18] He explained how the propaganda of the philosophes influenced every class in France, even the nobles and the clergy; and how it was this propaganda which brought the situation to a head in 1789.

In this controversy both sides failed to take into consideration the significance of the philosophes as an intelligentsia. As such they played a rôle that was new in revolutionary history. Popular uprisings are as old as history itself, but not until the French Revolution did a popular uprising in Europe succeed in overturning all of the existing institutions and in creating a new social and political order in harmony with the needs and desires of those who had overturned the old one. Before the French Revolution, popular uprisings had been desperate outbreaks against certain laws or certain practices, as were those of the peasants and of the townsmen during the Middle Ages. There had been no clear vision of a new society, at best only a vague longing for the reign of Christ upon earth, as in the Peasants Revolt in Germany during the Protestant Revolution. In the eighteenth century, when the educated became discontented and joined the masses, popular discontent became revolutionary, hence, dangerous to the existing order. The junction of the intellectuals and the masses gave a direction and a goal to popular discontent; and when the uprising took place in 1789 it was not in desperation, but in organized revolution under capable leadership. The French intellectuals of the eighteenth century waged uncompromising and relentless war against the Old Régime on the ground that its institutions, its ideals, its traditions, and its methods were violations of the rights of man. This wholesale repudiation was revolutionary; it plainly implied that if an existing order did not conform to the principles of the rights of man, it must be destroyed, and a new one set up on the basis of these rights. The "strange and concentrated glow" that burns in the pages of Rousseau's *Social Contract* came from the newly lighted fire of social revolution which, in the French Revolution, was to burst into devouring flames.

However, it must be borne in mind that the "people" of eighteenth-century France, for whom the philosophes wrote, were not the "masses" of today. The masses did not read the works of the philosophes for the simple reason that, in the main, they were illiterate. By the philosophes they were either despised as the *canaille* or altogether left out of consideration. It was to the bourgeois, who had wealth and influence but little political power, that the philosophes gave their intellectual leadership. And, for the most part, the philosophes "wrote for the discontented bourgeoisie; where their doctrines were agreeable to the mental habits of their readers and seemed to promise a fulfillment of popular social and economic aspirations, they were readily accepted and became the basis of Revolutionary change." [19] Without this leadership the discontent of the bourgeoisie might have been allayed by reform of the taxes and by favorable commercial policies. With it came the vision of a new system of government and society based upon freedom and equality, in which the "people" ruled. A narrow class interest gave way to universal principles, and popular discontent became revolutionary. In this sense only can it be said that the philosophes prepared the way for the French Revolution.

The success of the philosophes was amazing. In the middle of the eighteenth century they constituted a literary clique in Paris, barely known outside of its walls; by 1789 it might be said that virtually the entire body of educated opinion was on their side. A revolution in ideas had taken place in France during that short period. On the eve of the French Revolution the Old Régime seemed as powerful as ever. The king ruled as absolute monarch by divine right; the nobility maintained its privileges; the church held its sway over the faithful. The Old Régime was intact but its mind was gone.

In their war against the Old Régime the philosophes succeeded, in a remarkably short time, in completely discrediting its institutions and ideals. In religion they spread incredulity and indifference, even more than hostility. Openly

RISE OF PHILOSOPHES

or secretly revealed religion became a subject for mockery. "Theological disputes are beginning to be regarded like the quarrels of Punch and Judy at the fairs," declared Voltaire. Nobles, magistrates, and even the clergy were impregnated with "philosophy," as the philosophes had succeeded in creating an intellectual atmosphere which influenced even those hostile to them. Unbelief became a convention. Diderot tells the story of a dinner party at which two monks were present. One of them read to him a treatise in favor of atheism which, he declared, was common in the monastery. So outspoken was his denunciation of religion that a single phrase would have been sufficient to send him to the stake.[20] D'Argenson decried the influence of the philosophes; nevertheless, he hoped that the future would see "no priest, no sacerdotalism, no revelation, no mystery, and that God would be seen only in his great and good works."[21] The books of the philosophes "spread incredulity, or at least indifference, among large sections of the aristocracy, and this indifference deeply penetrated the clergy, made great headway among the middle classes, among the youth, and in the colleges."[22] This is the view of Mornet in his authoritative study of the movement.

In literature the influence of the philosophes was so great that they completely ruled the Republic of Letters. Never before and never since, in the literary history of France, was there so great an identification of literature with deliberate propaganda. The poets, novelists, and dramatists of eighteenth-century France who were not identified with this propaganda were not important. The philosophes laid siege to the French Academy itself, and succeeded in forcing their way into that conservative institution. Montesquieu was admitted in 1728; Voltaire, in 1746; D'Alembert, in 1754; and Condorcet, in 1782.

In the field of politics the philosophes succeeded in discrediting all arbitrary government. Whether they favored "enlightened despotism" like Voltaire, or parliamentary institutions like Montesquieu, Diderot, and Condorcet, or direct democracy like Rousseau, they all advocated government by laws based upon the rights of man. The adoption of these rights would, in their opinion, result in the abolition of the many complicated and vexatious laws and customs characteristic of the Old Régime, and in establishing a régime based on laws that were simple, universal, and uniform. "They all agreed that it was expedient to substitute simple and elementary rules, deduced from reason and natural law, for the complicated traditional customs which governed the society of their time." [23] As in religion, the influence of the philosophes in politics was all-prevailing. Louis XVI could assert that he ruled as an autocrat by divine right, but he spoke to a generation that had read the *Spirit of Laws* and the *Social Contract*, and his assertion, therefore, brought irritation instead of conviction.

Although not affiliated with the philosophes, the Physiocrats were, nevertheless, part of the intellectual movement of the day. In economics they profoundly influenced public opinion, though they did not succeed in converting many to their pet theory that agriculture was the only true source of wealth. The contemporaries of Quesnay and Turgot upheld their views regarding freedom of enterprise, freedom of labor, freedom of contract, individual initiative, and the reduction and simplification of the taxes. These policies, they believed, would solve the vexing problems created by the restrictions of the monopolistic corporations and guilds, by the feudal burdens of the peasants, and by the outrageous system of taxation under the Old Régime.

RISE OF PHILOSOPHES 37

Against the attacks of the philosophes the Old Régime defended itself feebly, or not at all. There was no mighty Bossuet, only a feeble Fréron,[24] to defend the church against the devastating Voltaire. There was no political philosopher in France of the stature of Burke to defend the state against the revolutionary doctrines of Rousseau. It was as though a powerful army had attacked a citadel which was magnificently fortified, but which had no defenders. The organs of public opinion, the press, books, lectures, and, most important of all, the famous Encyclopaedia were almost entirely in the hands of the philosophes. Their writings automatically became public opinion. Nothing so illustrates the blindness of the Old Régime as its failure to make any effort to direct this powerful influence in its favor. The government, being an absolute monarchy by divine right, had no need of popular support; therefore, it did not subsidize journals and reward writers to create public opinion in its favor.

In their war against the Old Régime the philosophes made effective use of satire. From Rabelais to Anatole France satire, even more than logic, has been the Frenchman's favorite weapon with which to attack abuses and prejudices. Montesquieu's *Persian Letters,* satirizing political conditions in France, and Voltaire's *Letters on the English,* satirizing religious practices, were supreme illustrations of the saying that, in France, laughter kills. As Voltaire put it, one cannot argue with a prophet; therefore, he did not enter into disputations with the theologians. Neither did Montesquieu or Diderot debate with those who favored the established political and social order. They came to the conclusion that all existing institutions were the outcome of man's prejudices, not of social progress, hence not to be judged in an historical spirit. Ignorance, stupidity, and fear, and nothing else, went into the making of the "cake of custom." The interest evinced by the philosophes to explain the origin of the institutions of the Old Régime, was inspired by a desire to discredit them by showing their origin to have been evil or absurd. As they did not regard the institutions as legitimate products of history, they resorted to ridicule and satire in order to expose them.

Finally, the philosophes appealed to *bon sens,* or common sense, which they succeeded in raising to the rank of a philosophy. By metaphysicians and poets, common sense had always been despised as a low form of mental activity which concerned itself with matters merely practical. In the higher reaches of the mind, only the imagination of the poet and the abstract thought of the philosopher were worthy of serious consideration. Common sense, as a philosophy, may be considered as a by-product of the scientific spirit which arose with the Scientific Revolution of the sixteenth and seventeenth centuries.[25] Scientific inquiry concerned itself with practical things, and sought to bring enlightenment by observing facts and deducing relations from them. The philosophes took over the scientific attitude, though not the scientific method of laborious investigation, and converted it into a new weapon, *bon sens,* which they used with deadly effect in their attack upon institutions and traditions that had only custom and antiquity as reasons for existence. It was a method that greatly appealed to the *honnêtes gens,* who were now surfeited with the mysteries of religion and with the obtuseness of metaphysics; and they hailed with delight discourses on general ideas that were presented so simply, so easily, and so appealingly. Especially did *bon sens* appeal to the bourgeois reading public; it was a philosophy that eminently suited a class that prided itself on being practical, virtuous, and kindly.

RISE OF PHILOSOPHES

There was a sharp reaction in the eighteenth century against metaphysics and theology which had occupied so much attention in the preceding century. People now readily accepted the maxim that the "proper study of mankind was man," especially in relation to his environment. The eighteenth-century writers, "dwell on man, on the observable man, and on his surroundings; in their eyes conclusions about the soul, its origin, and its destiny, must come afterwards and depend wholly, not on that which revelation, but on that which observation, furnishes. The moral sciences are divorced from theology and attach themselves, as if by a prolongation of them to the physical sciences." [26] This new attitude was the outcome of the Scientific Revolution of the sixteenth and seventeenth centuries. The vast change in the conception of the universe, and of man's relations to it, which was inaugurated by the scientists from Copernicus to Newton, had little popular influence in its day. The scientists did little to spread their ideas; they were only too happy when they were let alone by the authorities in church and state. Furthermore, the Protestant Revolution had the effect of distracting attention from the truly revolutionary thoughts of the scientists to the theology of the Protestant Reformers. And it was not until the eighteenth century, when religious strife was somewhat stilled, that the opportunity came to popularize the discoveries of the Scientific Revolution. That became the task of the philosophes.

The philosophes were propagandists, first and foremost. Their importance was due "not so much for the answers which they gave as for the questions which they asked; their real originality lay not in their thought, but in their spirit. They were the first great popularizers." [27] With the appearance of a large reading public and a professional literary class the question of censorship became acute. Freedom of thought was as much an economic necessity to the philosophes, as professional writers, as was freedom of trade to the merchants, and freedom of work to the laborers. The professional writer felt himself hampered by the restrictions of the censorship, as did the merchants by the restrictions of the Mercantilist system, and the laborer, by those of the guilds. Naturally, the entire profession became ardent advocates of freedom of speech and of the press. *Libre examen*, prodded on by an insatiable curiosity, became a veritable passion in the eighteenth century. Milton's noble plea for freedom of thought, a century before, had fallen on deaf ears; now it was the battle cry of a powerful class interest.

There existed, in France, a formidable system of censorship that fairly bristled with stringent regulations and severe penalties. Printers were licensed, and a book, before it was published, had to have the approval of the Director of Publications (*Directeur de la Librairie*), who was the chief of a body of censors. After publication a book often ran the gauntlet of various bodies that had either power or influence to suppress it. The sale of a book might be forbidden by a decree of the Council of State or by an order of the courts, the parlements. Denunciation of a book by the Sorbonne or by the clergy might result in its suppression. The king, if displeased with a book, might intervene directly, and a *lettre de cachet* would throw the author into the Bastille and his volume into the flames. The punishment of those responsible for a condemned book might be severe: prison for the author; loss of license for the publisher; and the galleys for the colporteur, or bookseller. An edict of 1757 decreed the death penalty for authors and printers of books attacking religion.[28]

RISE OF PHILOSOPHES

And yet, the philosophes openly defied the censorship, and boldly proclaimed their revolutionary doctrines! This was largely due to the fact that the censorship laws were enforced spasmodically, and then only half-heartedly. Considering the boldness of their attack the philosophes suffered but little because of their propaganda. In fact, the condemnation of a book was apt to bring publicity rather than punishment, and authors competed "for the honors of the bonfire" by deliberately violating the censorship. "A decree of parlement, a censure by the Sorbonne, the burning of a book by the public executioner, imprisonment for several days, these were considered sufficient 'lessons' to the philosophes." [29] Voltaire's *Letters on the English* was condemned by parlement, and he was obliged to keep in hiding. Diderot's *Letters on the Blind* and his *Philosophic Thoughts* were condemned by the government, and he was imprisoned several months at Vincennes. Helvétius' *On the Human Mind* was condemned by the government, and he was obliged to leave the country. Morellet's articles in the Encyclopaedia were condemned by the government, and he spent seven weeks in the Bastille. These were the most notable instances of the persecution of the philosophes, who were treated with deference by their jailers, and whose cells "were illuminated by literary fame." Nothing happened to Montesquieu, to d'Alembert, to Turgot, to Quesnay, to d'Holbach, to Condorcet, and to Raynal. Rousseau did, indeed, suffer from the censorship when *Social Contract* and *Emile* were condemned, and he was obliged to flee from place to place. It was due chiefly to the fact that Rousseau had a martyr complex, and refused to use the stratagems and subterfuges resorted to by the other philosophes in order to avoid prosecution.

The philosophes clearly realized that the forces of repression, powerful and terrible as they were, could yet be rendered innocuous by clever dissimulation. Conservatives, they knew, seldom understand the significance of new ideas, unless they are labeled as being dangerous. They are generally satisfied with forms and appearances, and the philosophes, whenever possible, adhered to them with mock seriousness, and even with subtle satire. Voltaire urged d'Alembert to write "in a dull manner and no one will be able to know your identity. One can say good things in a heavy style. You will then have the pleasure of enlightening the world without endangering yourself and that would be excellent, and entirely for a good cause. You would then be an apostle without being a martyr." [30] The philosophes were exceedingly adroit in their methods of attack. "They employed all methods," declared Condorcet, "from the humorous to the pathetic, from learned tomes to novel or pamphlet; covering the truth with a veil to hide it from those of feeble eyes, but which permitted others the pleasure of piercing it; shrewdly praising prejudices in order better to give them a mortal blow; never threatening any of them either singly or in the mass; sometimes quieting the enemies of reason by pretending to favor only partial toleration in religion and only partial liberty in politics; applauding despotism when it fought religious absurdities and applauding religion when it fought despotism; attacking both in their fundamental principles and yet appearing only to attack revolting or ridiculous abuses; in other words, striking at the roots of these baleful trees and seeming merely to prune a few stray branches; sometimes teaching the friends of liberty that superstition, which covered tyranny with an impenetrable shield, should be first attacked, the first chain to be broken; sometimes, on the contrary, denouncing superstition to the despots as their real enemy, and frightening them with pictures of their hypocritical conspiracies and their bloody turbulence, but always proclaiming the independence of reason and the freedom of thought as the salvation of mankind." [31]

The philosophes were not averse to using any subterfuge, legal and illegal, to evade the censorship: secret printing presses, as in the case of the Encyclopaedia; anonymous authorship, as in the case of Voltaire's many pamphlets against the church; pretended authorship, as in the case of Diderot's *Letters on the Blind* which pretended to explain the work of an Englishman; imaginary letters of travelers, a common device, the most notable example being Montesquieu's *Persian Letters;* and imaginary translations of foreign books, a method often resorted to by d'Holbach. The bootlegging of condemned books was as openly practiced in eighteenth-century Paris, as the bootlegging of liquor was in twentieth-century New York, and with similar attendant circumstances, spies, raids, and bribery of the police. Not infrequently did the philosophes have the secret sympathy of high officials in the office of the censor. A notable instance was that of Malesherbes, Director of Publication from 1750 to 1760, who himself hid the plates of the condemned Encyclopaedia during a police raid. "The whole trade in books was a sort of contraband, and was carried on with the stealth, subterfuge, daring, and knavery that are demanded in contraband dealings." [32] The sale of condemned books became an extensive industry in France. Everyone wanted to read them, and bootleggers reaped a rich harvest. The dangers of the trade were small, but the profits were large. Rousseau's *Social Contract* was openly sold under the very vestibule of the royal palace. The doctrine of freedom of thought found ready acceptance because it corresponded to actual, though illegal, conditions, in which the censorship laws were openly disregarded. In a way the situation was not unlike that which caused free trade to be favored because of widespread smuggling; and free labor, because of illegal manufactures outside the guilds. Radical theories corresponded with actual, though illegal, practices.

For resorting to subterfuges in their warfare against the Old Régime, the philosophes have been subjected to severe criticism. Unlike Bruno and Servitus they did not suffer death for their opinions. In fact, martyrdom was the one thing that they wished to avoid. "I indeed love truth well, but I do not at all love martyrdom," said Voltaire, and he expressed the attitude of nearly all of the philosophes. They were children of their age, men of the world with a keen zest for life, who lived in the easy and pleasant atmosphere of the salons, and basked in the sunshine of the rich and the powerful. The philosophes revolted against martyrdom as they did against asceticism, both of which they regarded as variations of Christian fanaticism. They were sufficiently realistic to understand that to go to the stake for an idea was not at all the final proof that the idea was true. "To suffer martyrdom in any cause proves nothing, except that our party is not the strongest," declared Diderot.

The laxity of the government in suppressing this subversive propaganda was chiefly due to the belief that it was not a movement against the established order, as the philosophes made no inflammatory attack on the constituted authorities. A revolution in opinion was not considered dangerous by the Old Régime because discontent "broke out only in words." [33] The philosophes were careful not to spread the idea that they were rebels. Quite the contrary. They were generally on good terms with the *gens en place,* especially with Louis XV and his gay and frivolous court, whom they flattered outrageously.[34] "The court did not realize," later wrote Mme. de Staël, "the intimate relation that exists between all prejudices. They believed that they could, at the same time, maintain themselves in power in a system founded upon error and adorn themselves with the spirit of philosophy."[35] Those in power were, if anything, in sympathy with the philosophes whose writings were attractive because of their wit and eloquence. "We thought it was only a warfare of pen and word, which to us appeared quite devoid of danger to the superior existence that we enjoyed."[36] The philosophes keenly realized that, generally, only the humble and the lowly are made to pay the penalties of heresy. Because of their literary abilities they constituted a power within the nation; they, too, could reward or punish by creating public opinion either in favor or against powerful personages. No matter how absolute the autocrat or how haughty the noble he had to bow before the power of the pen. Madame de Pompadour, no less than Catherine the Great, wished to be in the good graces of the philosophes. The powerful influence of the *gens en place* was, therefore, sought by the philosophes to break the force of the censorship. When Diderot was cast into prison, several highly influential aristocratic friends intervened to make his stay short and pleasant. It was due to the influence of Madame de Pompadour that the Encyclopaedia was, for a time, permitted to appear. When Helvétius' book was condemned it was Frederick the Great who offered him an asylum. When Rousseau's books were condemned he found refuge in the homes of influential friends.

The great problem that confronted the philosophes was, how the Old Régime, with its political despotism, its religious intolerance, its censorship, its privileged classes, its monopolies, and its feudal restrictions was to be abolished; and how a new régime of liberty and equality was to be established. The answer that they gave comprehended a system of political and social philosophy and a method of reform which, in the nineteenth century, became generally known as liberalism.

At the very basis of the philosophy of liberalism was the doctrine of natural rights, or the rights of man, which was the supreme political ideal of the eighteenth century. According to this doctrine every human being, by the mere fact of birth and by the mere fact of being human, without any special qualifications whatsoever, possessed certain fundamental political rights. These were summarized by the famous Declaration of the Rights of Man and of the Citizen as being, liberty, property, security, and resistance to oppression. The rights of man were derived from self-evident principles, and not from precedents, historical or traditional. They were created neither by positive nor divine law. They were "natural," that is, derived from the very nature of man, hence eternal, inviolable, and universal; they consequently applied to all human beings, man and woman, natives and foreigners, white and colored. Being natural, the rights of man antedated civil society, and the state came into existence for the chief purpose of maintaining and protecting them. It, therefore, logically followed that natural rights were superior to the state, which could not legitimately suppress them altogether, even in the case of an individual citizen. When the state deprived a citizen of his life or of his property, as for instance in decreeing the death penalty for a crime or in condemning property for public use, it had to do so according to rigid forms, prescribed by law, in order not to violate the principle of natural rights by arbitrary action. It was universally believed, in the eighteenth century, that natural rights were the only legitimate ones; all special advantages that individuals or classes derived from the state were condemned as "privileges," to be suppressed forthwith.

But the suppression of privileges involved a reconstruction of society. The argument of the philosophes to justify such a revolutionary procedure ran as follows: Man's environment was nature and society. Nature, which they considered beneficent in all its ways, was to be followed implicitly. But society was artificial, and its institutions, they believed, were designed to perpetuate abuses, to maintain despotism, corruption, inequality, prejudices, and, above all, to keep the masses in ignorance and superstition. How could society be made as beneficent as nature? The common answer of the philosophes was by reorganizing its institutions in accordance with the principles of the rights of man.

To argue as to the truth or falsehood of the doctrine of natural rights is now beside the point. Considered historically it was a powerful weapon in the liberal armory with which the philosophes attacked the abuses and privileges of the Old Régime. By demanding equality as a natural right they sought to create among the unprivileged masses a sense of human dignity by lifting them to a plane of equality with the upper classes. "Now, the meaning of this proclamation of the rights of man," declared a recent writer, "was none other than to lift human souls from their interior servitude and to implant within them a certain consciousness of mastery and dignity." [37]

Another weapon in the liberal armory was reason. According to the philosophes the rights of man came from reason, and only from reason. Respect for the reasoning faculty of man was as old as humanity itself, but the worship of reason was distinctively a phenomenon of the eighteenth century, especially so in France, where the institutions and ideas of the Old Régime appeared to all enlightened persons as the very negation of reason. None could be defended or justified on rational grounds, therefore, the philosophes repudiated them all as the evil fruit of the ages of prejudice. To worship reason was, in a sense, their way of showing contempt for the past. They exalted reason above facts because they identified the facts of history with the hateful institutions of the Old Régime. The Dark Ages, which historians have pushed back to the tenth and eleventh centuries, were pushed forward by the philosophes to the eighteenth, the Age of Reason. "All feel and say that they have emerged, not only from darkness, but from the twilight before dawn, that the sun of reason is high in the horizon, illuminating the intellect and irradiating it with most vivid light." [38] To the philosophes reason was a method of simplification that arose from assuming *a priori* general truths and deducing from them specific applications. The method of reason was not, therefore, the scientific method of research into the facts, and deducing from them a general theory. It was the age-old method of logic that was now applied to the social sciences. As the universe was governed by natural laws which resulted in harmony, so was reason governed by logic which resulted in the discovery of universal truth. An orderly universe found an echo in an orderly mind. Reason, as the sole means of discovering truth, was an idea inspired by Descartes, whose influence the philosophes repudiated, but whose method they, nevertheless, slavishly followed. Descartes' great maxim was, "I think, therefore I am." On this maxim was based the fundamental principle of Cartesian philosophy, namely, that man alone is a thinking animal, and that he should accept only those ideas that his mind clearly and distinctly conceives. Nothing should be accepted as true, unless it was known clearly and evidently to be such. In Cartesianism neither authority nor tradition has a dominant place; it boldly asserts the supreme confidence of the human mind in itself. Reason is immutable, universal, and innate. It is present, though dormant and undeveloped, even in children, in savages, and in the untutored. "There is no human being who is not rational; there is nothing rational which is not logical, there is nothing logical which does not appeal to common sense or to the minimum of intelligence and rationality which the majority of mankind possesses." [39] Everything was dismissed as a "prejudice" by *la raison raisonnante*, which could not justify itself rationally, namely, logically. By his method of reasoning, Descartes had endeavored to demonstrate the truths of religion, and, by the same method, the philosophes endeavored to establish the truths of the social sciences. "It is, essentially, an attempt to apply the principles of Cartesianism to human affairs." [40]

From the worship of reason arose the rationalistic movement that played so great a part in the intellectual history of the eighteenth and nineteenth centuries. By rationalism is meant "the mental habit of using reason for the destruction of religious belief." [41] It aimed to break down the wall between the sacred and the profane, and subject all matters, religious as well as non-religious, to the same rules of critical inquiry fashioned by reason. What was incredible was not to be accepted, no matter how great the prestige of its authority and tradition. Rationalism had arisen, in the seventeenth century, as a by-product of the Protestant Revolution. Christendom had been divided by Protestantism into many sects all of whom, no matter how small, asserted claims to a monopoly of religious truth, and were not averse to persecuting those who denied such claims. These claims had the effect of discrediting religious infallibility, anywhere and at any time, in the eyes of the pioneers of modern rationalism, Bayle, Spinoza, Descartes, Hobbes, and Locke. With them rationalism was merely an attitude of mind, but with the philosophes it became a passionate crusade against all revealed religion. Nearly all of the philosophes were convinced that revealed religion originated in the fears and superstitions of primitive men, which were deliberately exploited by knavish priests who invented gods, manufactured miracles, and announced revelations in order to maintain their power over the multitude. And they have continued to maintain their power throughout the centuries by these same methods. Consequently, all revealed religions were false and pernicious to the philosophes, whether they were deists, like Voltaire and Rousseau, or atheists like d'Holbach and Diderot. All of them, the cautious Montesquieu no less than the irrepressible Diderot, the prosaic Voltaire no less than the poetic Rousseau, were convinced that priests, dogmas, and churches, were a sore affliction of the human race. "Philosophy" became a battle cry in a war against revealed religion in the name of reason.[42]

Especially false and pernicious was Christianity, and still more so, Catholicism. Against the latter the philosophes vented their wrath in an unending stream because they were firmly convinced that the Catholic church was the institution, above all others, that consecrated all prejudices and all traditions, thereby making possible popular acceptance of age-old tyrannies in government and society. All the evils of mankind came from superstition, and all the good, from reason, declared d'Holbach.[43] The quickest way to destroy the psychology of consent to these tyrannies was by destroying the religious faith of the masses. Therein, lies the explanation of the uncompromising war that the philosophes waged against the church. To attack Catholicism, in the eighteenth century, meant to attack revealed religion entirely. Protestantism was regarded by the philosophes, not as an alternative to Catholicism, but as a weak imitation of it. By that time it had become evident that Lutheranism and Calvinism, the two outstanding expressions of Protestantism, were as hostile to toleration and to freedom of thought, as was Catholicism. When Voltaire, in his *Letters on the English*, praised the English Quakers; or when d'Alembert, in his article on Geneva in the Encyclopaedia, praised the Swiss Calvinists they did so, not indeed because they admired these sects, but because they regarded them as ridiculous or as insignificant. Praise of religion by these philosophes was merely a form of satire.

There was only one solution of the problem of religion, according to the philosophes, and that was universal toleration. They were convinced that the evils generated by religion, fanaticism, superstition, and persecution, would be dissipated if all faiths were permitted to exist unmolested. What would remain would be the universal love of God, namely, deism. The case for toleration was best stated by Voltaire in his characteristic manner, "If there had been in England only one religion," he declared, "its despotism would have been fearful. If there had been two religions they would have cut each other's throat. But as there are thirty they live peacefully and happily." [44]

To the philosophes the ideals and the practices of the church were even more pernicious than her policies and her privileges. They severely condemned, as a low view of human nature, the doctrine that all men were born in sin, and could not attain salvation without divine aid; the anti-social practice of monasticism; the renunciation of this world and the emphasis on life to come; the opposition of the church to free thought; and her intolerance. These ideals and practices of the church were opposed to the faith of the philosophes in the natural goodness of man; to their hatred of asceticism; to their insistence on making this world a better and happier place; to their belief that man, by his own efforts, and without supernatural guidance, can progress morally as well as socially; to their passion for free thought; and to their love of toleration. "Broadly stated," says Morley, "the great central moral of it all was this: that human nature is good, that the world is capable of being made a desirable abiding place, and that the evil of the world is the fruit of bad education and bad institutions." [45]

The bold aim of the philosophes was nothing less than to separate morality from religion. Morals were to have a purely secular basis, thereby repudiating "other worldliness" as the inspiration of human conduct. In their view wickedness arose from bad systems of government and society, and not from sinful humanity or from natural conditions. Both man and nature were good. Morality, based on religion, viewed man as the scene of a conflict between two spirits struggling within him, good and evil, or God and the devil. This struggle "in the cave," as Diderot put it, was, according to the philosophes, an artificial one created by the theologians. They shifted the struggle from "the cave" to one between the individual, who was good, and existing society, which was evil.[46] Social progress was to be the guiding principle of a secular system of morals in which human conduct was to be motivated by desires to be more free, more intelligent, and more prosperous.

The rationalism of the philosophes inspired the "secularism" of the liberals in the nineteenth and twentieth cen-

RISE OF PHILOSOPHES 53

turies. In all lands liberalism became the stout protagonist of the separation of church and state, of secular education, of civil marriage and divorce, and of civil registration of births and deaths. Naturally, France was the chief scene of the struggle to establish the "lay" state.

The secular spirit of the philosophes, inspired by rationalism, gave another direction to their thought. It was to assimilate man to nature, and to bring his activities under the reign of natural law. What "evolution" was to the nineteenth century the "natural order" was to the eighteenth; it influenced every phase of the thought of that century, political, economic, social, and religious. Natural law had been well understood in ancient times, especially by the Stoics and by the Roman jurists. During the Middle Ages it was regarded as part of divine law, and subordinate to it; still lower in the scale of values was positive, or human, law. The Scientific Revolution of the sixteenth and seventeenth centuries had the effect of establishing the reign of law in nature. In the "world machine" of Newton, whose influence swept the eighteenth century much as Darwin's did the nineteenth, the philosophes beheld a universe of order, of law, and of beneficence. And the result was a fusion of divine and natural law, a rapprochement between God and nature, which "deified nature and denatured God." [47]

Nothing was more bold or original than the attempt of the philosophes to establish a natural order in human society. As the physical order was subject to natural law so, they believed, the social order was subject to laws to which it must conform as unalterably as did the universe to the laws of gravitation. Man was definitely regarded as an animal, and, consequently, part of the natural order. "If one wishes to understand him (man) in respect to his natural qualities, one must class him as an animal," declared the Encyclopaedia.[48] But the philosophes were chiefly interested in man as a *social* animal. In the writings of Montesquieu and of Rousseau there appeared a concept of society as an organism, and, as such, subject to natural law, like all other organisms. Social institutions were organic expressions of human relations, and subject to social laws that were as universal and as immutable as the physical laws that governed the universe. But how was one to discover these laws that governed human society? In the physical world the way was indicated by scientific observation of physical phenomena and by experiment in the laboratory. As there were no human laboratories the philosophes seized upon primitive man who they believed had only those institutions that conformed to social laws. In a sense primitive life was a human laboratory in which a successful experiment had already been performed; and the outcome was a society where reigned virtue and happiness.[49] Primitive man was wiser—or perhaps more fortunate—in being free from the corruption of tradition and prejudice; unlike his civilized brother he permitted the unobstructive working of natural law in human society.

It, therefore, behooved civilized man to learn a great lesson taught by the untutored savage. This lesson was that just as harmony existed in nature through the working of natural laws, so would harmony exist in human society, if the social order were free from the obstructions of traditions, prejudices, privileges, and restrictions. Harmony in society could be attained only by setting the wellbeing of the community as a whole, "the public interest," above the interest of any class or of any section. This doctrine, so distinctive of liberalism, assumed that the various social, economic, and political elements had a common fundamental interest. If they but knew it and acted accordingly! Conflict arose from the ignorance of the laws that govern society, as disease arose from the ignorance of the laws of health. The knowledge that natural law was universal, necessary, and constant, argued the philosophes, has led to man's control of nature. And a knowledge of social laws that are equally universal, necessary, and constant would lead to man's control of society. This application of Newtonian principles to social, political, and moral matters, would result in establishing a society in which everything would be harmonious and happy. The idea of the "harmony of interests" in society came to the philosophes as a reaction against the caste-ridden, feudal order, whose privileges and discriminations were productive of as many conflicts and irritations. A change "from status to contract" would make the social order as harmonious as the physical order.

One of the laws that controlled human society was progress. "Perfectibility," or universal happiness, was considered, by the philosophes, to be the chief end of man. It was not to be, however, a heaven imposed from without by the "intervention" of a deity, but the outcome of man's own striving in accordance with his psychical and social nature. According to Bury, the historian of the idea of progress, it "involves a synthesis of the past and a prophecy of the future. It is based upon an interpretation of history which regards men slowly advancing in a definite and desirable direction, and infers that this progress will continue indefinitely." [50]

The idea of progress was enthusiastically embraced by the philosophes because it comprehended a secular and rational philosophy of life in opposition to the Christian attitude toward human life and destiny. According to the teachings of Christianity man was a sinful creature, evil in his nature, who could not attain salvation by his efforts alone, but had to resort to divine aid. And salvation came, not in this world, but in the next. This world was only a pilgrimage, a *via dolorosa,* and any concern that man might have for his welfare in this world was "worldliness," which might endanger his eternal salvation. Against the doctrine of salvation in the next world the philosophes put the idea of progress in this world. Human nature was good, and the world was a good place in which to live. Therefore, man's chief concern should be his welfare upon earth, and this welfare was to comprehend improvement in his material, intellectual, political, and social conditions. Concern for the next world, "otherworldliness," was regarded either with indifference or with derision.

In one sense the idea of progress was a rationalization of what the philosophes really desired, which was a better present rather than remote perfectibility. They repudiated the then existing order primarily because they could not live in it. As the protagonists of the new life of free enterprise, of free labor, and of free thought, which was pulsating in the eighteenth century, they felt themselves constricted and confined within the rigid framework of the Old Régime. It was the passionate desire of the philosophes to create, here and now, a world fit for rational and free men that inspired them to advocate the idea of progress.

Social progress would come, naturally and easily, in a free society, the philosophes believed, as a consequence of the acquisition of more knowledge which would be spread to the public by means of popular education and propaganda. "It is not a matter of indifference that the minds of people be enlightened. The prejudices of the rulers are derived from the prejudices of the people," said Montesquieu.[51] As in the natural sciences, the laws of nature could be discovered only by a study of the facts, so in the social sciences wise policies could be adopted only after the facts had been indisputably established as a result of investigation. Enlightenment would reveal the essential harmony of interests involved in the solution of any social problem.

The way of liberalism was the way of progress by pacific means, and the method was an appeal to reason. Therefore, there must exist freedom of thought, unhampered by any kind of censorship. Systems of popular education must be established to spread enlightenment among the masses. It was Locke, another magic name ever on the lips of the philosophes, who suggested to them this method of progress. According to Locke's famous theory of "sensationalism," the human mind was a blank sheet, a *tabula rasa;* and all ideas arose as a result of experience derived through the senses from the natural and social world, and of the reflection of the mind on these "sensations." Social institutions, namely, the social environment, consequently, determined the character and ideas of people. Men were not born sinful, but ignorant. The philosophes had an *"a priori* conception of society in all countries as a blank sheet for the pen of pure reason." [52] This psychological interpretation plainly implied that social progress could be achieved only by changing the social environment through the spreading of knowledge. Enlightened public opinion would demand reforms, and this demand would be answered by enlightened laws. Tyranny, privilege, and corruption were the result "less of viciousness than of stupidity, less of the deliberate malice of kings or ministers than of a long, ingrained tradition of narrow-mindedness and inhumanity in the principles of government. Their great object, therefore, was to produce, by means of their writings, such an awakening of public opinion as would cause an immense transformation in the whole spirit of national life." [53] Public opinion would become all-powerful because it would arise from a literate people who were being continually enlightened by new knowledge.

As convinced believers in the power of reason to bring about progress, the philosophes, one and all, strongly condemned popular uprisings. They believed that such movements were due to the religious fanaticism of the masses who were roused by priests to civil wars and massacres, as in the struggles between Catholics and Protestants. They also identified popular uprisings with the disturbances created by unruly nobles, as in the case of the *Fronde*, which almost ruined France. "The voice of reason," declared d'Holbach, "is neither seditious nor sanguinary. The reforms that it advocates are moderate, and consequently well planned. In becoming enlightened men become milder; they know the price of peace; they learn to tolerate abuses that cannot be destroyed all at once without danger to the state. . . . It is by rectifying opinion, by combating prejudice, and by showing both ruler and people the rewards of equity that reason can hope to cure the evils of the world and firmly establish the reign of liberty." [54] Violent revolution, as a method of progress, was something that the philosophes could not even imagine, and nothing would have so horrified them as to hear their names invoked during the violent scenes of the French Revolution.

The philosophes had an unbounded faith in the efficacy of legislation. All problems, of whatever kind, could be solved by enlightened laws, an idea which sprang from their unquestioned belief in the natural goodness of man. Evil in society, they contended, existed because of bad laws, and would vanish once good laws were established. Human nature was plastic material in the hands of the legislator who, if enlightened, could mold it in harmony with the beneficent laws of nature. But the state, as the philosophes knew it, was an undiluted despotism that comprehended all the prejudices of all the ages. This contradiction led them to give an interpretation of law which harmonized more with the idea of natural rights than with the actual facts. According to the philosophes, law was an expression of the "general will," and could, therefore, exist only in a free state in which legislation was the means to promote the liberties and the welfare of the people. In an autocratic state there really was no "law," but only arbitrary acts of the ruler, in his interest or in that of the privileged classes, which interfered with the liberties of the people and were contrary to public welfare. "The old laws of nearly all the nations," declared Condorcet, "are only a collection of attacks on justice by force, and of violations of the rights of all in favor of the interests of a few." [55]

From the reaction against the autocratic state of the eighteenth century, arose another liberal tenet, individualism. The philosophes were ardent champions of "liberty," by which they meant that the individual must be liberated from the church which hampered his freedom to believe; from the Mercantilist system which hampered his freedom to trade; from the guilds which hampered his freedom to labor; and from the censorship which hampered his freedom of self-expression. To the state they cried, "laissez faire," or "hands off" which, in truth, had a wider connotation than economic. It comprehended the complete liberty of the individual in all spheres of human activity, limited only by the rights of other individuals. To the state was assigned merely the function of protecting natural rights.

Revolutionary as were their aims, the philosophes, nevertheless, hoped to realize them through any but revolutionary methods. In their view the free society, of which they were dreaming, would be brought into existence by the granting of civil rights, such as equality before the law, no arbitrary imprisonment, freedom of speech and of the press, the protection of property rights, and religious toleration. In spite of their fervent devotion to the cause of freedom the philosophes had little interest in political rights, such as suffrage and election to office. Few of the philosophes were republicans. They accepted the dictum of Montesquieu that a republic was best suited to small states, like Geneva in modern Switzerland and Athens in ancient Greece; a kingdom, to middle-sized states, like France and England; and an empire, to very large states, like Russia and the Holy Roman Empire. Democracy was undesirable, even unthinkable. For the masses, *la canaille,* the philosophes had the most withering scorn and the utmost contempt. According to Voltaire they were cattle, and all that they required were a yoke, a goad, and fodder. The communistic Mably was no less severe in his hatred of democracy than was the bourgeois Voltaire. In a democracy "where every citizen has a right to translate his vagaries into laws," he declared, "where no reasonable precautions are taken to foil the plots of the wicked and to still the turbulent passions of the mob, it is plain that all decisions are made by madness."[56] D'Holbach hated the masses as "an imbecile populace who, having no intelligence and no common sense, is always ready to be the instrument and the accomplice of turbulent demagogues who wish to trouble society."[57] At best, even the most advanced of the philosophes, like Diderot and Condorcet, favored a parliamentary system controlled by property owners, such as existed in England before the Reform Bill of 1832.⁵⁸ Montesquieu did, indeed, believe that the English government, in his day, was the best of all possible governments, but it is an error to assume that he wanted to see it established in France. The transplantation of political systems from one country to another was against his political philosophy, the basis of which was that all institutions and laws bore a necessary relation to the special conditions in each country.

But how were civil rights to be established? By means of "enlightened despotism," answered most of the philosophes. Therefore, they strove with might and main to enlighten the rulers of their day because, as they believed, these rulers alone had the power to inaugurate necessary reforms. Tyranny, they believed, was due to the fact that the rulers followed the counsels of priests, the upholders of prejudices, by whom they were surrounded. It would cease to exist if the rulers surrounded themselves with philosophes. An absolute monarch, whose policies were guided by philosophes, would almost fulfill Plato's dream of an ideal government in which the rulers were philosophers. "A new generation will arise," declared Voltaire, "that will hold fanaticism in horror, and the seats of power will be occupied by philosophers, and the reign of reason will begin." ⁵⁹ When Louis XVI appointed Turgot, as his minister, and told him to go ahead with his proposed reforms, the philosophes were almost sure that Voltaire's prophecy had at last come to pass.

This belief of the philosophes, that an all-powerful ruler could, if he so willed, inaugurate an era of freedom and equality, appears rather naïve today. And yet it appealed most powerfully to the skeptical philosophes. Herein, lies a serious criticism of their political philosophy, which has subjected them to the charge of being superficial. Although they clearly enough understood the evils of their day, they did not realize the interdependence that existed between the economic, the social, and the political orders. An absolute monarch, no matter how powerful and enlightened, could not make fundamental reforms without risking his throne, and perhaps his life. The sad disappointment of Emperor Joseph II of Austria, when he attempted to make "philosophy the legislator," came a little too late to influence their views. And they never saw through the charlatanism and knavery of Frederick the Great and Catherine the Great, who used the renown that Voltaire and Diderot gave them, as "enlightened despots," to cover up their tyranny at home and their aggression abroad.

Sophisticated as the philosophes were in the ways of the world, their inveterate tendency to logical deduction from assumed premises prevented them from having a psychological insight into human motives and conduct. Therefore, they did not give the traditional ideas of the Old Régime their proper place in human psychology, but denounced them as "prejudices." To the philosophes the issue was simple. Reason and nature were on one side, and, on the other, were ignorance and superstition. Therefore, their sympathies were narrowed, and their imagination was dulled by a rationalism that was as hard as it was intense. "Theology, in fact," comments Morley, "was partly avenged of her assailants for she had in the struggle contrived to infect them with the bitter contagion of her own traditional spirit." [60] In their attacks on the church the philosophes were irreligious in more than a theological sense; they had neither understanding nor appreciation of the mystical state of mind which accompanies religious devotion. In a devout man at prayer they beheld an ignorant fool who was being imposed upon by a crafty knave,

RISE OF PHILOSOPHES

the priest. Of all the philosophes, only Rousseau had a religious sense. He did believe that, apart from dogma and ritual, there was a mystical craving in man which, he declared, was a natural love of God. In their attacks upon the political and social institutions of the Old Régime the philosophes were guilty of similar dogmatism. "What they could not see," justly remarks Morley, "was the great fact of social evolution; and here too, in the succession of social states, there has been a natural and observable order. In a word, they tried to understand society without the aid of history. Consequently they laid down the truths which they discovered as absolute and fixed, when they were no more than conditional and relative." [61]

The philosophes contracted the vice of false clarity, which is sometimes found among the French, as the vice of false profundity is sometimes found among the Germans. Oversimplification, by means of general ideas, became almost a disease. Voltaire avoided difficulties by rippling gayly over the surface; Rousseau, by attenuated logic or by glowing rhetoric; and Diderot, by sentimental moralism. Arguing from assumed premises gave them that peculiar sense of certainty that a mathematician has, when he constructs a logical theorem on the basis of axioms. Seldom did they apply themselves to investigate the foundations upon which they based their arguments in favor of the rights of man. "Some think," declared Diderot, "that a knowledge of history should precede views of morality. I am not of this opinion. It seems to me more useful and expedient to have the idea of the just and the unjust before having a knowledge of the actions of the men that are to be judged." [62] This *a priori* attitude, so characteristic of the philosophes, was the logical outcome of their passionate faith in the power of reason to solve all human problems. "In their love for pure reason, they relied too often on the swift processes of argument for the solution of difficult problems, and omitted that patient investigation of premises upon which the validity of all arguments depends. They were too fond of system, and those neatly constructed logical theories into which everything may be fitted admirably —except the facts." [63] Paradoxically, the method of reasoning, pursued by the philosophes, was the same as that of the theologians whom they so bitterly reviled; the theologians, too, came to logical conclusions from assumed premises. This is an excellent illustration of the substitution of absolutes which was so characteristic of eighteenth-century thought. For God, the philosophes substituted nature; for divine will, natural law; for revelation, enlightenment; and for preaching, propaganda. They did not seem to be aware of the influence of the social, political, and economic forces in society on opinion, because their eyes were glued to the thin veneer of reason that covered the vasty deep of human irrationality.

And yet because the problems that the philosophes dealt with were social, political, and economic, and because they favored complete freedom of inquiry, which the theologians did not, they deserve to be regarded as pioneers of modern thought. It must always be kept in mind that they were propagandist reformers intent upon creating a better world here and now; and this *a priori* method gave a religious fervor to their propaganda by pointing to every abuse in society as a violation of eternal principles. The social sciences and scientific history were still in their infancy, and the philosophes were, therefore, forced to use what weapons they had in their struggle with the Old Régime. "And though the French philosophers of the middle of the eighteenth century do not always impress us as possessing intellectual superiority, though, on account of their eager attempts to simplify and popularize, they often make the great small, and profane which is really sublime, yet behind their dogmatism, their short-sightedness, and their trivialities lies a fervent faith in light, in progress, and in humanity, for the sake of which they must be forgiven much." [64]

CHAPTER FOUR

CONDORCET BEFORE THE FRENCH REVOLUTION

It would be difficult to find another philosophe who so completely exemplified the intellectual movement in France, as did Marie-Jean-Antoine-Nicolas Caritat, Marquis de Condorcet.[1] He was born on September 17, 1743, at Ribemont in Picardy, now the Department of the Aisne. The family seat, originally, was the Château of Condorcet, in Dauphiné, hence the noble title. As a younger son the father, Antoine, had entered the army, and was a cavalry officer stationed at a garrison in Ribemont. There he met a wealthy young widow, of the bourgeois class, whom he married. The marriage of a poor army officer of noble birth and a rich bourgeoise was as common in eighteenth-century France, as in nineteenth-century Germany. About four years after the birth of Condorcet, his father died. His mother, now twice a widow, was deeply attached to her only child, and her mother love was intensified by the fact that he was delicate in health. Deeply religious she consecrated the child to the Virgin in order to preserve him from evil. And to preserve him from rough handling at play, she sought to isolate him from other boys by dressing him in girl's clothes until he was nine years of age.[2] This overzealous care of the mother undoubtedly had an influence in determining the character, the temperament, and even the physique of Condorcet. As a boy he was shy, diffident, and averse to physical exercise. As a man he "was extremely refined with a craving for intimacy and affection to which was joined indecision, a certain timidity, and a dangerous impressionability." [3]

Condorcet's education was in charge of his paternal uncle, who was a bishop. First, he was sent to a Jesuit preparatory school at Rheims; later, in 1758, to the Jesuit College of Navarre in Paris. The man who was to become a skeptic in religion, a pacifist, and a democrat was brought up in an environment of priests, soldiers, and nobles, so typical of aristocratic France of the Old Régime. As a student Condorcet's life was *triste et solitaire*. He kept very much to himself, and his associates were chiefly his teachers. He became deeply interested in mathematics, and, at the age of sixteen, he brilliantly defended a mathematical thesis before a body of mathematicians among whom was d'Alembert. When Condorcet left school he decided to follow the career of a mathematician, which created a storm of opposition in his family, who regarded such a career as being unsuitable to a noble. They wanted him to be a soldier, like his father. But Condorcet detested the profession of arms, and determined to pursue the profession that he had chosen for himself. In 1762 he left home and settled in Paris, where he lived modestly from a small allowance given to him by his mother. His departure was not due to a break with his family who, though they disapproved of his choice, yet loved him too well to cut him off.

Once in Paris Condorcet was irresistibly drawn into the intellectual society of the salons. His mentor was d'Alembert, who remembered the youthful mathematician whom he regarded as a prodigy. The salons of Paris were open to anyone of talent, and Condorcet was welcomed as a rising young intellectual. Through d'Alembert he met Julie de Lespinasse who took the serious-minded, studious young man under her wing, and introduced him to the circle of philosophes who came to her salon. But, like Rousseau, Condorcet did not shine in the brilliant and gay society of the salon. He was too serious, too shy, too silent among people who were gay, daring, and quick at witty repartee. "This tall youth, awkward, timid, and embarrassed, who walked with a stoop and bit his nails, who was silent or spoke rapidly in a low voice, inclining his head and blushing, must have found himself out of place in the elegant and carefree salons among the bold and clever wits of his day."[4]

Naturally Condorcet sought more serious circles. He became a friend of Helvétius, at whose house he met men who deeply influenced his life and his ideas, Lafayette, Franklin, the Duke de la Rochefoucauld, and, above all, Turgot. For the last Condorcet conceived a tremendous admiration, and the two became intimate friends. They had similar temperaments; both were earnest, studious men, and rather grave and retiring in disposition. In Turgot young Condorcet beheld his model and his master whose ideas on economics roused new interests in the young mathematician.

Condorcet continued his mathematical studies, and, in 1765 at the age of twenty-two, he published his first work, *Essay on Integral Calculus*. A few years later he published several other mathematical works, which elicited the enthusiastic admiration of mathematicians like d'Alembert and Lagrange.[5] Condorcet's contribution to mathematics was recognized in 1769 when, at the age of twenty-six, he was elected to the Academy of Science. A few years later he acted as perpetual secretary of that body, a position that he officially assumed in 1785, and filled until his death.

As secretary of the Academy of Science it was Condorcet's duty to write eulogies of the dead members of the Academy, who were chiefly scientists.[6] The eulogies that he wrote were grave, dignified, and somewhat stilted disquisitions on the contributions to science of the men eulogized, a sort of history of science in biographical form. These literary contributions of Condorcet were well received by the academic public. Voltaire, who ever kept an encouraging eye on promising young disciples, wrote Condorcet that "the public wishes that an academician might die every week so that you might have the opportunity of writing about him."[7]

At the early age of twenty-eight Condorcet was already a fairly prominent figure in the intellectual life of Paris of that day. His prominence was due chiefly to his ability as a mathematician; his admirers saw him on the road toward becoming a mathematician of the rank of Descartes and Pascal.[8] Yet, at this very time, Condorcet definitely gave up his career as a mathematician, and devoted himself to the social sciences, which became his absorbing interest to the end of his life. There were powerful influences which were drawing him in this direction, and no one, who was intellectually alive in those days, could resist these influences, especially the impressionable Condorcet. All about him were the brilliant philosophes discussing the questions of the day which were absorbing everyone's interest. Perhaps Condorcet came to doubt whether he had the genius to make original contributions to mathematics. Perhaps he came to believe that, with his mathematical bent of mind, he could contribute a new and different solution to the problems which everyone was discussing. Moreover, the example of Turgot, whom he admired as a man "whose existence was necessary to humanity," was ever before him. It inspired the young disciple to emulate his master in a career of bold speculation and enlightened public service. Curiously enough the skeptical eighteenth century believed in myths of its own contriving: the wise philosopher-lawgiver of ancient times, the noble savage in the state of nature, and the sage emperors of China. In Turgot Condorcet beheld the Legislator of ancient Greece and Rome, the inspired philosopher-statesman come to life, giving wise laws to his fellow-countrymen. In 1775 he wrote to Turgot that from his early youth he had been meditating on the ideas of justice and virtue and on the problem of how our individual interest commands us to be just and virtuous.[9]

Then there was another influence, that of Voltaire, which no one, living in the eighteenth century, could escape. A journey to Ferney during that period became what a journey to Italy had been in the sixteenth century, the beginning of a new life in a world of new ideas. In 1770 Condorcet made his pilgrimage to the Patriarch of Ferney. Voltaire received him cordially, and promptly enrolled him into the philosophe army as a young warrior who would wield a mighty sword against the obscurantists. In his correspondence with Turgot and with Voltaire, Condorcet frequently showed his unbounded love and admiration for his masters. However, he was a faithful, but not a slavish, disciple. An incident in his relations with Voltaire illustrates Condorcet's independence of character. Voltaire disliked Montesquieu, and wrote an attack on the *Spirit of Laws*, which he wanted Condorcet to have published. The young disciple considered his master's attack unjust, and refused to have anything to do with it. "My affection for you," he wrote Voltaire, "causes me to tell you what is best for you, not what would please you. If I loved you less, I would not have the courage to gainsay you." Voltaire took the reproof of his young disciple in good part. "One always sees badly," he wrote to Condorcet, "when things are far away. We should never blush to go to school even at the age of Methuselah." [10] Condorcet wrote biographies of both Turgot and Voltaire which, like the *éloges* that he wrote as secretary of the Academy of Science, were less personal biographies and more discussions of the ideas which these philosophes championed.[11] He also wrote commentaries on some of Voltaire's works, in which he defended his master against those who charged Voltaire with being superficial. Many say, declared Condorcet, "that Voltaire is a superficial philosopher, and that is because he is neither rhetorical nor enigmatic." [12]

Condorcet now plunged fully and ardently into the career of a philosophe, both as a writer and as a reformer. It is not surprising that the first pamphlet that he wrote, in his new capacity, was an anonymous attack on religion. It was in the form of imaginary letters by a theologian, and contained a scathing attack on theology written in the vein of Voltaire.[13] A time will come, and perhaps was already near, was Condorcet's belief, when theology would no longer be of sufficient importance to be the subject even of ridicule. The pamphlet was promptly ascribed to Voltaire, much to the latter's annoyance, who, because he so frequently denied his authorship of attacks on religion, was accused of being the author of anti-religious pamphlets that were written by others.

The philosophes welcomed Condorcet, partly because of his abilities, partly because his noble origin gave social prestige to their group. He became intimately associated with Diderot, d'Holbach, Helvétius, Quesnay, and Morellet. His most intimate friends, however, were the Suards, husband and wife.

Suard was a journalist who was connected, socially and professionally, with the intellectual groups that met in the various salons. Madame Suard was an attractive, kindly, impressionable woman, the type of *femme sensible*, that Rousseau did so much to popularize. Neglected by her husband she sought, and received, attention from other intellectuals. Condorcet became a frequent visitor to the Suard home, and, in 1772, he left his lodgings and took up his residence in that household. Unlike the other philosophes Condorcet was exceedingly puritanic in his life; no woman of the salon could boast of having been his mistress. The *ménage à trois* of the Suards and Condorcet was curious in that it was the lover, not the husband, who played the platonic rôle. Condorcet's shy nature craved for intimacy and affection which the kindly Madame Suard bestowed freely upon him. To her he came for advice as to his career; for comfort when he was disappointed in love with a Madame de Melun; and to air his views on public matters. This family group and a few intimate friends fulfilled all of Condorcet's needs for social life.[14] He cared very little for the brilliant social circles to which he was welcome because of his rank and intellectual standing. Retiring and studious he was averse to a continuous round of social duties which he described as "dissipation without pleasure, vanity without motive, and idleness without repose." [15] Another intimate of the Suards was the critic, La Harpe, who came to visit them frequently. Madame Suard's cup of happiness now overflowed; she had her three men. "You are the three objects from whom my heart receives all its joys and over whom it spreads a profusion of loving qualities with which nature has endowed me." [16]

What broke up the happy *ménage à trois* was the appointment of Condorcet, in 1774, as Inspector of the Mint, by

Turgot, when the latter was made Minister of Finance by Louis XVI. Condorcet left the Suard household, and took up his living quarters at the Hotel des Monnaies, a government house that went with his position. This change threatened to end the *roman d'amitié*. Madame Suard was almost heartbroken, but she was consoled by the fact that her husband also received an appointment under Turgot. As Condorcet became immersed in his official duties, his visits to the Suards became less and less frequent, although he never ceased to have friendly feelings for the couple.

Condorcet now entered upon his rôle as economist. As the faithful disciple of Turgot he espoused his master's Physiocratic views, and warmly defended his reforms in abolishing the *corvée*, in suppressing the guilds, and in establishing internal freedom of trade in foodstuffs. The war against the restrictions on trade, imposed by the Mercantilist system, was fought in the literary as well as in the political field. As a Physiocrat Condorcet was strongly opposed to the system, and his writings helped to prepare the way for Turgot's reforms. He wrote a number of pamphlets and articles for the Encyclopaedia, advocating the complete suppression of all restrictions on trade, on labor, and on land.[17] Turgot's reforms had no stronger supporter than Condorcet who engaged in a bitter controversy, on their behalf, with Necker who advocated internal tariffs on foodstuffs. When, in 1776, Necker succeeded Turgot as Minister of Finance, Condorcet was disconsolate. He resigned his position rather than serve under one whose views he so violently condemned. The dismissal of Turgot brought great disappointment into the camp of the philosophes. "We have had a beautiful dream, but it has been brief. I am going back to geometry and philosophy," Condorcet wrote to Voltaire.[18]

But he was now too deeply immersed in public affairs to go back to mathematics. Instead, he plunged even more deeply into the problems of his day, both as pamphleteer and as an active reformer. He became interested in the condition of the Negro slaves in the French colonies, and, in 1781, he published a pamphlet denouncing slavery and the slave trade.[19] In the same year he wrote another pamphlet on the status of the French Protestants, in which he denounced the legal discriminations which put them in the position of semi-outlaws.[20]

Condorcet had now achieved sufficient prominence in the literary, social, and political world to be a candidate for the French Academy. There was a movement among the philosophes to capture that citadel of conservatism, a movement headed by d'Alembert and encouraged by Voltaire. And when Condorcet became a candidate he received the powerful support of the philosophes, especially that of d'Alembert, who was secretary of the Academy. "We have need of men in the Academy that think like you," wrote Voltaire to Condorcet.[21] In 1782 Condorcet, at the age of thirty-nine, was elected by majority of only one vote over Bailly, the famous astronomer.

Entrance into that distinguished body did not cool Condorcet's ardor as a reformer. The intervention of Voltaire in the famous Calas and de la Barre cases started a tradition in France that it was the special duty of the intellectual to expose a miscarriage of justice due to popular prejudice, a tradition upheld by Emile Zola and Anatole France during the Dreyfus Affair. In 1786 another affair took place that threatened to become as famous as that of de la Barre. Three peasants were accused of burglary, and were condemned to be broken on the wheel. Their trial revealed clearly, not their guilt, but the vicious system of justice and the barbarous methods of punishment then prevailing in France. Public sentiment was aroused on behalf of the accused, and the three unfortunates found a champion in Dupaty, a distinguished judge who was a liberal and a friend of the philosophes. Dupaty began an agitation in favor of the condemned, as a result of which he was driven from his position by his associates. Condorcet threw himself into the case. Anonymous pamphlets appeared, known to be written by him, which defended Dupaty, and denounced the court that had condemned the three peasants.[22] The case ended in a royal pardon of the accused, and in the restoration of Dupaty to his position.

The incident had an unexpected outcome, so far as Condorcet was concerned. It led to his marriage. As a result of his relations with Dupaty he came to know the latter's niece, Sophie de Grouchy. A young woman of noble family, the daughter of the Marquis de Grouchy, Sophie was beautiful, refined, intelligent, enlightened, rich, and twenty-two. Condorcet was distinguished, learned, admired, respected, and forty-three. They fell madly in love with each other, and were married in 1786. The marriage of Condorcet created a sort of scandal in philosophe circles. Family life was not considered becoming in a true philosophe; a mistress, not a wife, was more in keeping with the gay and elegant literary world of the eighteenth century. It was also somewhat disconcerting to Condorcet's noble associates because he had not asked for a dowry from his wealthy father-in-law.

The married life of the Condorcets was supremely happy. Their successful marriage, despite the difference in their ages, was not a little due to the fact that they were friends and co-workers as well as husband and wife. The Condorcets were interested in education, and they helped to organize a school, called the "Lycée," where writers and scholars gave lectures on all sorts of subjects to the fashionable and cultured society of Paris. Condorcet lectured on mathematics, and among his students was his wife. The home of the Condorcets became a salon in which the brilliant young wife shone. *Elle était toute lumière.* Thither came the new generation of literary men and philosophes, Beaumarchais, Chénier, Morellet, Volney, and Grimm. Englishmen and Americans were warmly welcomed, as both the Condorcets knew English very well. Thomas Paine, Jefferson, and Adam Smith became intimates in the Condorcet household. Madame Condorcet translated Adam Smith's *Theory of Moral Sentiments* into French. Later, during the French Revolution, she also translated Paine's speeches to the National Convention. Under the influence of his wife Condorcet became more sociable; her charm, her tact, and her goodness had the effect of making her rather grave and shy husband more easy and affable. One child blessed their union, a girl who was born in 1790 and baptized Alexandrine-Louise-Sophie, to whom the parents gave their entire devotion.[23]

In appearance Condorcet was tall, broad-shouldered, with a rather large head and slender legs. In public he gave the impression of being cold and reserved because of his natural shyness; but with his intimates he was easy, friendly, and even gay. Now and then he would burst forth in passionate admiration or bitter denunciation which betrayed a highly emotional temperament. Condorcet possessed a natural and spontaneous goodness which overflowed in the intimacy of close friends. *Le bon* Condorcet was the appellation given to him by Julie de Lespinasse who knew him well. "Condorcet's face plainly showed that goodness was the most distinctive and the most decisive characteristic of the man's soul."[24] His kindness and gentleness extended even to animals. He gave up hunting, of which he was very fond, because the cruelty of that sport shocked his sensitive nature. In a letter of advice to his daughter, written when he was nearing his tragic end, he enjoined upon her to preserve "in all its purity and strength the sentiment which makes us sensitive to the pain of all living things. Do not limit yourself to sympathy for human suffering but let that sympathy extend to the suffering of animals." [25] In a sketch of Condorcet Julie de Lespinasse gave the following description of him. "His usual calmness and moderation was transformed into fiery ardor when it was a question of defending the oppressed or of defending what was even more dear to him, human liberty and unrewarded virtue. His zeal became a veritable passion. . . . He suffers; he acts; he talks and writes with all the energy of a soul on fire." [26]

In his early life Condorcet had undergone so much repression that he never entirely recovered from its effects. As a child his mother and his relatives had pressed him into the mold of the aristocratic conventions of his family. As a boy he had suffered ridicule at the hands of his playmates because he was dressed in girl's clothes. As a youth he had been under the severe discipline of Jesuit teachers. Although he completely repudiated all the influences of his early life Condorcet never was entirely free from them. They vanished into his unconscious. As a consequence his naturally ardent and enthusiastic temperament was held in restraint by a strong reserve. Condorcet's reserve, however, was not aristocratic hauteur, but a shyness and modesty which seemed like timidity, and which became all the more pronounced because of his habit of calm and deliberate reflection before he came to a decision. Condorcet is "a volcano covered with snow," said his friends. He is "a sheep in a passion" (*mouton enragé*) said his enemies. Gentle and retiring this *reformateur exalté* performed brave deeds quietly and without heroics. Before the French Revolution he boldly attacked the evils of the Old Régime. During the Revolution he was always resolutely in the forefront of those elements that were seeking to establish France as a complete democracy.

Condorcet was, in many respects, a typical philosophe. He was widely read, thoughtful, suggestive, free-minded, but without concentration in any particular field. He was too curious and too versatile to apply himself consistently to a special subject of study. Condorcet was an omnivorous reader, and he possessed an amazing memory. The range of his reading showed remarkable versatility, even for a philosophe. "He has read all things," wrote a contemporary, "from the *fabliaux* to the publicists of the eleventh century; from the novel of the hour to the collections of the Academy of Belles Lettres. He reads with equal pleasure Euler (the mathematician) and Ariosto (the poet), Hippocrates, Voltaire, the researches on wealth of nations, and la Nouvelle Heloïse." [27] In some other respects, however, he did not at all resemble his fellow-philosophes: he lacked style and humor, hence his writings had few readers. Condorcet was aware of his lack of style, which he rationalized into a scrupulous regard for truthful statement. "When one writes on subjects that require exact analysis and rigid precision," he declared, "there is danger of injuring these qualities if the writer endeavors to drape them with unsuitable ornaments or to stimulate an interest in his readers which does not arise from the subject itself." [28]

Condorcet completely assimilated the libertarian philosophy of the intellectual movement in France, and he conse-

BEFORE THE FRENCH REVOLUTION 79

quently repudiated the institutions and laws of the Old Régime as violations of the rights of man. But he was not content merely to denounce abuses in books and in pamphlets; he also associated himself with the men of his day who were actively interested in reforming conditions. Condorcet became a leading member of a famous Masonic lodge in Paris, called the "Lodge of the Nine Sisters," which numbered among its members, Voltaire, Franklin, who was regarded as its patron saint, Sièyes, Pétion, Brissot, Lalande, Greuze, and Danton. This organization was the Fabian Society of its day. It was composed of intellectuals, and became an influential center of reform agitation against the abuses of the Old Régime.[29] Condorcet disliked the mysteries and secrecy connected with Freemasonry, but excused them on the ground that they were "necessary precautions in a period of ignorance to enable the members of these societies freely to exercise their reason."[30] Along with Brissot, Mirabeau, and Lafayette, he was active in organizing the Society of the Friends of the Negroes, an anti-slavery society of which he later became president.[31] The Society carried on an active propaganda against slavery and the slave trade, and advocated the suppression of the slave trade and the emancipation of the Negroes.[32]

What were Condorcet's political views before the French Revolution? In the main, they were those of a constitutional monarchist. "France will remain a monarchy," he declared, "because this is the only system of government suitable to her wealth, to her population, to her extent, and to the existing political system of Europe."[33] But France was to be a constitutional, not an absolute monarchy; the power of the king was to be limited by the establishment of a national parliament. Who were to be the electors to this parliament? As a Physiocrat Condorcet firmly believed that only land constituted the true source of the wealth of a nation, hence only the possessors of land should be qualified as electors. The non-propertied inhabitants, he argued, lived in the country only because the landowners gave them a habitation.[34] It was land that made the citizen. Those who had more land than was required to be an elector were to have one vote and no more; and those, who had less, were to be grouped in sufficient numbers to choose an elector.[35] He presented ingenious arguments in favor of a propertied suffrage by showing that universal suffrage would result in establishing a government by the rich. It was property that made a man truly free, he declared, and giving votes to the poor would mean that they would be controlled by the rich elector. Property owners, great and small, according to Condorcet, had the same interest in having good government as non-property owners. And, in fiscal matters, they had an even greater interest in having good laws than the non-propertied, since it was they who paid the taxes. "There is then no danger in making them (the property owners) the guardians of the interests of society."[36] Condorcet also favored indirect elections because he believed that the voters were better able to judge who was fit to choose a representative than to choose one themselves. Those, chosen as electors, would be the educated, enlightened citizens of the locality who would acquire public esteem through the success of those whom they chose as representatives. These political views of Condorcet indicate that he was but little in advance of enlightened opinion of the day. However, even before 1789, he showed distinct tendencies in favor of far more radical reforms. In 1787 he published a pamphlet consisting of imaginary letters of a citizen of New Haven, in which he boldly advocated woman suffrage and a unicameral legislature.[37]

Another aspect of Condorcet's political views, before 1789, was his emphasis on the importance, in a free state, of local self-government. The French monarchy attempted to quiet the agitation for political reform by establishing provincial assemblies, consisting chiefly of members appointed by the king to represent the clergy, the nobility, and the Third Estate. The assemblies were given limited powers of local self-government, such as the building of roads, the maintenance of charitable institutions, and the assessing of certain taxes. The first provincial assembly was instituted in 1778, in the province of Berry; later, more were established in other provinces.[38] Condorcet warmly championed local self-government in his *Essay on the Constitution and the Functions of the Provincial Assemblies,* a work dealing with a wide range of constitutional law and government.[39] Local self-government, he argued, would solve the age-old antagonism between city and country. In order to create a balance between them the country villages should be grouped into self-governing communes. Through such bodies public spirit would be created in the countryside by rousing the political interests of the peasants.[40] In a publication, *Le Moniteur,* Condorcet also advocated self-government for the cities through the establishment of municipal communes. These bodies, he believed, would perform a double function: as powerful agencies with which to destroy feudalism; and as a basis of representation in case a national parliament was called by the king.[41]

On the eve of the French Revolution Condorcet had achieved a distinctive place in the intellectual movement in France. His writings did not have a wide appeal, but his views were respected and admired by the cultivated people in society. His distinguished family connection, his broad liberal views on public policy, his learning, and his well-known uprightness of character gave him a distinction far beyond his talents as a writer. Among those who hailed the calling of the Estates-General as the beginning of a new era, wrote a contemporary, "no one was more disinterested, more free from prejudice, more averse to intrigues, and more free from passion than the modest Condorcet. He brought as tribute to the country that he loved and to humanity that he loved still more, a character that was most unaffected, a power of reason that was highly trained, and a disinterestedness so natural and so simple that it was less a virtue in him than an ideal." [42]

CHAPTER FIVE

CONDORCET DURING THE FRENCH REVOLUTION

EVERYONE who reads about the French Revolution comes across the name, Condorcet. And that is about all. Aulard and Jaurès devote more space to him than do the other historians of the Revolution, chiefly because of their sympathy with his views.[1] In truth Condorcet was not a great Revolutionary figure, like Mirabeau, Danton, and Robespierre, nor even a figure of secondary importance, like Sieyès, Lafayette, and Desmoulins, despite the heroic effort of his enthusiastic biographer, Alengry, to establish him as the mentor of the French Revolution.[2] Nevertheless, Condorcet's rôle was an interesting and significant one because he was the only philosophe who was an active participant in the French Revolution. From his views and actions during the Revolution one can get some idea of what might have been the attitude of Voltaire, Rousseau, Montesquieu, Turgot, and the other philosophes when they saw the Old Régime fall into a heap of ruins, and beheld a new system of society and government arise that was inspired, according to the Revolutionists, by their teachings.

As an active reformer Condorcet was naturally interested in the agitation that led to the calling of the Estates-General in 1789. Always in advance of the liberal opinion of his day he opposed the calling of that feudal body, controlled by the privileged classes, because its very existence was a violation of natural rights. What he demanded was a popularly elected national assembly with power to issue a declaration of rights and to formulate a constitution.[3] When the Third Estate seceded from the Estates-General and established itself as the National Assembly Condorcet's demands were unexpectedly realized. At last, after centuries of oppression, the rights of man could be proclaimed by the representatives of the people. As a student of political science Condorcet aimed to be the preceptor of the newly organized Constituent Assembly. Therefore, in 1789, he drew up a model Declaration of Rights which he urged the Assembly to follow.[4] It was a long, and rather precise document, very different in style, though not in spirit, from the crisp yet vivid Declaration of the Rights of Man and of the Citizen, adopted by the Assembly. Unlike that famous document and the American Declaration of Independence, Condorcet's Declaration was entirely secular in spirit; there was no mention of God. In the main, it contained the same provisions as the Declaration of the Rights of Man and of the Citizen. However, it included several significant provisions, not contained in the latter: the abolition of capital punishment for private crimes; the preservation of natural rights in times of war as in times of peace; equality of inheritance as between children of different ages and of different sexes; and the periodic revision of the Declaration itself.

Condorcet followed the activities of the Constituent Assembly with the greatest interest, though he was not a member of that body. As a journalist and pamphleteer he was active in creating public opinion in favor of the reforms that were proposed. He visited the Assembly regularly, and reported its debates. In 1790 he became a member of the municipal council of Paris, and drew up many of the petitions of that body to the Assembly.[5] Condorcet's political views were still those of a constitutional monarchist. Like Mirabeau and Lafayette he was highly regarded as a liberal-minded noble who had left his class to take up the cause of the people. Condorcet found a fellow spirit in Abbé Sieyès with whom he became very intimate. Together they founded a new club, called the Society of 1789 (*Société de 1789*), which attracted the liberal minded among the nobility. The object of the Society was to provide a forum for discussing the problems of the day, from all points of view, in order to aid in the pacific transformation of France from despotism to freedom. The Society had an organ, *Journal de la Société de 1789*, which was edited by Condorcet and to which he was a frequent contributor.[6]

Condorcet's attitude toward the great reforms, inaugurated by the Constituent Assembly, was critical, not because the Assembly did too much or too little, but because, in his opinion, the reforms did not harmonize completely with the theories by which they were inspired. Primarily a political philosopher, he had a feeling of disdain for the practical politician whose work seldom has symmetry and form. In pamphlets, in articles, in petitions, Condorcet kept up a deluge of criticism and advice to the Assembly. He criticized the Declaration of the Rights of Man and of the Citizen as being vague and incomplete; the Civil Constitution of the Clergy as being too bold and too timid at the same time; and the constitution of 1791 as undemocratic because of the great powers given to the king, because of the property qualification for voting, and because of the failure to submit the constitution to a referendum.[7] Already, in the first stage of his career as a revolutionist, he exhibited that devotion to abstract principles which, later, was to result in making him pathetically ineffective when dealing with concrete situations. His was not the temper of a Mirabeau to whom principles were suggestions, not hard-and-fast rules, for practical statesmanship. Nor was his the temper of a Robespierre to whom principles were a battle cry to the masses to mobilize for swift and ruthless action. His was the temper of the doctrinaire liberal who earnestly sought to create a political order in harmony with abstract principles of government that were as inevitable and as eternal as natural laws.

Typically liberal was Condorcet's attitude toward the laws of the Constituent against the church. As a devout disciple of Voltaire he outdid even his master in his hatred of Catholicism. But he distinguished between religion as a private opinion, which should be fully and freely allowed, and the church as a political power which should not be tolerated under any circumstances. He opposed the Civil Constitution of the Clergy because it recognized the clergy as state officials. But he criticized the spoliation of the church, and demanded that compensation should be given for its confiscated property. Especially should the monks and nuns, left helpless by the suppression of their orders, receive pensions sufficient for their needs according to the rules of their order.[8]

As an economist and financier Condorcet was deeply interested in the financial experiments of France during the Revolution. He was appointed chairman of a Commission of the Treasury which drew up the plan of financing the administration, adopted on September 17, 1791, by the Constituent Assembly. France was embarking on a policy of inflation through the printing of the *assignats,* or paper money. As the assignats fell in value gold and silver began to disappear, and, in a short time, France was in the full swing of inflation and the resulting financial crises. Condorcet wrote a series of pamphlets on the subject of money and inflation, in which he criticized the financial policy of the Constituent Assembly.[9] He argued that, according to Gresham's law, the cheaper money would inevitably drive out the dearer money.[10] Great confusion arose, due to the uncertainty of the amount of assignats to be issued, and of the amount to be sold of the confiscated church lands, on which the assignats were based. This uncertainty, Condorcet declared, lowered the value of the paper money.[11] He strongly opposed the policy of the wholesale issuing of assignats, as it did not correspond to the needs of commerce and industry. Such a policy, he declared, would undermine the confidence of the masses in the government, which was more necessary in revolutionary than in normal times.[12] What Condorcet favored was controlled inflation, or the issuing of a limited amount of assignats.[13]

During the period of the Constituent Assembly (1789-91) Condorcet's political views underwent a change that again put him in the forefront of the advanced opinion of his day. He ceased to be a constitutional monarchist, and became an ardent advocate of a democratic republic, based on universal, equal suffrage. As was usual with him Condorcet did not champion half reforms; he favored woman suffrage as well as manhood suffrage. In 1790 he wrote a pamphlet, *On the Admission of Women to the Right of Suffrage,* which created a sensation.[14] It boldly advocated votes for women on the ground that women, like men, were human beings and therefore had the same natural rights. Condorcet expressed his astonishment that the Constituent Assembly, zealously engaged in establishing human equality, should tranquilly deprive half the human race of political rights.[15]

It was the taking of the Bastille that had converted Condorcet to popular suffrage. By this act, he declared, an inert, ignorant superstitious populace, the tool of the rich and the well-born, was suddenly transformed into a people that bravely and vigorously asserted its rights.[16] Henceforth, Condorcet consistently and enthusiastically advocated all new institutions that favored "the class which is the most poor and the most numerous."[17] He vigorously criticized the constitution of 1791 for establishing a property qualification for voting, and an especially high property qualification for election to the legislature. Property qualification exists in England, he declared, but it has not prevented political corruption; it exists in America, but, as in that country everyone has property, no one is excluded. "There, the land lacks men, not men lack land."[18] He keenly realized that the propertied suffrage, established by the constitution of 1791, would shift political control from the aristocracy to the bourgeois, and not to the people. Speaking of the Third Estate, he declared, that their interest "is to establish a bourgeois aristocracy, such as obtains in some of the Swiss cantons, where the nobility has been humiliated but where the people have become enslaved to the bourgeois."[19]

Condorcet's interest in the American experiment undoubtedly had much to do with converting him to a republican form of government.[20] Republicanism, in the eighteenth century, was identified with the ancient city states or with the Swiss cantons. The dictum of Montesquieu that a republic was suited only to small states was universally accepted. But the appearance of a great republic on the other side of the Atlantic caused many to consider the possibility of a large state having a republican form of government.[21] Since 1787 Condorcet had formed an intimate friendship with Thomas Paine who greatly influenced his views in favor of republicanism. Together, in 1791, they founded a new journal, *Le Républicain*, to advocate their views, but it lasted only a few weeks.[22] The home of the Condorcets became known as *le foyer de la République*, where republican opinions were freely expressed by radical thinkers. Distinguished foreigners, such as Paine and Mackintosh, came to the Salon Condorcet which became "the natural center of thinking Europe." [23]

However, it was the flight of Louis XVI, in 1791, that was the immediate occasion for the conversion of Condorcet to republicanism. Shortly after the Flight to Varennes he delivered an address in which he denounced "the corrupt and dangerous institution of monarchy," and boldly announced himself in favor of a republic.[24] He declared that constitutional monarchy, regarded as a barrier to tyranny, was no longer necessary. New barriers had been erected by the constitution, especially freedom of speech. "All who have read attentively the history of the usurpation of Cromwell, know full well that a single newspaper would have been sufficient to have prevented it." Had the English read other books besides the Bible, Cromwell would not have been dangerous, sarcastically commented the philosophe. Barriers could be erected against a usurping legislature, argued Condorcet, by frequent elections, by elected executives, and by periodic constitutional conventions. "We no longer live in the days when, to assure the power of the laws, we must depend on the impious superstition which makes of the king a kind of divinity." He severely denounced King Louis for endeavoring to flee from France. By running away Louis had abdicated his throne, and he was now "free of us as we are free of him." [25] In an imaginary letter of a young mechanic, Condorcet ridiculed a constitutional monarch as a kind of mechanism in which a dummy king could function as well as a live one.[26] The young mechanic proposed to produce, in a short time, a robot monarch who would "rule constitutionally." "It was an event," writes Aulard, "to hear the greatest thinker of that day, the disciple and heir of the Encyclopaedists, preach the republic which all the philosophes, his masters, had declared impossible or dangerous to establish in France." [27] Condorcet's pronouncement had considerable influence in the formation of a republican party, which felt itself "legitimatized by the stirring intervention of the heir of the philosophes." [28] But it lost him his aristocratic friends, the Duke de la Rochefoucauld and Malesherbes, who now beheld a traitor in the man whom they had revered as a guide and philosopher.

If Condorcet can at all be said to have played a prominent rôle in the French Revolution, it was during the short period of the Legislative Assembly (October 1, 1791-September 20, 1792). He was elected to this body not, as might be supposed, as a republican, but as a distinguished citizen whose democratic views had made him popular with the liberal minded bourgeois voters. His importance was recognized by the Assembly, which chose him, first as one of its secretaries, then, vice-president, and, finally, president. The majority of that body was monarchist. In opposition, on the left, was a group, later known as the Girondins, led by Brissot. Like Lamartine in 1848 Condorcet sat neither to the right nor to the left, but, as Lamartine put it, "on the ceiling." He boasted of belonging to no faction, of being "a stranger to all parties, concerned with judging men and measures with my reason, not with my passions." [29] Generally he acted with the Brissotins who, though republicans like himself, accepted the constitution of 1791 for all practical purposes.

Students of the French Revolution well know the ineptness of the Legislative Assembly when it came to action. But it is famous for proclamations, orations, reports, and addresses. In such a body Condorcet was in his element, and it was he who wrote most of the addresses and proclamations.[30] As an orator, however, Condorcet was a complete failure. His speeches were rhetorical, even declamatory, but they lacked warmth and eloquence. His manner of speaking was "cold and awkward; his gestures restrained and weary; and his lack of spontaneity and variety" [31] made him the very antithesis of a French Revolutionary orator. Condorcet's abstract eloquence was addressed to posterity not to an audience. Nevertheless his speeches, which were often read by him to the Assembly, were listened to with the greatest attention, because the members regarded the rather reserved and diffident orator as a liberty-intoxicated man, zealous for every reform that would make humanity more enlightened, more free, more happy. "On these hesitating and cold lips," writes Aulard, "hung the Assembly, France, and even Europe eager to know how the friend of Voltaire, d'Alembert, and Turgot judged the Revolution." [32]

The most important document, issued by the Assembly, was the report of the committee on public education. It was written by Condorcet, its chairman, and is undoubtedly his chief Revolutionary contribution.[33] The report is a landmark in the history of education; many of its provisions are quite startling in their modernness. It recommended the establishment of a national system of primary, secondary, and higher education, which was to be free, secular, and equal as between men and women. For long, declared Condorcet, he had meditated on these educational ideas as dreams to be realized in the long distant future. But "a happy event (the French Revolution) suddenly gave an immense impulse to human hopes; a single instance put a century of distance between the man of today and the man of tomorrow." [34] But an unhappy event intervened between Condorcet's scheme and its immediate realization. That was the war with Austria, in 1792, which began a series of conflicts between revolutionary France and the rest of Europe that lasted until 1815. Due to the exigencies of the coming struggle, Condorcet's report was tabled by the Assembly.

What was the attitude of Condorcet toward the war that was looming up between France and the monarchies of Europe? In a declaration, authorized by the Assembly, he denounced Austria as the protector of the émigrés and as the enemy of the free constitution established in France. If the choice lay between war and a shameful peace he would choose war.[35] However, with the insight of a true liberal, he feared that a war begun to defend liberty might become one of imperialistic aggression. Therefore, Condorcet inserted a clause in the constitution, which he later drew up for the French Republic, which declared that the French Republic renounced annexation of territory except as a result of a free vote of the inhabitants, and only when such territory was under autocratic rule.[36]

France was at war with both Austria and Prussia, who were despatching their forces. The émigrés were hovering on the frontier, secretly aided by the traitorous Louis XVI. In this revolutionary crisis Condorcet exposed his weakness as a revolutionist because he lacked the ruthlessness which seems to be essential to the success of a revolution in dealing with internal enemies. He proposed a plan to the Assembly, dealing with the émigrés, in which he distinguished those who renounced the laws of their country from those who conspired against them.[37] The émigrés who refused to take the oath of allegiance to the constitution, but who did not serve in foreign armies, were to be treated as foreigners, with all the rights of foreigners; only those émigrés who served in foreign armies were to be punished as traitors. Condorcet's plan was considered impractical, and it was, therefore, disregarded by the Assembly.

A crucial problem of the Assembly was what to do with Louis XVI. Condorcet proposed a solution of this problem which, again, illustrated his inability to see a crisis demanding extraordinary action. As a consequence of the defeat of the French troops and of the Manifesto of the Duke of Brunswick, popular feeling against the traitorous court became so menacing that the Assembly appointed a committee to consider the suspension of Louis XVI. Condorcet was made a member of this committee, and wrote its report. It was largely a technical discussion of constitutional limitations concerning abdication and suspension. To suspend Louis would be unconstitutional, it argued, therefore the report advised against any action in the matter.[38] Condorcet then proposed a vague scheme of educating the people on the exercise of their sovereign rights.[39] This report was read on the eve of August 10. "He heard the rumbling of the popular storm, and he sought a shelter in the constitution." [40] The report was tabled.

On the following day, the terrible August 10, *le peuple* appeared with Danton and his mob in the attack on the Tuileries. The uprising of the Parisians caused the Assembly to decree the suspension of Louis XVI. A provisional executive council was appointed, all the members of which were Brissotins, except Danton. Curiously enough, Danton's inclusion was due to Condorcet. Of the three most prominent leaders of the Paris mob, Marat, Robespierre, and Danton, he preferred the last, though he hated the violent methods of all of them. Robespierre he considered a fanatic. Marat he hated and despised as a lunatic who was mistaken for a prophet by an erring people. Danton's expansive temperament might, however, cause him to be more malleable. "It was necessary," Condorcet later explained, "to have a man in the council who had the confidence of these very people whose agitation had just overturned the monarchy . . . who, by his leadership, could restrain the very contemptible tools of a revolution that was useful, glorious, and necessary." [41] The burly figure of Danton was to stand between the mob and the representatives of the nation.

Condorcet's career in the Legislative Assembly, begun so auspiciously, ended in utter futility. His policies had been repudiated; and his reports, tabled. Perhaps he had dreamed of being the Turgot of the Revolution, who would achieve success where his master had failed, because he would have the support of a powerful, enlightened people, not that, as in the case of Turgot, of a weak and dull monarch. But when *le peuple* became a reality, instead of an abstraction, Condorcet experienced a sense of painful confusion. He "mourned deeply over the violations of the majesty of the laws, over the outrages against natural rights." [42] But his faith in progress and his devotion to his ideas were too great to cause him to turn reactionary. On the contrary, he held on to his abstractions all the more firmly, believing that the violent scenes of the attack on the Tuileries and of the September Massacres were the work of agitators who "give the name 'people' to those corrupt or mistaken men that they assemble in mobs." [43]

Despite his repeated failures Condorcet's prestige was now, if anything, higher than it had been since the outbreak of the Revolution. His career in the Legislative Assembly had given him the reputation of being a champion of the people, without being tainted by violent demagoguery. When, at the end of 1792, elections took place for the National Convention, five departments contended for the honor of being represented by him. He selected the department of the Aisne, and one of his colleagues, from that region, was his old friend, Thomas Paine.

As a member of the Convention, Condorcet was affiliated neither with the Girondins nor with the Jacobins. He criticized the Girondins because of their federalism, and he criticized the Jacobins because they were more violent than enlightened. Generally, he acted with the Girondins. In the Legislative Assembly Condorcet's part had been futile; but in the Convention it was pathetic. The tumultuous atmosphere of that body, with menacing mobs outside—and sometimes inside— was not the deliberative assembly, dreamed of by the philosophe, that was to draw up a republican constitution. The Republic, proclaimed by the Convention on September 21, 1792, was the direct and immediate outcome of the popular insurrection of August 10. Condorcet, the pioneer republican, stood aghast. He had imagined that it would be established by statesmen and philosophers after calmly deliberating, long and earnestly, on the problems of government and society. But the first French Republic was created overnight amidst wild disorder, mob violence, and fearful massacres. It was a red specter instead of a glorious vision. Those who created the Republic regarded republicanism, less as a theory of political science, than as a weapon with which to smite kings, aristocrats, and priests. However, Condorcet accepted the Republic whole-heartedly, and sought to guide it into peaceful paths. He even defended the insurrection of August 10 on the ground that the French people could not see their liberties assailed *sans inquiétude*.[44] The safety of the Republic demanded extraordinary measures against its enemies, but such measures must be strictly limited to safeguarding the Republic, as security, not violence, was their aim.

The Convention soon became the scene of terrific clashes of hostile interests and of ruthless ambitions. In the fierce party strife between Girondins and Jacobins Condorcet found that there was no "public," and he was in a position of dangerous isolation, like all true liberals in a time of crisis. Ingenuous and disinterested he was suddenly plunged "in the mêlée of ambitions and of interests in which his naturally fine social instincts and great delicacy were useless, as they prevented him from unraveling the threads of so many intrigues."[45] By Girondin chieftains, like the Rolands, he was despised as a weak reed at best, and as a tool of the Jacobins at worst. "One could describe Condorcet's intelligence in relation to his personality," declared Madame Roland, "as that of a fine liqueur soaked in cotton. . . . He is as feeble of heart as he is of health. The timidity, which is so characteristic of him, is noticeable in his face, in his manner, and in his deportment. It is not merely a vice of his temperament, but is inherent in his very soul; and his enlightenment has not enabled him to overcome it. After deducing a principle and demonstrating a truth, he will twist them into their very opposites when he appears before a turbulent assembly that is discontented and menacing. He is in his rightful place as secretary of the Academy."[46] Espousing the Republic had earned Condorcet the hatred of his aristocratic friends, but had not won him popular acclaim. By the Jacobins he was regarded with suspicion because of his noble origin, or with contempt because of his academic standing. He is "a great mathematician in the opinion of literary men," said Robespierre, "and a great literary man in the opinion of mathematicians. Condorcet is a timid conspirator, despised by all parties, who works ceaselessly to darken the light of philosophy by means of the perfidious rubbish of his paid-for rhapsodies."[47] Marat denounced Condorcet in his customary violent manner. Condorcet, he fulminated, is "a consummate Tartufe wearing the mask of frankness, an adroit intriguer who has the talent to grab everything in sight, a shameless impostor who endeavors to reconcile opposites. He had the unblushing effrontery to proclaim republican views . . . after having edited for so long a monarchical journal."[48]

Condorcet rarely addressed the Convention, and whenever he did so he was received with contemptuous silence. His attitude toward the trial of Louis XVI roused against him the hostility of the Jacobins. It was his opinion that the Convention was not legally competent to try the King because it could not be legislature, accuser, and judge at the same time. He was so naïve that he actually feared that the Convention would be prejudiced against Louis, and would consequently find him guilty.[49] To Condorcet, Louis was now an ordinary citizen, and, therefore, endowed with natural rights which were valid in times of crises no less than in normal times. A crisis to Condorcet was, like any other event, *sub specie aeternitatis;* for natural rights were universal, absolute truths, therefore valid at all times and in all places. He regarded revolution as a mathematical problem which could be solved by the formula of natural rights. Condorcet recommended that Louis be tried by a national jury chosen by the electoral bodies in the departments. In sharp contrast to the views of Condorcet were those of Robespierre. "Louis," said the latter to the Convention, "is not an accused. You are not judges. You cannot be other than statesmen and representatives of the nation." To consider Louis an ordinary citizen, entitled to a regular court trial, was to confuse the situation of a people in a state of revolution with one having a stable government. Louis was not to be tried but was to be condemned as a traitor by the Convention.[50] In reporting the sessions of the Convention for the *Chronique de Paris* Condorcet denounced Robespierre's view as "the right to assassinate without preliminary investigation those whom popular clamor had judged. To act on this view would be to destroy the very basis of political society whose primary object is to substitute the calm will of the law for the uncertain, tumultuous will of some people, even of a great number." [51]

Needless to say the Convention rejected Condorcet's plea and placed the King on trial. When the vote was taken Condorcet voted that the King was guilty; but he, together with Paine, refused to vote for the death penalty. "Execute the king but not the man," they declared. The execution of Charles I during the English Revolution, they reasoned, did not result in the abolition of monarchy; on the contrary, it resulted in its restoration. Paine voted for the imprisonment of Louis while the war with Austria and Prussia was in progress; and for his perpetual banishment after the war. Condorcet voted for "the severest punishment in the penal code short of death" on the ground that he was opposed, on principle, to capital punishment.[52] When the Convention voted the death penalty, Condorcet demanded a respite for the condemned monarch on the ground that the execution of Louis would rouse popular sentiment in Europe against

France. "Foreign rulers," he wrote, "will be compelled to inspire their subjects with hatred for France, and thereby receive national support for the war that they have declared." To conciliate the nations of Europe, Condorcet advised the Convention to pass social reform laws, such as the abolition of capital punishment, the establishment of public charities, the suppression of lotteries, and the abolition of imprisonment for debt.[53] But Condorcet's plea to conciliate foreign nations by social reform did not persuade the Convention to grant a respite to Louis XVI.

The chief work of Condorcet in the Convention was a draft of a constitution for the French Republic. In 1792 the Convention appointed a commission to draft a constitution, consisting of Sieyès, Pétion, Paine, Vergniaud, Brissot, Gensonné, Barère, Condorcet, and Danton. The majority was Girondin; Danton was the only Jacobin on the commission. Condorcet was made chairman because of his reputation as an authority on political science. This was the greatest opportunity of his life. "For thirty years I have hardly passed a day without meditating on political science,"[54] he had once declared. He felt that he was now like a legendary Legislator of ancient times who was called upon to give laws to his fellow citizens. The constitution, proposed by the committee, was sponsored by the Girondins, and was, therefore, known as *La Girondine*. It was the work chiefly of Condorcet, assisted by Paine. Danton never attended the sessions of the commission. Accustomed to the easy triumphs of eloquent oratory, he was temperamentally averse to the hard and concentrated work of committees. The other members participated but little, perhaps because Condorcet's zeal had the effect of increasing their confidence in his ability, and so decreasing their own activity. The Girondin constitution of

1793 was almost entirely the outcome of the meditations of Condorcet.

La Girondine is a very long document, and fills eighty-five pages of Condorcet's collected works.[55] It is exceedingly detailed and specific in its desire to make definite and positive the application of abstract political ideas to a scheme of government. "By its very mass, by its complexities, by its many details the Girondin project was bound to provoke hostility." [56]

The constitution was prefaced by a Declaration of Rights which followed the famous Declaration of the Rights of Man and of the Citizen. The government of France was to be that of a republic "one and indivisible." Legislative power was vested in a parliament of one house, elected by direct, universal, male suffrage. Curiously enough Condorcet, the pioneer of woman suffrage, did not include votes for women. The only possible explanation is that, just as he was dismayed when *le peuple* appeared in the mobs of Paris, he was disgusted when *la femme* appeared in the *Faubouriennes*, or mobs of market women, who were mobilized by Marat to disturb the sittings of the Convention. Executive power was to be exercised by a popularly elected committee. There was to be a popular censorship of acts of parliament by the means of the initiative and referendum. The constitution itself was to be submitted to a referendum for ratification. There were many articles designed to protect the liberties of the individual against arbitrary acts of the government. Public officials of all kinds, local and national, executive and legislative, were to be popularly elected for short terms. An extensive system of local self-government was provided which would have had the effect of decentralizing France.[57]

As chairman of the committee to draw up a constitution, Condorcet made his first report to the Convention on February 15-16, 1793.[58] It received little attention from that body which, in that critical time, was more concerned with the threatening foreign armies on the frontiers and with the uprisings of the royalists in La Vendée. On April 17 the Convention turned its attention to Condorcet's draft; and a debate began which continued intermittently for about fourteen weeks. Curiously enough this document, drawn up by its author as a model for all mankind, became a bitter partisan issue between the Jacobins and the Girondins. The former charged that it was a scheme devised in the interest of the propertied classes in the provinces, the strongholds of the Girondins. They feared that Paris, their stronghold, would lose control of the nation through Condorcet's provision for local self-government. The draft called forth Robespierre's famous speech on property, in which he argued that property was not primarily a natural right but a social institution created by law, therefore, it was subject to limitations imposed by law. "You have numerous articles," he told Condorcet, "to assure the greatest liberty to property and not a single word to determine its nature and legitimacy, a method followed by your Declaration which evidently is designed not for mankind, but for the rich, for monopolists, for stock jobbers, and for tyrants."[59] The system of frequent elections, favored by Condorcet, was denounced by his opponents as a system in the interest of the rich who had plenty of time to indulge themselves in this pastime, and therefore truly Girondin. The poor will be unable to participate in them, declared François Robert, hence popular sovereignty will become an illusion. "The rich who do not labor will become the supreme masters of these assemblies, and, as a consequence of an excess of democracy badly understood, there will arise a new and terrible aristocracy, an almost absolute aristocracy of wealth." [60]

Neither the scheme nor its author made a favorable impression on the Convention. According to Mathiez, the scheme was "of interminable length and the preliminary discourses of Condorcet were dull and dry. . . . It exhausted the patience of even those who were most ready to applaud the work of the last of the Encyclopaedists." [61] Its adoption was constantly postponed, and debate lagged. As the Convention became the scene of hostility between Girondin and Jacobin, Condorcet became concerned with the fate of his constitution. Was it to be put aside like his report on education in the Legislative Assembly? He issued a pamphlet in which he declared that the adoption of a constitution was necessary in order to establish stable institutions, without which there could be neither liberty, equality, nor property; the country would oscillate between tyranny and anarchy.[62] On May 13, 1793, Condorcet demanded of the Convention that it either submit his scheme to a referendum of the people or order the election of a new Convention.[63] But no attention was paid to his demand.

After the expulsion of the Girondins from the Convention, Condorcet's constitution was doomed. It was rudely thrown aside by the Jacobins who were more concerned with having a government than a constitution. A new committee was appointed by the Committee of Public Safety to draft a constitution. Its chairman was Hérault-Sèchelles, who drew up a plan in less than a week.[64] On June 10 it was presented to the Convention; and on June 24 it was adopted with hardly any debate. In order to mollify Girondin sentiments in the provinces the Jacobin constitution of 1793 (Year I) took over many features of Condorcet's project. It provided for a unicameral legislature to be elected by universal, manhood suffrage; for an executive council of twenty-four members to be chosen from a list of candidates, nominated by the departments; and for referenda on laws passed by the legislature. "Thus, although they had nothing but criticism for the Girondin plan, the Jacobins now in their pressing need virtually purloined it, revamping it a little, but not changing it in essentials."[65] The constitution was then submitted to a referendum, and was accepted by the people.

Condorcet's amour-propre was deeply hurt by the rejection of his scheme. The greatest effort of his public life had been frustrated by men whom he despised as demagogues and ignoramuses. They had contemptuously thrown aside his constitution, the product of years of study of political science, and had put through a hastily concocted document which, he declared, was a caricature of his project. Again, Condorcet failed to sense the critical situation in France. In the tumultuous Paris of 1793 he imagined that he was in quiet Philadelphia in 1787. America needed a constitution to achieve a more perfect union and to have a national Bill of Rights. France, in 1793, had achieved a more perfect union and had acquired a Declaration of Rights. She now needed a constitution to give a popular sanction to a dictatorship in order to tide over a crisis. That was the function of the constitution of 1793; once the crisis was over it was not even applied.

The expulsion of the Girondins from the Convention by a Jacobin mob, as well as the rejection of his constitution, roused Condorcet to a high pitch of indignation. During the referendum he issued an anonymous pamphlet, *Advice to the French on the New Constitution*,[66] in which he challenged the triumphant Jacobins by exhorting the citizens to reject their constitution. The integrity of national representation, he declared, was undermined by the violent ousting of the Girondin members. To Condorcet there was something sacred in a representative body in which resided the mystical "general will." The expulsion of the Girondins was an act of violence, not merely against individuals, but against the nation itself, which could not be justified at any time and under any circumstances. He bitterly denounced the Jacobin constitution as a perversion and a corruption of his project. It was brief, he said, because it surmounted difficulties by avoiding them. Among the many defects of the new constitution the most serious one was, according to Condorcet, a lack of sufficient guarantees to insure individual liberty.

It became known that Condorcet was the author of the pamphlet which the Convention stigmatized as an act of high treason. In denouncing the Jacobin constitution Condorcet openly identified himself with the Girondins. Although he was the author of the Girondin constitution, he was not considered a member of that party, and had, therefore, not been expelled from the Convention. Knowing his honesty and his political incapacity the Jacobins would have suffered him to live, had he not roused their ire by attacking their constitution. On July 8, 1793, Chabot, a Jacobin deputy, bitterly denounced Condorcet's pamphlet as seditious, and moved for the arrest of its author. "This man," declared Chabot, "who because he has sat among the learned in the Academy imagines that he has the right to give laws to the French Republic." [67] The Convention passed the motion of Chabot, adding Condorcet's name to the list of the proscribed.

The last days of Condorcet were pathetic, tragic, and unexpectedly fruitful. Friends of the proscribed man found a place of refuge for him in a pension kept by a Madame

Vernet, where he was hidden for nine months. The family was now in dire need, and Madame Condorcet supported herself, her husband, and their daughter by painting miniatures and by selling lingerie.

In his retreat, at Madame Vernet's, Condorcet began writing a justification of his acts during the Revolution. But he was dissuaded from continuing it by his wife, and the document remains an incompleted fragment.[68] It seemed petty and personal to the large-souled philosophe to justify himself before mankind; rather would he justify mankind itself. Inspired by this motive Condorcet wrote, with little aid from books and notes, the work for which he is chiefly remembered, *Sketch of the Intellectual Progress of Mankind*,[69] the leading motif of which is the idea of social progress, or the unlimited perfectibility of mankind. If anyone wishes a modern instance comparable to Socrates calmly discoursing philosophy, while awaiting death in his prison cell, he could find it in Condorcet calmly writing on the perfectibility of mankind under the shadow of the guillotine. The true greatness of the philosophe was never more evident than in his attitude toward the Revolution which now threatened to destroy him. "I have the good fortune," he declared, "to write in a country in which neither fear, nor expectation, nor respect for national prejudices has the power to suppress or to veil any universal truth. . . . There now exists a country where philosophy can offer to truth a homage pure and free, a worship purged of all superstition, hence a description of the progress of mankind can be written with complete freedom." [70]

Condorcet did not turn reactionary because the French Revolution had not gone his way. Although he hated terrorism and violence with all his heart, he knew what had raised the specter, "what passion and weakness gave to it substance, and he knew that presently reason would banish it and restore men to a right mind. The scientific spirit implanted in such a character as Condorcet's and made robust by social meditation builds up an impregnable fortitude in the face of incessant rebuffs and discouragements." [71]

When Condorcet received news of the execution of the Girondins he became concerned, not about himself, but about his benefactress, Madame Vernet, who was violating the law in harboring a refugee. If he was discovered in her house she, as well as he, would be dragged to the guillotine. Condorcet told Madame Vernet that he would leave her pension. But that brave and generous woman refused to hear of it. "The Convention has the power to put you outside the law (*hors de loi*), but it has not the power to put you outside of humanity. You will remain," she told him.[72]

As the situation became more serious Condorcet was determined not to endanger his benefactress by remaining any longer under her roof. He made efforts to escape from his retreat, which were, however, foiled by Madame Vernet who kept a watchful eye on her guest. The eighteenth-century belief in the essential goodness of human nature was strikingly illustrated by Condorcet and Madame Vernet under the Terror. He wanted to leave the pension because of the danger to *her;* and she refused to let him do so because of the danger to *him.*

One day Condorcet managed to elude his watchful benefactress, and escaped from her house in disguise. For several days he wandered about the quarries in Clamart, outside of Paris, half-starved, footsore, with a copy of Horace in his pocket. Famished he entered an inn and asked for food. His plight and his unusual appearance aroused suspicion. He was arrested as a suspect, and lodged in the prison of Bourgla-Reine. The next morning (March 28, 1794) Condorcet was found dead. According to his biographer, Arago, he had cheated the guillotine by swallowing poison which, it was said, he had carried in a ring.[73] But the medical officer, who examined his body, certified that Condorcet had died of a blood congestion which might have been brought on by exposure, hunger, and mental anguish.

The news of Condorcet's pathetic end caused considerable feeling in the Convention, which was now stirred to compassion for the *philosophe infortuné*. Perhaps to atone for its act in proscribing him the Convention ordered the publication and the distribution of Condorcet's last work, *Sketch of the Intellectual Progress of Mankind*. The book seemed like a legacy which the last of the philosophes had left to his fellow countrymen.

Judged by the standard of definite accomplishment Condorcet's career during the French Revolution was a failure. "None of his views were accepted by his contemporaries; neither was his constitution, nor his system of education. He was able neither to control the Girondins nor to prevent their proscription." [74] This is the judgment of his authoritative biographer, Léon Cahen. Condorcet's attitude toward the great questions that confronted him was typical of the philosophe mentality in that he endeavored to solve practical problems, not by the logic of events, but by the logic of abstract ideas. The French Revolution was, to Condorcet, a struggle between enlightened opinion and unreasoning prejudice, and it would begin and end with the spoken and written word, now at last unshackled. He never really understood the nature of the irreconcilable conflict of interests that the French Revolution had roused, nor the mad passions that it had unleashed. In the very midst of the swift and tumultuous events of the Revolution, Condorcet played an individual part; he had neither a party in the legislature nor a mob in the street to support him.

There was another cause for Condorcet's failure as a revolutionist, and that was his lack of psychological insight into human motives and conduct. He was as impersonal in his human relations as he was abstract in his thought, and therefore he had no understanding of the personal side of the internecine struggle among the leaders of the Revolution, Danton, Marat, Robespierre, and Hébert. The French Revolution, like all revolutions, was fertile in producing leaders whose will to power was their primal urge, and who did not hesitate to destroy ruthlessly anyone who barred their way.

It was Condorcet's altruism, not his revolutionary propensities, that caused him to forward the agitation which led to the Revolution. It was again his altruism which caused him to become active in the Revolution during its pacific stages. Never in all his life did he visualize the Goddess of Liberty as a mad fury, and he was, therefore, bewildered at the turn of events during the Reign of Terror. The attitude of the royalists he could understand; they were just "unenlightened." But the Jacobins completely puzzled him because they, like himself, were children of the Age of Reason, and devout believers in the rights of man.

As a true liberal, Condorcet was willing to go any distance under the guidance of reason, even to the establishment of a completely democratic republic. But terrorism could have no place in any scheme of things motivated by reason. When, in 1793, the French Revolution became an open conflict between class interests, common action on the part of those who believed in the abstract principles of the rights of man became impossible. As a consequence Condorcet and the Girondins, who had proclaimed the revolutionary Republic, were destroyed by the Jacobins to whom the Republic was primarily a weapon with which to destroy the aristocrats, not an ideal state to be erected as a model for mankind. In commenting on Condorcet's revolutionary career, Sainte-Beuve, in his essay on the philosophe, says truly that Condorcet was "one of those who make revolutions, who advance their progress, who hope everything from them, and who do not halt, except at the last moment, on the brink of the precipice, and who finally fall over it." [75]

CHAPTER SIX

POLITICAL LIBERALISM

AMONG the pioneers of political liberalism in eighteenth-century France, Condorcet was a notable, if not a great, figure. He was fully abreast of the most advanced of his contemporaries by advocating freedom of speech, constitutional government, religious toleration, freedom of labor and of industry, abolition of slavery, and universal peace. But of him only, of all the philosophes, can it be said that he anticipated the advanced liberalism of the nineteenth and twentieth centuries by advocating the rights of women, universal free education in all grades, universal suffrage, proportional representation, republicanism, separation of church and state, and social legislation. And it is by reading Condorcet "more than by reading Voltaire, and even Montesquieu and Rousseau, that we can get an idea to what extent we are still profoundly the intellectual children of his age." [1]

The political task of the eighteenth century was to establish a system of government in harmony with the changing conditions in society. The demand for freedom of enterprise in the new economic order, which was arising, could be satisfied only by a system in which there was elasticity in the making of laws. Absolute monarchy, bound by custom and tradi-

POLITICAL LIBERALISM 111

tion, was unsuited to the task. Only a parliamentary system, chosen in demand to the changing wishes of the people, could function in harmony with the needs of the day.

Equality was the demand of the rising bourgeoisie. In a political system dominated by the landed aristocracy, as was the Old Régime, the bourgeois, having no privileges, could not attain supreme power. Only by establishing equality before the law, which meant the abolition of aristocratic privileges, could the bourgeois, as masters of the new economic order, attain power commensurate with their wealth.

In the writings of Condorcet can be found a system of political thought, elaborate and complete, which answered fully to the needs of his day. Like the other philosophes Condorcet sought to solve the great question that faced the eighteenth century, namely, how the Old Régime was to be abolished and how a new régime was to be established that would be enlightened and free. Like all the other philosophes he was opposed to violent revolution, but, unlike most of them, he had no faith in "enlightened despotism." In his essays, addresses, books, and projects Condorcet developed a logical and well-integrated system of political thought that comprehended political liberalism in all its aspects.[2]

There were three important elements in Condorcet's political system. First, was the adoption, by a national assembly, of a declaration of rights which would safeguard the liberties of the individual. Second, was the adoption of a constitution by a convention, especially chosen for that purpose, establishing a new system of government. Thirdly, a regular and periodic method of amending the constitution was to be adopted in order to assure the peaceful progress of the nation.

To Condorcet, as well as to his contemporaries, a declaration of rights was regarded as a political charm with which to ward off despotism. And such a declaration, to be potent, must be adopted by a national assembly representing the sovereign people. It was essential, according to Condorcet, that a declaration of rights should proclaim as inviolable:

1. Security of person. There must be no violent interference with the right of every individual to exercise all his faculties freely, provided he does not infringe upon the rights of others.

2. Security and free enjoyment of property.

3. No arbitrary interference with the course of justice. Every individual must obey those laws binding upon all.

4. The right to share in the making of laws, directly or indirectly, through representation.[3]

"From the moment," declared Condorcet, "man becomes a sentient being, able to reason and to form moral ideas, it inevitably and necessarily follows that he should enjoy these rights, which cannot be taken away from him without injustice."[4] In other words, man sprang from nature a political animal, fully endowed with rights that needed only to be declared, as, in a biological sense, he was born with capacities that needed only to be developed.

Condorcet fully shared the general belief of his day in the doctrine of natural rights, or the rights of man. "If there is a question of establishing liberty on the ruins of despotism, and equality on the ruins of aristocracy," he declared, "we would show wisdom in not looking for our rights in the Capitularies of Charlemagne or in the Ripuarian Code but we should look for them in the eternal laws of reason and of nature."[5] The doctrine of natural rights was concerned with the freedom of the individual who, it was believed, was endowed by nature with pure reason and by God with free will.

POLITICAL LIBERALISM 113

In the feudal scheme of society which, legally and philosophically, lasted until the French Revolution, the individual was recognized only as a member of a group: a corporation, a guild, an order, a class, each with its privileges and restrictions. To liberate the individual from the group Condorcet became the protagonist of individual freedom in all its aspects, political, economic, social, religious, and cultural. The individual was regarded by him as the depository of natural liberty whose rights were inviolable, "before whom the power of the state halts and in some way ceases to exist." [6]

As civil society was instituted to conserve natural rights the individual could realize his greatest good, liberty, only in society. And liberty increased with the spread of civilization through the greater use of reason.[7] Condorcet regarded civilization as "natural" as savagery; it was another, and higher, form of organization than savagery because civilized man was conscious of his rights. In the centuries of ignorance and prejudice that had succeeded the savage state, declared Condorcet, the rights of man had been forgotten; they were rediscovered and proclaimed by the scientists and philosophers of the era of enlightenment. To know when and where its liberties were being attacked, a people must possess a declaration of rights which, if "complete, well organized, and precise" was "the most useful work that could be offered to mankind." [8] According to Condorcet it was highly essential that the ideas, proclaimed by a declaration, should be clear and definite, and the language, precise and convincing. He complained that the language of the social sciences was imperfect, and he aimed to give a scientific character to these studies by giving them a precise language. He was very careful to define personal, social, and political liberty, adding discussions and explanations.[9]

According to Condorcet the edifice of a society of free and equal men should be built on reason, on rights that all have been endowed with by nature, and, finally, on the maxims of universal justice.[10] Wherever there was no declaration of rights and no representative assembly there was despotism, either direct or indirect.[11]

A declaration of rights was, moreover, to serve as the foundation on which to build a constitutional structure, the second pillar of Condorcet's political system. The adoption of a constitution meant not only a change from one system of government to another; it was also the opportunity of establishing a new political and social régime in harmony with the most enlightened thought of the day. Therefore, a constitution should be adopted by a body especially elected for that purpose, a constitutional convention. In this way the abstract doctrine of popular sovereignty would find concrete expression in an assembly that issued directly from the people with a mandate to establish a new government. Influenced by the American state and federal constitutions, and by the quickened pace of democracy during the French Revolution, Condorcet developed ideas of constitutional law, and worked out a scheme of constitutional government that anticipated the most advanced political thought of the nineteenth century.[12]

Fundamental in all his political thinking was the doctrine of popular sovereignty, proclaimed by Rousseau's *Social Contract*. Once this doctrine was accepted, Condorcet reasoned, the age-old distinction between the rulers and the ruled would disappear, and the reign of freedom would begin. Direct government by an assembly of citizens, as in the ancient city states, was impossible in large states like France; therefore, a representative assembly was the only method of popular government under modern conditions. Before the French Revolution Condorcet had criticized the Estates-General as not being a representative body because it was divided into orders. This division, he asserted, signified that the Estates-General was a body that represented the conquerors, the nobility, and the conquered, the commons.[13] The individual with his rights, not the order with its privileges, was the only basis of free government. Therefore, he favored a unicameral legislature, chosen by universal, equal suffrage. However, democratic government was not to be a mechanism to obtain a majority which would impose its will on the minority, a system which would continue the distinction between the rulers and the ruled. But, according to Condorcet, it was to be a mechanism, in his system of political science, to discover the right policies governments were to pursue in order to be in harmony with the fundamental laws that governed human relations.

Nothing was more characteristic of Condorcet than his search for absolute political truth. He was a Cartesian in that he believed that all men had the same universal reason implanted in their minds, and all that was necessary in order to arrive at the truth was a method of logical deduction from assumed premises. Therefore, he sought for absolute reason in what is perhaps the most irrational of all human activities, namely, popular elections. The unanimous decision of an enlightened representative body, chosen by an intelligent, literate, honest electorate, composed of all adult men and women, was to him the surest means of establishing the truth in government. However, there were certain essential conditions: those who had the right to decide must be enlightened, and the method to be applied must be simple.[14] Such an assembly, in Condorcet's constitution, was not to be brought into existence as a result of the struggle of political parties, the outcome of which gave evidence of superior strength, not of greater enlightenment. A representative assembly was to be the outcome of a full and free expression of opinion by the citizens who, in voting for representatives, indicated their view of what was the highest public good.

Condorcet sought to give mathematical precision to a system of voting by proposing a scheme of proportional representation which would give exact electoral strength to every shade of opinion.[15] A legislature, representing every shade of opinion, chosen by virtuous, intelligent citizens, would govern the nation. Obviously, a unanimous vote would not be possible. According to Condorcet, a majority vote was an approximation to the truth, and the larger the majority, the nearer the approximation. "A proposition upheld by fifteen persons," he declared, "is more probably right than an opposing proposition upheld by only ten."[16] A minority submitted to a majority solely because the latter was more likely to be "right." It was highly essential, therefore, that both the elector and the legislator should be motivated by public interests only. If they were motivated by special interests or by personal corruption, their decision would be deflected from the path of truth, and was, consequently, not valid. In this sense, the elector and the legislator were priests who, by voting, performed a political sacrament; and this sacrament was not valid when performed by polluted hands.

This method of arriving at political "truth" was prompted by Condorcet's passionate faith in the supremacy of public interest. He was convinced that the advancement of the public interest would inevitably result in the advancement of the

POLITICAL LIBERALISM

interest of every individual, hence the welfare of the nation should be the primary object of all citizens. In fact, the true interests of the individual and society were one and inseparable. By a "law of the moral world," the efforts of every individual to better himself inevitably conduced to the good of the whole, which required that each man should understand his interest and be permitted to pursue it freely. And a system of society should be established whose laws and institutions would bring into harmony the welfare of the nation and the interests of the individuals composing it.[17]

Nothing was a better illustration of eighteenth-century thought than Condorcet's search for absolute truth in the social sciences. "Considering the nature of the moral (social) sciences," he declared, "one cannot help seeing that, if based, like the natural sciences, on the observation of facts they would follow the same method, acquire a vocabulary equally precise, and attain an equal degree of certitude. One, not of our species, would be able to study human society as unemotionally as we study the society of beavers or of bees. A great difficulty arises in the fact that the observer is part of what he observes, and truth cannot be judged by those who are prejudiced or corrupt. That is why the progress of the social sciences has been slower than that of the physical sciences."[18] However, there was a way out of the difficulty, according to Condorcet, and that was to discover the fundamental laws of society by a method known, in the eighteenth century, as social mathematics, or "political arithmetic," and in the nineteenth century, as statistics.

Mathematics appealed powerfully to the eighteenth-century mind because it was abstract, scientific, and capable of arriving at absolute truth. "I turn to geometry for complete nourishment. There is the only place in the world where everything goes well," wrote Condorcet to Turgot.[19] His early training as a mathematician may, in all likelihood, have inclined Condorcet to apply mathematical methods to the study of the social sciences. Reason, Condorcet believed, was insufficient as a guide to truth when different conclusions could be drawn from a given set of circumstances, hence the element of probability required the aid of mathematics.[20] He was greatly interested in the theory of probability, a subject for speculation in his day, and even before, notably by Sir William Petty, Pascal, Jacques Bernoulli, and Quesnay.[21] In his two essays, *Essai sur l'application de l'analyse* and *Tableau générale de la Science*,[22] Condorcet worked out a highly complicated mathematical system to determine the probability of the "truth" of decisions arrived at by public bodies. "Whatever certitude one can have," he declared, "is based on the natural tendency to regard as constant what one sees repeated a great number of times." [23] He was convinced that all judgments rested on the degree of the probability of these judgments being right. "The reason for believing that, out of 6,000,000 white balls and one black one, it will not be the black one that I would draw first is the same as the reason for believing that the sun will not fail to rise tomorrow. They differ only in being more or less probable." [24] The welfare of the nation was not to be left subject to chance policies, the outcome often of enthusiasm or of prejudice. Wise policies could be determined mathematically on the theory of probability. Given citizens and legislators, purged of ignorance by knowledge, of prejudice by enlightenment, and of selfishness by altruism, and the way would be clear for absolute truth to dictate their decisions.

Especially important was general enlightenment. If the "people are enlightened their representatives, under some circumstances, are sure to be right."[25] How about the possibility of corrupt and prejudiced men participating in this decision? The answer of Condorcet was to increase the size of the deciding body in order to diminish their influence, which would maintain the degree of probability of the truth of the decision by that body.[26] "It is plainly an infallible council that he divined and sought to convoke."[27]

The application of probability was not to be limited to political decisions. Condorcet clearly indicated that the function of statistics was to discover the social laws that governed all human relations. Some of the things that might be determined in this way would be the death rate, longevity, and rates for marine insurance.[28] Without the scientific precision given by mathematics, he declared, new errors were likely to be created because of enthusiasm for a cause.

In the light of his views on probability, Condorcet's emphasis on the importance of precision in defining abstract political ideas and in formulating declarations of rights becomes clear. To him such definitions and declarations were like the definitions of scientific terms and the statement of scientific laws. Like the laws of nature, the laws of man were universal "as truth, reason, justice, the rights of man, the interest of property, of liberty of security are everywhere the same. One cannot see why every nation should not have the same civil, the same criminal, and the same commercial laws. A good law ought to be good for all men as an axiom is true for all men."[29]

In his search for absolute truth in the sphere of government, Condorcet came upon the problem of representation. What constituted a representative assembly? One answer was given by the English parliament, with its hereditary House of Lords, and its House of Commons, elected by a narrow, propertied suffrage. This answer did not at all suit the democrat Condorcet. If he was opposed to a limited suffrage, he was even more opposed to an hereditary legislature which, in his view, was the very quintessence of privilege, hence a violation of natural rights.[30] In his Declaration of Rights he denounced heredity in office as absurd and tyrannical.[31] All public officials should be salaried, he declared, otherwise the rich would have the advantage of getting honorable distinction. "To serve without pay is not always a proof of disinterestedness," he observed.[32]

In a pamphlet, written in 1789, he came out flatly in favor of a unicameral legislature in his scheme of constitutional government.[33] If both houses are chosen the same way, he argued, a bicameral legislature confuses the popular will. He demonstrated, by a series of mathematical computations, that a majority in the smaller house could defeat legislation, favored by a majority in the larger house. A law, passed by a majority in each house, might be enacted by a minority of the members of both the smaller and the larger houses. A bicameral legislature facilitated corruption because it was easy to bribe a few members in the smaller house in order to get a majority. If the upper house was hereditary or made up of rich men, it would result in perpetual abuses; and if made up of distinguished citizens, it would eventually become a self-perpetuating oligarchy.[34] An upper house, in his opinion, merely clogged the wheels of legislation or constituted a dangerous aristocratic irritation.

Condorcet's political views were wholly democratic, but his temperament, like that of many another liberal, was moderate and cautious. He desired some check on a popular legislature in order to prevent hasty action, and, therefore, favored the establishment of a council of state, composed of distinguished citizens, which would have a suspensive veto over measures passed by the legislature, but for a limited time. This council would have the power to withhold its approval of measures for two successive times, and no more, in order to compel the legislature to reconsider them. Such a body, Condorcet believed, would have all the good, but none of the evil, of an upper house. Curiously enough, the position of the British House of Lords, as defined by the Parliament Act of 1911, is in harmony with Condorcet's views as to the powers of an upper house.[35] Opposition to a unicameral legislature, asserted Condorcet, was based on the fear that the unlimited power vested in one body might constitute a danger to the rights of the individual, but this evil could be avoided by a declaration of rights, by periodic revisions of the constitution, and by a referendum. A unicameral legislature, elected by universal, equal suffrage, was a method by which representative government could be reconciled with direct government which, according to Rousseau, was the only true way of expressing the general will.

Condorcet's advocacy of a unicameral parliament was in harmony with the advanced political thought in France. In the clash of interests between the aristocracy and the bourgeoisie, a bicameral parliament would give power to the former in the upper house to thwart the will of the latter in the lower house. This was evident when the Estates-General convened in 1789. It was the desire to wield supreme power in legislation which caused the Third Estate to set itself up as a single-chamber Constituent Assembly. And both the constitution of 1791 and that of 1793 provided for unicameral parliaments.

An ideal constitution, according to Condorcet, would not only provide for a unicameral legislature, but also for the union of the legislative, executive, and judicial powers of government. His views were directly opposed to the doctrine of the separation of powers, enunciated by Montesquieu, which attained immense influence in eighteenth-century political thought. It was then almost universally regarded as the very touchstone of political freedom. England which, according to Montesquieu, was the only nation that had a system of government based on this doctrine, was hailed as the Promised Land wherein liberty and authority were reconciled. However, Condorcet saw in the system of checks and balances a method of checking popular will through its complexity and clumsiness. Each power in the government, he argued, was, in this system, reduced to inertia by the mutual resistance of all of the separated powers. He compared the system of checks and balances to a slave serving two masters when he would be happier with only one.[36] Condorcet attributed the clumsiness of the system to the unconscious desire of its creators to control it by confusing the people. "Every profession has its own peculiar type of charlatan," he observed. "Some politicians appear to regard their ideas and methods as a sort of occult knowledge which they alone understand. It is self-interest which inspires them to take this attitude. The more complicated the constitution the more opportunities they have for sophistry and intrigue." [37] The declared object of the system of separation of powers was to establish equilibrium in the government; to defend its special interests, each power became the defender of liberty against the usurpations of the others. But, argued Condorcet, experience "has proved that either the machine becomes so complicated that its actions are clogged or that alongside the legally established system there arises another one based on intrigue, corruption, and indifference. In a sense there are now two constitutions: one, public and legal, that exists in law books only; and another one, secret but real, which is the outcome of a silent understanding among the powers that be." [38]

This observation of Condorcet was astonishingly keen.[39] It came from an understanding of the English political system in the eighteenth century that was far more profound than that of Montesquieu. In his *Spirit of Laws*, Montesquieu had held up the English government as a model of political liberty because, as he believed, it maintained a system of separation of powers and "checks and balances." In respect to England as a Promised Land Condorcet was a heretic among the philosophes. He caustically pointed out the weak spots in the English political system, which became only too clear to his fellow-countrymen during the French Revolution. In his view the parliamentary system in England was a façade, behind which an oligarchy ruled the nation, and was an illustration of what he termed "indirect despotism." The Commons which "legally represents the people," he declared, "really does not do so because it is an aristocratic assembly which is controlled by forty or fifty ministers, peers, and commoners." [40] The system of "checks and balances" and separation of powers safeguarded, not liberty, but the "authority of the rich, the noble, the magistrate, and the priest." [41] It was established to balance the conflicting interests of the landed aristocracy and the commercial class. The English nation was not aware of the fact, he asserted, that when its government functioned, despite the checks and balances, it was because harmony had been established between these interests.[42] And this harmony arose from parliamentary corruption. In order to have parliament do his bidding the king, through his ministers, used bribery and patronage to influence the votes of the members, thereby creating harmony between the executive and legislative powers. This system of "indirect despotism" was upheld by the English because they were self-enslaved by "a superstitious respect for their constitution and for certain laws to which they attribute their national prosperity. A servile worship of certain principles, which are in the interests of the rich and the powerful, forms part of English education, and is maintained by all who aspire to fortune and to power. These principles have become a sort of political religion which makes almost impossible a reform of the constitution and the laws of England." [43] Condorcet made a sarcastic comment on the relation between Bible reading and the government in England. "The habit of adoring the mysteries of the Bible has fortified the faith of the English in the mysteries of their constitution." [44] The politicians of both political parties pretended to have respect for the established faith, and encouraged religious fanaticism in order to use it, each in turn, for their purposes.[45]

It is quite astonishing that so complete an ideologue, as Condorcet, should have entertained such realistic views of a political system that was the hope of libertarian France. It may be explained on the ground that he was not only a political philosopher, but also an active reformer and revolutionist, which Montesquieu was not. Condorcet's activities, before and during the French Revolution, had the effect of giving him an insight into the practical workings of political systems that, not infrequently, gave a realistic turn to his abstract ideas.

There was another aspect of the system of separation of powers that drew sharp criticism from Condorcet, and that was the power of the judiciary. "Judicial despotism," he declared, "is the most odious of all despotisms because it makes use of the most respectable means, the law, to maintain itself." [46] Other despotisms may become tolerable in lands where customs are mild, but not so judicial despotism "which maintains outrageous laws even in those lands where customs are mild and tolerant." The judges, therefore, should be elected for definite terms of office.[47] He saw clearly that where the judiciary constituted one of the powers of government, they did not restrict themselves to jurisprudence, but "sought to encroach on the other powers of government by pretending that their sanction is necessary for the validity of laws. This legislative power, joined to their extensive judicial functions, would create a situation incompatible with liberty." [48] These views of Condorcet on the tendency of the judiciary to arrogate to itself legislative powers exhibit again his political clairvoyance. The history of the judicial review in the United States goes far to substantiate the soundness of his judgment.

Condorcet's hostility to the judiciary arose from his opposition to the parlements of the Old Régime, the body of judges who had originally purchased their judicial office from the king and whose tenure was hereditary. The parlements often attracted attention by refusing to register royal decrees and issuing protests, explaining their refusals on the ground that such decrees were a violation of the "fundamental laws" of the kingdom. The king could, however, override their veto by summoning the judges to a *lit de justice*, and commanding them to register an objectionable decree.[49] In a sense the parlements constituted an independent judiciary, but their independence was generally exercised when the king proposed to lay taxes that would come out of the pockets of the class to which they belonged, the upper bourgeoisie. Their opposition to royal despotism often made popu lar heroes of a judicial oligarchy that was dominated by narrow class interests, by religious intolerance, and by hatred of freedom of thought. The parlements were bitterly hated by the philosophes as narrow-minded Jansenists who had sent Calas and de la Barre to their deaths; who had condemned famous books, such as Voltaire's *Letters on the English,* Diderot's *Letters on the Blind,* Buffon's *Natural History* and Rousseau's *Emile.* "These parlements," declared d'Alembert, "are very unworthy of the favorable opinion that foreigners have formed of them. They are, if possible, more degraded than even the clergy in that they are governed by an intolerant and persecuting spirit." [50]

Condorcet shared, in full, the hatred of the philosophes for the judicial oligarchy. He denounced them as an hereditary caste that lived from justice as from a business; and as a narrow, greedy oligarchy that exercised a terrible power in the nation. Unlike Montesquieu, Condorcet saw in the parlements, not a body of judges, but a power in the government of France that was strong enough to defy an autocratic divine-right monarch.

Profoundly influenced by the idea of progress, Condorcet strove to establish a system of government which provided, above all other things, for a peaceful mechanism of change. This was the third pillar of his political structure. The problem that faced him was how to initiate change, not how to maintain stability which he identified with the evils of the Old Régime. Condorcet feared that the enlightened system which he proposed would, in time, become another old régime unless it was continually being reformed. The right to change the system of government, he declared, was the most important guarantee of progress, otherwise mankind would be "condemned to eternal infancy." [51] In the

POLITICAL LIBERALISM

past, men had regarded all change with apprehension, therefore they aimed "to establish systems which would prevent change rather than those which would provide for it." This attitude, due to fear of innovation, was one of the greatest evils that had afflicted mankind. Fear of change had caused man to regard systems of government with superstitious reverence. But mankind has now lost "the art of the ancient legislators to produce miracles and to inspire oracles. The Delphic oracle and the thunders of Sinai have long since been reduced to silence. Today, lawgivers are only men who can give to their fellow-men laws that are as transient as themselves." [52]

In framing a constitution it was, therefore, vitally important to provide for methods of revising it, in whole and in part, otherwise future generations would become the victims of the errors of their predecessors or of changing conditions.[53] Therefore, methods of amending a constitution were as important as the systems of government which were already established. In constitutional amendments Condorcet saw the peaceful equivalent of violent revolution. *C'était là son évangile,* remarks his biographer, Arago.[54] The mob violence during the French Revolution convinced Condorcet that the masses were interested in political questions, but constitutional methods were lacking whereby they could express their views peaceably, hence they resorted to rioting. Above all, he aimed "to establish a system of government by means of which the nation could express its desires on the need of any reform whatsoever, so that never would insurrection be necessary." [55] America, Condorcet believed, gave the conclusive answer to this question by providing for constitutional conventions, especially elected for the purpose of establishing and revising the fundamental law of the land.

Because of Condorcet's insistence on peaceful progress he has been erroneously characterized as a political evolutionist. The idea of evolution comprehends regular and necessary steps in progress, an idea which was not clearly formulated until the nineteenth century, largely as a result of the influence of Darwinism. Condorcet was a revolutionist of the eighteenth-century pattern in that he did not propose regular and necessary steps in the transition from the absolutism of the Old Régime to the libertarianism of a new régime. He shared the common view of the philosophes that an enlightened nation, by merely taking thought, could deliberately and quickly establish new laws and institutions. Such a change did not imply to Condorcet a violent break with the "past," but an adjustment of society to conform with universal reason and natural law.[56]

Condorcet's studies in political science contain many discussions which, today, would be described as constitutional law. He discusses such topics as delegated, reserved, and derived powers of government; the relations between the executive, the legislature, and the judiciary; individual rights; the right of suffrage; and constitutional limitations. It is possible that his study of the American state and federal constitutions, which he so greatly admired, may have been influential in casting his political ideas in the mold of constitutional law. Although his contributions to this subject have been exaggerated by his enthusiastic biographer, Alengry, Condorcet was undoubtedly one of the pioneers of constitutional law in France.[57]

Unlike his fellow philosophes Condorcet had an opportunity to apply his theories when the National Convention

POLITICAL LIBERALISM

appointed him chairman of a committee to draw up a constitution for the Republic. His political ideas, in their most mature form, took definite shape in the ill-starred Girondin constitution, into which went the political speculations of a lifetime.[58] Although it was rejected by the Convention its influence was plainly evident in the constitutions of 1793 and of the Year III.[59] Condorcet's project holds an important place in the history of political theories, as it contains innovations that anticipated some of the advanced political methods of the nineteenth and twentieth centuries.

What Condorcet aimed to do in this constitution, was: (1) to harmonize the direct democracy of ancient times with the representative democracy of modern times; (2) to protect the civil rights of the citizen by the most careful and precise guarantees; and (3) to maintain popular government in all its purity by all possible methods that political science could devise.

The constitution was preceded by a Declaration of Rights which, in the main, followed the Declaration of the Rights of Man and of the Citizen. But Condorcet's Declaration contained "rights" not envisioned by its famous predecessor. He emphatically states that: "Elementary education is the need of all, and society owes it equally to all its members." "Public assistance is a sacred debt of society; law should determine its extent and its application." "A nation has always the right to revise and to reform its constitution. One generation has not the right to subject future generations to its laws. Heredity in office is absurd and tyrannical." [60]

France was to be a republic of the most advanced democratic type. Supreme power in the government was to be exercised by a unicameral legislature, the Assembly, elected by direct, universal, manhood suffrage for a term of one year.

This provision was a great advance over the suffrage provision in the constitution of 1791, which established indirect suffrage, based upon property qualifications. To each department in France was assigned a number of seats in proportion to population, one for every 50,000 inhabitants; and a reapportionment was to take place every ten years, a provision which, quite evidently, followed American precedent.

The electors were to be grouped into Primary Assemblies, each consisting of not less than 450 and not more than 900 members. These bodies were to be the bases of the political life of France, the "people," organized legally and functioning constitutionally. It was the deliberate intention of Condorcet to have the Primary Assemblies as a substitute for the violent, anarchic mobs which he so heartily detested. Every Assembly was to have the power of naturalizing foreigners by simply adding their names to the list of citizens; any foreigner who had lived in France for one year was eligible to citizenship.[61] By this liberal provision Condorcet emphasized the modern conception of nationality, proclaimed by the French Revolution, that it is an attribute of the inhabitants of a given territory not of a given racial group.

Nominations and elections for the national legislature were to be by the Primary Assemblies in each department. A list of candidates, three times the number of seats to be filled, was to be drawn up by a central office of the department, on the nomination of the Assemblies, and presented to the electors in each Primary Assembly in two columns, one being marked first choice, and the other, second choice. By a system of preferential voting, an innovation of Condorcet, the required number of representatives was to be elected.

Neither in the constitution itself nor in his speeches expounding it, did Condorcet suggest party government. In the eighteenth century there was no conception of party government, as it is understood today, neither in England nor on the Continent. The English Whigs and Tories were regarded as two cliques of nobles who ruled parliamentary England by means of public corruption, as, in absolutist France, court cliques ruled through intrigue and royal favor.

To the national legislature was given, not only complete power in the making of laws, but also complete control over foreign affairs. Every step in diplomatic relations from preliminary negotiations to the drafting of treaties, was to have the approval of the legislature; and to it, alone, was given the right to declare war. According to these provisions secret diplomacy, which had reached its apogée in the eighteenth century, was to be entirely abolished.

There was an important provision regarding local self-government of which Condorcet had long been a champion. The departments were to be divided into Great Communes, consisting of groupings of towns and villages, which were to be the local units of government, being given a large degree of autonomy. The scheme of the Great Communes was another innovation of Condorcet. It constituted his solution of the question that agitated France in 1793, whether the newly created Republic was to be federal, according to the Girondins, or centralized, according to the Jacobins.

The administration of the laws was confided to an Executive Council of thirteen members, elected by the people for two years. Each department was to recommend a number of candidates to the national legislature. From all the names the national legislature was to select a list of candidates who were to be voted for in the Primary Assemblies according to a system of preferential balloting. Condorcet was opposed to a single executive.[62] His proposal of an executive council, another innovation, was adopted by the constitution of 1793 and by that of Year III.

In effect, this scheme of a popularly elected executive provided for the separation of powers, and consequently, for a system of checks and balances which Condorcet had so often severely condemned. To justify it he made a subtle and rather strained distinction between a "power" and an "agent" in the sphere of government. The Executive Council, according to Condorcet, would not constitute a "power," separate from that of the Assembly, but would be merely its agent "in administering the laws."

Control over the finances was to be exercised by a special body of three members, the Treasury Commission, independent of the Executive Council, but elected in the same manner for a term of three years. Condorcet feared to give the Executive Council control over the finances, lest it use this control to increase its power. "It is important in a free government," he declared, "that the executive should not be concerned with the finances, except to receive the amount given to it by the legislature in order to meet the expenses of the government." [63]

Condorcet instituted another innovation, the *Droit de Censure,* or a popular veto of the acts of the national legislature. According to his scheme, any citizen, in a Primary Assembly, by getting the support of fifty fellow citizens, could initiate a referendum on any existing law, or on the promulgation of a new law, or on a constitutional change. If adopted by the Primary Assembly, the proposal was then submitted to the other Primary Assemblies in the Great Commune; and then to the Primary Assemblies of the department. If accepted by them, the proposal went to the national legislature which was to accept or to reject it. If rejected, and the rejection was opposed by a department other than the one that had initiated the proposal, all the Primary Assemblies in France were to be convoked in a referendum on it. Direct and representative government were reconciled by Condorcet through the people delegating legislative and executive power to elected bodies but maintaining a veto power by means of the *Droit de Censure*.[64]

The constitution was to be subjected to periodic amendment every twenty years by conventions especially elected for this purpose. Special constitutional conventions could be called, at any time, by the national legislature, supported by a referendum, or on the initiative of a citizen according to the procedure of the *Droit de Censure*.[65] All proposed constitutional changes were to be submitted to a referendum, which would conserve the complete sovereignty of the people; Condorcet's project itself was to be submitted to a referendum. By these methods constitutional changes could be made easily, and as rapidly as the people desired. To make the constitution difficult of amendment was to invite judicial interpretation, which Condorcet vehemently rejected. His constitution contained the following significant article: "The courts shall not participate in the exercise of the legislative power. They shall neither interpret the laws, nor extend them, nor veto them, nor suspend their execution. Neither shall they encroach on the executive nor cite officials before them on matters pertaining to their functions."[66] Constitutions, submitted to referenda, and laws, submitted to the "censure of the people," would constitute, according to Condorcet, the "legal means" of "resistance to oppression."

There were many provisions guaranteeing and protecting individual rights. These provisions were exceedingly detailed and were based largely upon American and English practices.

In this sphere, also, Condorcet made several innovations, such as the abolition of capital punishment for private crimes; and the convening of a popularly elected national jury to try high officers of state, accused of treason. To Condorcet a constitution was inconceivable without a Bill of Rights as an integral part of it. The function of a constitution was not merely to establish a free government; it was also to create free citizens. Like the fathers of the American constitution he unconsciously identified all government with despotism, and he was, therefore, careful to circumscribe its sphere and to enlarge that of the individual citizen.

Permeated by the cosmopolitan spirit of the eighteenth century, Condorcet designed his constitution as a model for any country at any time; only incidentally was it drawn up for France in 1793. It was utterly unlike the American constitution, with its compromises and its dependence on colonial practices; or even like the French constitution of 1791, with its class bias and monarchical compromise. The downfall of feudalism and of the monarchy had created France into a political *tabula rasa* upon which Condorcet felt free to write a model constitution. His project exhibited, in full, the peculiar qualities of its author: passionate adherence to abstract principles and a mathematical rigidity in applying them. The Cartesian method, applied to politics, found its legitimate exponent in the mathematician Condorcet, whose political principles were as abstract in their formulation, as inevitable in their logic, and as universal in their application as a theorem in geometry.

Condorcet's political philosophy, of which his constitution was the supreme example, was motivated by the idea that a mortal combat existed between prejudice, which is artificial and local, and reason, which is natural and universal. Political truths were as universal as moral truths, hence all nations should have the same laws. The methods of abolishing old laws and institutions, based on prejudices, might vary in different countries because prejudices varied in origin and in influence among different nations. But laws, which established an enlightened system, should be the same everywhere because they are based "on the nature of man and on his rights which are everywhere the same." [67] In other words, according to Condorcet, there were different kinds of prejudices but only one kind of enlightenment. In the dark past, men were divided, because of their prejudices; but in the glorious future they would be united through their enlightenment. And the glorious future of mankind began with the French Revolution with its vision of humanity living under institutions inspired by Liberty, Equality and Fraternity.

CHAPTER SEVEN

INTELLECTUAL AND SOCIAL LIBERALISM

CONSTITUTIONAL government was essentially government by public opinion. The machinery of representative institutions, elections, candidates, platforms, and political parties, obviously demanded freedom of speech and of the press. What is called "public opinion" arose to a considerable degree during the eighteenth century. The new libertarian spirit, created by the Intellectual Revolution, could not find full expression under the system of censorship of the Old Régime. Therefore, the philosophes sought to destroy this system, and to create another one in which a new ruler, public opinion, would arise as a consequence of complete intellectual freedom.

None of the philosophes was more convinced than was Condorcet that a liberal, political and economic order could arise only among people who were intellectually free, and whose social institutions were based on egalitarian principles. All institutions, according to Condorcet, owed their existence to "opinion"; the bad ones to "prejudice," or perverted opinion; and the good ones to "reason," or enlightened opinion. Even in autocratic countries opinion directed the policies of the monarch who could not institute reforms against popular prejudices and ancient customs.¹ What was most essential to human progress, therefore, was not to enlighten the ruler but to enlighten the people. A thorough and consistent democrat Condorcet repudiated the belief in "enlightened despotism," the bourgeois ideal so common among his fellow philosophes.

The formation of public opinion was, therefore, all important in Condorcet's scheme of things. And the chief function of writers, as a class, was to enlighten the masses because "every society which is not enlightened by philosophers is deceived by charlatans." ² Condorcet forcefully upheld the propagandist function of literature. "To spread important discoveries," he declared, "and to put them at the service of the greatest number, to direct to useful purposes the work of scholars should be the ambition of most authors." ³ When it was a question of attacking abuses and prejudices the author should present the truth "often and in different ways" in order to make an impression on the masses. "A single book suffices to establish the reputation of an author, but several are necessary to bring about a revolution in general opinion." ⁴ Voltaire was the great man who typified to Condorcet the new rôle of the writer as a reformer. Had it not been for Voltaire, he declared, liberty would have remained as it had been hitherto, "a secret among the wise." ⁵

Violent revolution as a method of progress Condorcet did not envisage at all. With an enlightened public opinion, he reasoned, progress becomes inevitable, so why resort to bloodshed and make uncertain the reforms which "time must surely bring without any sacrifices"? When a ruler violated the natural rights of the citizens had they the right to resist? Condorcet evaded the question by saying that while it was always useful to know one's rights, it was "not always wise to vindicate them, and every method of doing so was not legitimate." [6] His views on the Puritan Revolution and on the Revolution of 1688, in England, are instructive on this point. In his opinion the former was a movement, led by religious fanatics, against a moderate and enlightened monarch. Cromwell, it should be noted, is only a recent acquisition to the hall of famous libertarians. During the eighteenth century he was generally regarded as a usurping tyrant and superstitious fanatic. Let one consider the two revolutions, declared Condorcet, that of fanatical and that of enlightened England. "On the one hand were the contemporaries of Prynne and Knox who, while boasting that they were fighting for God and freedom, drenched their unhappy country with blood in order to establish the tyranny of the hypocrite Cromwell; and, on the other hand, were the contemporaries of Boyle and Newton whose pacific wisdom established the freest constitution that has yet existed in the world." [7] Hence, according to Condorcet, the bloodless Revolution of 1688 was the legitimate way of vindicating natural rights, whereas the violent uprising of the Puritans was not the legitimate way inasmuch as it resulted in tyranny and fanaticism.

The ideas and methods of Turgot were, to Condorcet, the very model of progressive statesmanship. In his biography of that eminent reformer he outlined a policy of liberalism. Those who desired to advance progress, he declared, should avoid: (1) everything which might disturb public tranquillity; (2) everything which might disturb, too violently, the condition of a large body of people; and (3) everything which would attack prejudices too openly and too violently.[8] It would doubtless be well to destroy all errors at once, but as it is impossible to do so "we ought to imitate a wise architect who, desiring to demolish a building and knowing how its parts are held together, demolishes it in such a manner that its

INTELLECTUAL, SOCIAL LIBERALISM 139

destruction does not prove dangerous." *Il ne suffit pas de faire le bien, il faut le bien faire.*[9]

However, Condorcet's liberalism did not entirely eschew violence. He made a distinction between a people vindicating its natural rights against oppressors, and a people who, having established their rights, desired to advance further on the road to freedom. In the first instance, insurrection was a sacred duty because there were no other means open to the citizens. During the French Revolution Condorcet applauded the taking of the Bastille, and defended the Parisian uprising of August 10, 1792, against the traitorous Louis XVI. But once representative institutions had been established, and the question was of "passing from a free system of government to a freer one. . . . When it is a question of giving to a people, already in possession of their fundamental rights the full enjoyment of the fruits of these rights . . . should not this transition, which is a matter of pure reason, be as peaceful as pure reason itself"?[10] A nation that has an assembly, with power to take all the necessary measures for its protection, plunged to its ruin if it resorted to violent methods. To make changes, no matter how drastic, in a constitutional manner, once a free régime was established, has been the distinctively liberal way of progress.

There was one guarantee of peaceful progress, according to Condorcet, and that was liberty of speech and of the press. Once freedom of opinion is granted, Condorcet declared, "the truth inevitably succeeds in establishing itself. It is in the very nature of things that error is transitory, and truth, eternal."[11] The only way to ameliorate the lot of mankind was to accelerate the progress of enlightenment. All other means produced results that were only transient and limited. A free press, Condorcet declared, was the only means that a legislator possessed "of being served by those who are enlightened." [12] As a rule more harm was done by those who governed through their ignorance than by those who governed through their wickedness. And it was especially necessary that the government should know the views of the opposition; and for this purpose "books are better than spies." [13]

With the advent of printing, argued Condorcet, censorship became impossible because it could be easily evaded in all sorts of ways. The official burning of a book did not destroy it; on the contrary, it advertised the author. "The actual danger (of the censorship) is so little that it frightens no one; but the seeming danger is sufficient to give publicity." And to have their books suppressed was the great ambition of mediocre writers, who were the ones to flourish under a censorship. Furthermore, the censorship really helped to spread those very doctrines that it wished to suppress. "So popular are attacks on conservative views that authors frequently turn aside from their special subject in order to make such attacks, and, as a consequence, many readers become familiar with radical views who, otherwise, might never have heard of them." [14] Another evil, produced by censorship, was that it encouraged extreme views. The wider publicity, generally given to extreme views, acted as an inducement to express them. Freedom of speech, on the contrary, tended to promote moderation. In his biography of Voltaire, Condorcet excused Voltaire's practice of disavowing his books in order to evade the censorship on the ground that the blame really lay on "those unjust men who make such a disavowal necessary to the safety of the author, who is thereby compelled to make it." [15]

There should be no limitations to freedom of speech when

addressed to reason. According to Condorcet, anyone should have a perfect right to criticize and to question, not only the laws, but the system of government itself. But when the writer appealed to the passions by inciting his readers to revolt he should be punished for sedition. Condorcet commended Queen Elizabeth for prohibiting unlicensed preaching on the ground that these preachers incited their hearers to rebellion.[16]

Condorcet's liberalism was nowhere more clearly manifested than in his plea for the same freedom of thought in the social sciences as in the natural sciences. No one is forbidden, he argued, to attack the theories of geometry, of mining, and of anatomy; to say that arsenic is not a poison; and that inoculation is not useful. Why, then, should not the same tolerance be extended to religion, to politics, and to morals? "Is it because that truth in these matters is not susceptible to proof? Or is there a tacit avowal that, in these matters, one does not himself believe the opinions that he wishes to see accepted?"[17] From his day to our own the same pleas have been made by liberals who see in economics, history, politics, and sociology merely fields of scientific investigation. In the struggle for freedom of thought, Condorcet failed to realize that it was primarily a weapon of attack, not an abstract ideal. In the eighteenth century the social sciences were the battlefield of opposing interests. Under the Old Régime freedom of speech meant freedom to destroy the social and political order; and every class and every group that derived benefit from it was opposed to freedom of speech. Free investigation and discussion would reveal not, as the philosophes believed, the basic harmony but the basic conflict of the interests in the caste-ridden autocratically governed Old Régime. There could be freedom of thought in geometry, but, as Hobbes has so well observed "if it had been a thing contrary to any man's right of dominion, That the three Angles of a Triangle should be equall to two Angles of a Square; that doctrine should have been, if not disputed, yet by the burning of all books of Geometry, surpressed, as farre as he whom it concerned was able." [18]

Intellectual freedom, to Condorcet, was the best method of promoting social reforms of all kinds, in which he was intensely interested. There was hardly an evil in his day that did not rouse him to war against it. That man was naturally good, and that evil came as a result of bad institutions and laws, it will be recalled, was a cardinal doctrine of the philosophes. What about the criminal who deliberately committed evil deeds? Was he, too, a product of bad institutions and laws? The answer was an unqualified "yes." In the writings of the famous criminal law reformers, Montesquieu, Beccaria, and Bentham, the burden of the attack is on the criminal code, not on the criminal. The savage punishments, meted out to criminals in the eighteenth century, were out of all proportion to the crimes that they had committed. Hundreds of crimes were made capital offenses. The methods of trial were borrowed from the tribunals of the Inquisition. "Confessions" were extorted by means of torture; secret accusations and arbitrary arrests were permitted; and in the prisons were men who did not even know with what crimes they had been charged.

In his views on crime and punishment, Condorcet echoed those of Montesquieu and Beccaria.[19] Punishment, he declared, was legitimate only when it was sufficient to deter crime; its severity must, therefore, be measured by the seriousness of the offense. "Certainty of punishment makes a greater impression on one who is tempted to commit a crime . . .

than the severity of the code and the cruelty of the punishment." [20] To Condorcet the criminal code was based, like the other evils of the Old Régime, "on the idea that the poor and weak should be punished in order that the rich and powerful should live in tranquillity." [21] One of the striking reforms that he advocated was the establishment of a "public defender" for those, accused of crime, who had no means to engage an advocate.[22] Condorcet inveighed against the severity of the laws against the smuggling of salt (*faux saunier*) which, he declared, did not prevent the practice because the laws, not the violators, were popularly regarded as evil. "There were many violators because those who smuggled salt felt fairly certain of escaping punishment because they had all the citizens as protectors or as fellow conspirators." [23]

Condorcet was an ardent and eloquent champion of the abolition of capital punishment for private crimes. All punishment, he argued, should be capable of extension and contraction, such as imprisonment and forced labor. But the death penalty was absolute, and, therefore, made possible an act of irreparable injustice; there was always a possibility that the condemned might be innocent. The abolition of capital punishment would be "one of the most efficacious methods in the process of perfecting mankind; it would destroy the tendency to ferocity that, for so long, has dishonored it." [24] His project of a constitution for the French Republic contained a provision abolishing the death penalty for all private crimes.

Even more important than the abolition of capital punishment, as a step in the progress of mankind, was the abolition of war. During the eighteenth century wars of all kinds took place, dynastic, territorial, commercial, and colonial. These conflicts culminated in the Seven Years' War, which was a world war involving Europe, Asia, and America. The wars of the eighteenth century were not national and popular, like those of the nineteenth and twentieth centuries. They were generally waged by small professional armies who fought for pay and booty; the people at home were ignorant of what was going on at the front, and often indifferent as to the outcome. A defeat was considered a setback for the monarch who suffered it, not a national humiliation.

However, the wars were costly, and the people were taxed to support them. Discontent was widespread, and the monarchs were blamed for engaging in wars that were ruinous to their subjects. A pacifist movement appeared in the eighteenth century which found expression in many plans for universal peace, the most famous of which were Abbé Saint-Pierre's *Abrégé du projet paix perpétuelle*, Rousseau's *Jugement sur la Paix Perpétuelle*, and Kant's *Ewige Friede*. Anti-war sentiment was widespread in Europe, especially among the educated classes who were cosmopolitan in spirit. Although nations had appeared, the spirit of nationalism among the peoples of the Continent was almost as weak in united countries, like France and Spain, as in divided countries, like Germany and Italy. The inhabitants of the various provinces in united France had their own laws, their own customs, their own tariffs, and distinctive characteristics, much as did the inhabitants of the various states in divided Germany. To be a Frenchman in the eighteenth century meant merely a civil status, that one was a subject of the king of France. It did not mean, as it does today, a state of exaltation and mystic communion with the Fatherland. The Frenchman, Voltaire, had as little nationalistic sentiment as did the German, Goethe.

Although of old French noble stock, Condorcet's loves and hates centered about systems and ideas, not about nations

INTELLECTUAL, SOCIAL LIBERALISM 145

and races. Hardly a trace of nationalistic sentiment is to be found in all of his writings. On the contrary, they are saturated with a cosmopolitan outlook, and even with distrust of patriotism itself. "If hatred for foreigners is mingled with patriotism," he declared, "it encourages continuous warfare. If one mingles the love of old customs with national views, patriotism becomes a source of opposition to useful reforms, hence an instrument in the hands of the secret enemies of the nation." [25] Temperamentally grave, almost to the point of solemnity, Condorcet was yet stirred to sarcasm when speaking of nationalism. Some believe, he declared, that it is useful to employ superstitions in order to advance the national cause; for example, the superstition that one who dies for his country is eternally happy. "Strong drink has the same power, yet it would be ridiculous to make drunkenness as a political principle. However, it might be a lesser evil, for drunkenness is less shameful than superstition. Drunken soldiers on the day of battle can be reasonable men on the day after, but fanatical soldiers will never be anything else than dangerous lunatics." [26]

The cosmopolitan spirit of the eighteenth century made it easier to spread sentiments of universal peace. Among the philosophes there was an intense hatred of war and of militarism. "The military spirit," declared Condorcet, "is not a passion to defend unto death our friends and Fatherland; it is rather a science to destroy men. It inspires slaves to kill anyone, when commanded, at the first sound of the drum; it destroys all moral sentiments, and substitutes, in their place, mechanical obedience." [27] War was a relic of barbarism that found favor only among those who were not enlightened. Even the most legitimate and the most just war would inspire all men with horror and repugnance, "were it not for the fact that prejudices had enfeebled the natural sentiments of humanity and the power of reason." [28] Despite his horror of war, Condorcet realized the necessity of having armed forces to defend the nation. But, in his opinion, a standing army was incompatible with popular government. The solution that he favored was a system of popular militia, such as existed in America where, he believed, militarism was unknown. A nation, having only a popular militia, would temporarily be at a disadvantage in fighting an opponent with a standing army. In the end, however, the enthusiasm and patriotism of a volunteer army would be more than a match for disciplined regular forces.[29] The truth of these views was borne out in the great victories of the volunteers of the French Revolution over the regular armies of Prussia and Austria.

Condorcet's pacifism was inspired by his economic views as well as by his humanitarianism. As a Physiocrat he favored universal free trade which had, as its corollary, universal peace. Like the free traders in the nineteenth century, Cobden and Bright, the Physiocrats believed that wars were due to national trade rivalries which were engendered by restrictive policies, based on the theory that one nation's prosperity meant another nation's adversity. "It is not in a nation's interest," declared Condorcet, "to attack another nation, to restrict its liberty, and to seize part of its commerce. In general, it may be said that the interest of one nation is in harmony with the common interest of all nations, just as the enlightened interest of an individual is in harmony with the common interest of society." [30]

Unlike Saint-Pierre and Rousseau, Condorcet proposed no general peace plan. On the contrary, he derided those who did so as men who were incapable of a statesmanlike approach to the problem. What was necessary, he declared, were not projects of perpetual peace, "which have occupied the leisure and consoled the souls of some philosophers," but new institutions and a sentiment of internationalism which would bind nations together.[31] The idea must be spread that no one, except a few generals and ministers, gain anything as a result of even the most successful war. In order to decide territorial disputes, which were the cause of the dynastic wars in the eighteenth century, Condorcet suggested that a plebiscite of the inhabitants, not dynastic claims, should determine the fate of disputed territory.[32] He also suggested the establishment of a world court with power to judge international disputes. Such a court "would destroy the seeds of war by establishing strong bonds among the nations in times of peace."[33] Condorcet's views on the value of a world court anticipated the views of those who, today, believe that the greatest value of the existing World Court and the League of Nations lies in the strengthening of the bonds of union among the nations by accustoming them to common action, no matter how unimportant. In times of crisis, these bodies could function as an honorable alternative to war or to the loss of national dignity.

As a leading member of the Legislative Assembly, in 1792, when France declared war against Austria, the pacifist Condorcet was suddenly placed in a quandary. He had always believed that a nation was justified in going to war to defend itself against invasion. But it was France who now took the aggressive step of declaring war. He came to the conclusion that France was waging war to defend the French Revolution, and was, therefore, justified in declaring war against Austria who was preparing to come to the aid of Louis XVI. "I voted for war, though detesting it, because war was the only means of foiling the plots of a conspiring court."[34]

If war, to Condorcet, was a relic of barbarism, even more so was slavery. One of the unfortunate results of the discovery of the New World was the revival of slavery, which had long been extinct in western Europe. The need for a large number of men, accustomed to living in a tropical climate, to labor on the sugar and tobacco plantations of America was responsible for a flourishing slave trade that was as lucrative as it was nefarious. Slavers seized or bought Negroes on the western coast of Africa, and shipped them to America where they were sold to the planters.

Slavery and the slave trade shocked the humanitarian conscience of the eighteenth century. Anti-slavery societies were formed in England and in France that agitated in favor of the emancipation of the Negro. Condorcet was active in this agitation, and became the president of a French anti-slavery association, the Friends of the Negro. In 1781 he published a pamphlet, *Reflections on Negro Slavery*,[35] which was an eloquent and devastating indictment of slavery. When the elections for the Estates-General were taking place, Condorcet issued an appeal to the voters to demand the abolition of slavery in San Domingo, then a French possession.[36] When the National Assembly was organized, he appealed to that body to exclude the representatives from San Domingo on the ground that they, as masters, could not represent their slaves.[37]

Condorcet's arguments against slavery were both humanitarian and economic. The Negro was a human being, and, therefore, entitled to natural rights; otherwise, the Declaration of the Rights of Man should be changed to say "that all *white* men are free and equal in rights, and give a rule on determining the degree of whiteness required."[38] Slavery was a crime against humanity, and was no more justified than was the theft of a horse on the ground that the thief needed the horse more than did the owner.

But Condorcet's economic arguments against slavery are more interesting.[39] First he presented the arguments of the plantation owner: (1) a large number of laborers were necessary to work under tropical conditions, who could not be recruited in sufficient numbers from European immigration, and, therefore, the sugar industry could not be developed without slave labor; (2) the Negro, if free, would not be a steady worker as he is naturally lazy, hence the sugar crop would be in constant danger of being ruined. Condorcet made telling replies to these arguments. The planters, he argued, were interested primarily in profits, not in production. Under slave labor they believed that they could make more profit because (1) they paid no wages; and (2) they could fix monopoly prices, as there was little competition in a slave industry. Admitting that Negroes might be necessary to the sugar industry, it did not follow that Negro slavery was necessary. Was it not true that the wheat fields and vineyards of Europe had, in ancient times, been cultivated by slaves, and were they not now cultivated by free peasants? Laziness was not characteristic of Negroes only, but of all people who worked under an evil system and were hampered by restrictions and prohibitions. If the Negroes were lazy it was because they saw no need of working more than they were obliged to work. What could one gain by being industrious under such a system? Condorcet then made a significant statement, which recalls the economic argument against slavery in the United States. "It is certain that cultivation by free Negroes, far from ruining either the quality or quantity of the product, would, on the contrary, help to make the quantity larger, and the quality better." [40] Free labor would introduce competition among the planters, which would result in increasing the crop. And the labor cost would not be more than under slavery. The free Negroes would always be in a position of the poorest laborers, competing with one another, and their wages would consequently be very low, never above the minimum necessary for existence. The abolition of slavery "would ruin neither the colonies nor commerce; on the contrary it would have the effect of making the colonies more prosperous and of increasing commerce." [41]

Emancipation was, therefore, morally right and economically wise. As slavery was not a property right, declared Condorcet, the natural right of property would not be violated by the immediate emancipation of the Negroes without compensation to their masters. But his cautious liberalism was opposed to such a plan because it would arouse so much opposition that it could not be put through. He, therefore, proposed a plan of gradual emancipation which would make the transition from slavery to freedom more easy. The plan was as follows: (1) immediate abolition of the slave trade; (2) all newly born children of slaves to be free, provided that the master did not object, otherwise they were to become automatically free on reaching the age of thirty-five; (3) all slaves, under fifteen, were to become automatically free at the age of forty; (4) all slaves over fifteen should, at the age of fifty, have the choice of becoming free or remaining slaves; and (5) a price was to be fixed for every slave, and anyone wishing to free a slave could do so by offering the purchase price to his master, who would be compelled to accept it.[42] This plan of gradual emancipation would, according to Condorcet, give the masters an opportunity to introduce a system of free labor by hiring the freedmen as wage laborers and by encouraging white immigration. Condorcet's defense of his plan of gradual emancipation was that the evils of slavery from which the Negro suffered, ignorance, brutality, and immorality, did not fit him to become a free citizen immediately. He must be prepared for freedom as an invalid is prepared for health by gradual healing.[43]

Slavery was a dramatic violation of the rights of man, and, as such, it roused all liberal sentiment against it. But what about the less dramatic, but no less evil, conditions of the lower classes at home, doomed to poverty and misery? It is a common charge against the philosophes that they preached abstract and illusory notions of freedom and equality. Nothing was further from the truth. These pioneers of the social sciences saw clearly enough the importance of favorable economic conditions in their schemes for realizing human equality. Condorcet expressed the views of the philosophes, generally, concerning the problem of poverty. The impoverishment of the masses was due, he declared, to (1) the concentration of property in land because of primogeniture and entail; (2) the concentration of property in industry because of the restrictions of the Mercantilist system; and (3) the unjust and unfair system of taxation. The one cause of poverty, not due to evil institutions, according to Condorcet, was due to the progress of invention. Machines displaced men by destroying the handicrafts; instead of skilled artisans there were poorly paid unskilled workmen who performed only simple tasks. However, Condorcet recognized that technological unemployment was temporary. Machine production produced great quantities of cheap goods which created larger markets. A larger demand for labor then followed. He had the curious idea that invention would, in time, slow up, and then the problem would be merely one of perfecting existing machinery.[44]

How was poverty to be abolished? The answer of the philosophes was through a wide distribution of property. The emphasis that they placed on the natural right of property came from their convictions that the universal possession of property would guarantee all the other natural rights. A monopoly of wealth guaranteed the privileges of the few, but a wide distribution of wealth would guarantee the liberties of the many. The abolition of feudalism would, at one stroke, create millions of small peasant proprietors. The abolition of the guilds and corporations and of the restrictions on trade would give everyone the opportunity to engage in business and in the professions, the outcome of which would be the creation of a great body of urban proprietors. The establishment of a just system of taxation would shift great burdens from the poor to the rich, and thereby enable many to keep what property they had acquired. If these reforms were accomplished, inequality of fortune would still remain, but such inequality would not be very great and would arise, fairly, as a result of some having superior abilities or superior education. "Considering the physical, mental, and other human attributes," remarked Quesnay, "there exist great inequalities among individuals in relation to natural rights. These inequalities take no account of the principles of justice, but are the outcome of natural laws. As man cannot know God's purpose in constructing the universe, he cannot rise to the height of understanding the purpose of immutable laws constituted by God in the creation and preservation of His work." [45]

Condorcet entertained pronounced views in favor of economic equality. "I know that the existence of great fortunes is an evil," he declared, "and that a fair degree of economic equality is desirable. Without it, even equality of rights cannot be complete and real." He keenly realized the distinction that existed between *égalité formelle* and *égalité réelle*. But economic equality should not be brought about by sudden and wholesale confiscations, which would only result in the disorganization of commerce and industry and condemn several generations to poverty and misery.[46] "Inequality of fortune is a great evil," he declared, "but it is a political evil (*mal politique*), like all other evils. Injustice is no cure; only just laws can remedy this evil."[47] In other words, legislation was not to confiscate the property of the rich and give it to the poor, but was to create a condition in society whereby economic equality would arise as a result of everyone having an opportunity to acquire property. "Public welfare," Condorcet declared, "demands a wide distribution of wealth, but it also demands that it should come about by methods other than mere accumulation, and, above all, that each individual should have security in enjoying his portion."[48] In other words, Condorcet's conception of economic equality was to reconcile the rights of property with its widest possible distribution. Great differences in fortune, he believed, were maintained by laws, especially designed for this purpose. The "natural order," however, favored a wide distribution of wealth, as, under free enterprise, great fortunes tended to be divided and dissipated.[49]

Once established, the system favorable to economic equality was to be maintained through freedom of commerce and industry; through freedom of marriage by discouraging marriage for money; and, above all, through equal inheritance. Nothing was more evil, in Condorcet's opinion, than the aristocratic system of primogeniture and inequality of inheritance, which continually upset the social equilibrium and perpetuated inequality of wealth.[50] Freedom to testate would give a father the right to partition his estate, which would result in the greater division of property.[51] Condorcet's Declaration of Rights contained provisions establishing equality of inheritance by all the children of both sexes.[52]

In favoring the wide distribution of property Condorcet was fully abreast of the most advanced opinion of his day. In one respect, however, he was far ahead of it, and that was in his attitude toward social reform. His passionate love of equality and his fervent humanitarianism led him to anticipate social legislation, the preoccupation of twentieth-century liberalism. "A free, rich nation," he declared, "owes those of its citizens endowed with equal rights, but deprived of advantages . . . by unforeseen misfortunes, such assistance as will aid them in establishing equality."[53] The danger of ruin was ever present in those families, whose head had only his labor with which to maintain his dependents. When he grew old and could no longer work, his family faced starvation. Condorcet suggested two schemes for the amelioration of the lot of the poor that are startlingly modern, namely, coöperative banking and old age pensions. Credit, he declared, has, hitherto, been the privilege of great wealth. A fund should be established, "under the protection of society," from which loans were to be made to those who were of age to start in business for themselves, but who lacked the necessary capital. With the organization of these coöperative credit associations, industry and commerce would be less dependent upon the great capitalists.[54] To assist the helpless, Condorcet recommended the establishment of a fund, consisting of contributions from its members, which would be based on an actuarial computation of the probabilities of life. From this fund would come old age pensions and allowances for widows and orphans.[55]

Condorcet's advocacy of social legislation, at the very dawn of laissez faire liberalism, marks him as a bold pioneer of the contemporary movement for social reform. Possessing a social imagination, far greater than that of his fellow-philosophes, he envisaged the problems of the democratic society of which they were all dreaming. As a rule the humanitarianism of the philosophes comprehended such evils as slavery, war, and the cruel treatment of prisoners and the insane, which they believed could be abolished by enlightened legislation. Condorcet went much further by including poverty as an evil that could be abolished, like the others, by enlightened legislation.

CHAPTER EIGHT

ECONOMIC LIBERALISM

THE challenge of the libertarian spirit of the eighteenth century was directed not only against the political, religious, and social restrictions on individual liberty, but also against the economic restrictions on individual enterprise. The Mercantilist system was now outworn and antiquated; it could not answer the needs of the new economic life, based on free enterprise, that was surging forward.[1] A great demand for capital arose to finance the new commerce and industry, and, naturally, eyes were turned in the direction of what was then the greatest source of wealth, land.

Under the Old Régime, in France, a vast amount of land was virtually withdrawn from "circulation" by primogeniture, according to which the eldest son inherited the entire estate; by mortmain, according to which the lands of religious bodies could not be alienated; by the system of "noble" lands which commoners could not acquire; and by all sorts of feudal restrictions and exactions. The problem was how to release the land from the grip of feudalism so that it might become (1) a basis for capitalistic enterprise; and (2) a source for the investment of capital.

About the middle of the eighteenth century France became

greatly interested in agriculture, and in country life generally. This was wittily described by Voltaire. "About 1750," he wrote, "the nation, satiated with poetry, tragedies, comedies, operas, novels, imaginative romances, and with moral views, even more imaginative, and with theological views concerning grace and religious convulsions, at last began to reason about wheat." [2] This interest in agriculture was due in part to the success of the agricultural experiments conducted in England by Jethro Tull who invented a "drill" that deposited seeds in straight furrows; by Viscount Townshend who devised a scheme of rotating crops; and by Robert Bakewell who increased the size of cattle by new methods of breeding. As agriculture in France during the first half of the eighteenth century had shown, in some years, a precipitous decline it was believed that more progressive methods would be effective in making farming more prosperous.[3]

There was another aspect to this interest in agriculture, and that was the attitude toward land shown by the wealthy bourgeois who had acquired estates. The aristocrats of the Old Régime regarded land as a means of livelihood and as a basis for social position, not as a means of profit-making. A good harvest, like a bad one, was an act of God, not the result of a good or a bad investment. But the new bourgeois landowners brought a capitalistic attitude toward land. They saw the possibilities of large profits as a result of a judicious investment of capital in land, which would assure the proprietor the steadiest and largest income possible.

A school of economic writers arose, known as the Economists or Physiocrats, who gave intellectual expression to the new economic tendencies in France. The founder, and chief of the school, was Doctor François Quesnay whose views on economics were regarded as those of an oracle. His famous

Economic Table, explaining the circulation of wealth, was acclaimed by his followers as one of the three greatest inventions of mankind, the other two being, writing and money. Quesnay's most famous disciples were Count Mirabeau, father of the famous statesman, whose book *L'Ami des Hommes* created a sensation; Mercier de la Rivière whose book *L'Ordre naturel et essentiel des sociétés politiques* gave the clearest account of Physiocratic doctrines; Abbé Baudeau whose book, *Première introduction à la philosophie économique* was likewise a clear and concise statement; Du Pont de Nemours, whose book *Physiocratie* meaning "the rule of nature," gave the name to the school; and the statesman, Turgot. The last was of them, but not with them; he carefully held himself aloof from the Physiocrats, as he did from all literary and philosophic sects. In the main Turgot's economic views were those of the Physiocrats, and they are to be found chiefly in his *Eloge de Gournay* and *Réflexions sur la formation et distribution des richesses* (1769).[4]

In his economic views Condorcet was a follower of the Physiocrats, especially of Turgot, whom he regarded as his supreme master in economics as well as in politics. "One must not look for original ideas (in economics) in Condorcet. Primarily he was, in this field, an ingenious and elegant popularizer, but a popularizer who was thoroughly familiar with his subject."[5]

The Physiocrats may be described as the first "school" of economists in that they constituted a group which adhered to a coherent body of economic doctrines. As the intellectual spokesmen of the nascent capitalism of their time, they definitely and uncompromisingly favored the creation of a "free market" in which buyers and sellers would be completely free to conduct business, unhampered by feudal law and custom and by the restrictions and regulations of the guilds and monopolies. The guiding principles of the Physiocratic school were derived from the doctrine, known as the Natural Order (*Ordre naturel*). According to this doctrine, economic activity, such as buying, selling, producing, distributing, and consuming, were not haphazard affairs, but were regulated by economic laws that were as inexorable, as immutable, as universal as were the natural laws that regulated the physical universe. Prosperity attended those who obeyed the economic laws, and adversity, those who disobeyed them. Therefore, it was essential that the economic laws of the *Ordre naturel* should not be contravened by the "artificial" laws of the political order (*Ordre positive*). The Physiocrats, as a rule, were not much interested in the "state of nature" anterior to organized society, and in the doctrine of natural rights as over against the state. The only right that interested them was the right to make a living, in the best possible way, by having free access to every form of economic activity.

From belief in the Natural Order followed logically the famous doctrine of laissez faire. It is attributed to the economist Gournay, who is said to have remarked, *Laissez faire et laissez passer: voilà toute la police du commerce.*[6] According to this doctrine all economic activity was to be entirely free, unhampered by privileges, restrictions, requirements, and controls which were regarded as artificial interferences with the natural economic laws. The natural law of supply and demand would regulate automatically all economic life. Every individual was to be at liberty to engage in any trade, profession, or business, a policy directly opposed to the system of guilds and corporations under the Old Régime. Prices and wages were to be determined as a result of freedom of contract between buyer and seller. The promptings of self-interest were regarded as a surer guide to prosperity than codes of business laws, no matter how enlightened. "The wisest system of regulations," declared Condorcet, "would, at most, do what liberty alone could do, and do it more slowly and less perfectly." [7]

Condorcet severely attacked the monopolistic guilds and corporations as violations of the rights of labor and of property because they restricted the individual in disposing of the products of his labor. By artificially increasing prices, they raised the cost of living of the necessities of life. They produced a vicious tendency in every buyer, he declared, to see an enemy in every seller. The privileges, accorded to manufacturers, promoted intrigue and political corruption.[8] To Condorcet the very existence of the guilds and corporations was a menace to public interests. "Corporate solidarity," he declared, "is more dangerous than personal self-interest because the members act as a group, and are not restrained by decency or by the fear of blame." In contrast was the self-interest of individuals, which was not "opposed to general interest, except in rare and transient circumstances." [9]

Laissez faire was a reaction against one aspect of the Mercantilist system, the meticulous regulation of industry. Another reaction against the system was free trade. The Physiocrats denounced the restrictions upon commerce imposed by Mercantilism: (1) the tariffs, export and import, internal and external; and (2) government regulation of prices, of transport, and of markets. So varied and complicated were these regulations that, as Condorcet declared, a merchant never knew whether "the laws under which he has bought are the same as those under which he will sell." [10] The Physiocrats advocated free trade, by which they meant primarily,

ECONOMIC LIBERALISM

not free imports, but free exports and the free movement of agricultural products within the country through the abolition of the provincial tariffs. They were interested in foreign trade only as a means of selling surplus crops at good prices. According to Mercier de la Rivière foreign trade at best was a necessary evil as a nation was forced to buy what it could not produce.[11] Nevertheless, the Physiocrats also favored the abolition of tariffs on imports on the ground that, without free imports, free exports might lead to scarcity and to dearness.

Condorcet advocated the complete program of free trade.[12] As an economist, he was motivated by the same ideal of individual freedom that inspired his political and religious views. So enthusiastic was Condorcet in his championship of economic freedom that he came to regard Colbert, the great Mercantilist statesman, as the father of all that was evil in the economic condition of France during the eighteenth century. The ardent reformer in him made it impossible for Condorcet to understand the historic rôle of the Mercantilist system, as the economic expression of the nascent national state that had arisen as a result of the breakdown of feudalism in the seventeenth century. The leading exponent of Mercantilism in his day, was Necker, whom Condorcet hated as the living incarnation of Colbertism. He replied to Necker's defense of internal tariffs on foodstuffs by a direct, frontal attack on the *régime prohibitif*.[13]

According to Condorcet international free trade would be the logical outcome of internal free trade. It would bring about a situation whereby each country would produce only those products for which it was best fitted, hence every nation would be benefited.[14] This argument has become classical among free trade champions. International free trade would also bring about an approximation of prices in each country to a common European level.

Ironically enough, the Physiocrats advocated laissez faire and free trade because they believed that it would result, not in competition, but in harmonious coöperation between individuals, classes, and nations. Due to the principle of the division of labor, each individual was dependent upon the other; likewise, there was a community of interest between class and class, and between nation and nation.[15] Enlightened self-interest would dictate to each individual and to each group policies favoring their common interest; strife, whether in the form of individual competition, class struggles, or wars between nations, would disrupt this essential harmony and all would consequently be the sufferers. The idea of harmony of interests, so characteristic of the Physiocratic school, was well described by Condorcet in his analysis of the natural law that governed economic activity. "What are the laws," he asked, "according to which wealth is created or dissipated, saved or consumed, increased or diminished? What also are the laws that control the equilibrium which always tends to establish itself between demand and supply, from which arises a greater ability to satisfy needs and consequently greater well-being?" Despite the apparent chaos of production, there existed a "general law of the moral world which causes the efforts of everyone in his own behalf to serve the interests of all; and which, despite apparent conflict, the common interest demands that everyone should understand his own interest and be permitted to pursue it without opposition." [16]

The clash of special interests was, to Condorcet, an indication of a lack of enlightenment. "This pretended opposition between nations, between sections of each nation, between the capital and the provinces, between city and county, between mother country and colony, between commerce and agriculture, between capitalists and landowners, between rich and poor, has been until now the chief obstacle to progress, liberty, peace, and true equality." [17] Conflicts between rich and poor, argued Condorcet, arose as the result of living under social institutions dominated by privilege; there was no natural conflict of interests between them. The interest of the poor lay in having an opportunity to work, and the interest of the rich lay in creating this opportunity by investing in industry. If a vicious system of society condemned the masses to poverty, the property of the rich would be in constant danger. To save themselves the rich would be obliged to support the poor by means of charity, as they did in England through the poor laws. And the cost of charity was greater than the prevention of poverty.[18]

The fundamental difference between the Physiocrats and the Mercantilists was over the question, What constituted the wealth of a nation? The Mercantilists maintained that it was the amount of gold and silver that a nation possessed. The Physiocrats maintained that it was the surplus produced by agriculture. Commerce and industry, according to the Physiocrats, were "sterile" because they produced no surplus; only agriculture (including fishing and mining) was truly productive. Commerce multiplied buying and selling without multiplying goods.[19] Essentially it was an exchange of articles of equal value, therefore unproductive. The merchants were the intermediaries between buyer and seller, and their profits merely paid for the expense of their transactions. If one merchant made more, another necessarily made less. Business was, in fact, a form of gambling in which the sum always remained the same, though some of the players won, and others lost. Foreign, as well as domestic, commerce was "sterile." All foreign trade in manufactures was precarious. If one country gained it resulted in rousing competition in another country, with the result that the trade was shared between them.

Like commerce, industry produced no surplus. All that industry did was to "transform" raw material into finished products. The difference in value went to pay wages to the laborers and interest to the capitalists, who coöperated to produce the finished articles. Industry no more added to the wealth of a nation than did a cook who prepared dinner from raw food. The value of industrial production was in proportion to the value of the subsistence consumed by the workers and merchants; therefore, the artisan destroyed as much as he produced. The fact that, according to the Physiocrats, commerce and industry were "sterile" did not mean that they were useless. They were indeed useful, even necessary, in carrying on the work of a nation.

In agriculture alone, according to the Physiocrats, lay the wealth of a nation. Due to the bounty of nature, farming gave a return far greater than what was expended on it for the maintenance of the farmer and for the return on the capital invested. "The farmer," declared Turgot, "produces, beyond what is necessary for his subsistence, an amount of food . . . which he has not bought and which he sells. This is the only source of wealth which, by circulating, animates all the activities of society. The farmer is the only one whose labor produces more than is necessary for his wages."[20] In other words, the bounty of nature produced not only enough to nourish the farmer, but a surplus to nourish all the other classes. And this surplus, less the expense necessary for production, was the famous Net Product (*Produit net*). The necessary expenses for production consisted of (1) *avances primitives,* or the capital supplied originally to clear the ground and to provide houses, tools, and animals; and (2) *avances annuelles,* or capital spent on the necessary upkeep of the land, on wages, on seed, on repairs, etc. The Net Product was, therefore, the gross product less the necessary expenses of the annual outlay and the interest on the investment. The prosperity of the nation depended upon the distribution of the Net Product, or the "circulation of wealth" among the various classes. Because agriculture alone produced a Net Product it was, therefore, the only true source of a nation's wealth. Hence, those nations that lived on commerce and industry were always in the precarious position of living on their capital. Only those nations that lived on their agriculture were truly prosperous because they lived on their income.

The views of the Physiocrats concerning the "sterility" of commerce and industry and the productivity of agriculture was the economic variation of the *leitmotif* of the eighteenth century, namely, that all that came from nature was beneficent, and all that came from the hand of man was evil at worst, and valueless at best. Economic conditions, too, help to explain their views. Before the Industrial Revolution industry was, in a sense, sterile because its reproductive powers were greatly limited by the handicraft methods of manufacture; whereas, in agriculture, nature would sometimes produce a bountiful harvest, despite the primitive methods of cultivation then used by the peasants. The advent of the machine in the Industrial Revolution made industry, visibly and obviously, productive, and far more so than agriculture which was left far behind as a source of wealth. A new theory of production came with Adam Smith whose idea was that the wealth of nations consisted in the creation of utilities that satisfied human wants, whether from agriculture, commerce, or industry; and that a surplus could be created by saving in any of these pursuits.

As a Physiocrat Condorcet accepted the theory of the sole productivity of agriculture. "The true wealth of a nation," he declared, "consists in the surplus produced by agriculture after the expense of producing it is paid." [21] The wealth of a nation could be increased by increasing the investment in land in order to obtain a larger surplus. He advised the rich landlords to invest money in agriculture which would greatly enhance the value of their lands.[22] Condorcet regarded foreign commerce as a *richesse précaire,* and he had forebodings concerning England because she depended so much upon foreign commerce for her prosperity. "The gradual destruction of her precarious wealth," he declared, "must end by enfeebling England's power. When, in time, greater industrial equality will exist among the nations, the same fate will overtake England that overtook Holland and Venice, and that overtakes every nation which puts the source of her prosperity and power outside of her borders." [23] This prophecy sounds very much like the argument of the present day tariff reformers in England, who wish to revive English agriculture. To create an agricultural surplus, argued Condorcet, should be the aim of a nation's economic policy. It would result, not merely in national self-sufficiency, but in peopling the land with a healthy, hardy race. Like Jefferson, Condorcet believed that prosperous farmers constituted the best class of citizens in a free nation. It is the farmers "who nourish the state and defend it; it is their sweat that fertilizes the soil; it is their blood which flows in the defense of the Fatherland." [24] The other classes were less interested in the welfare of their country because they were less intimately tied to it than were

ECONOMIC LIBERALISM 167

the farmers. Least tied to it were the financiers, who had "no interest whatever in their country because, by the means of a bank operation, they can instantly become Englishmen, Dutchmen or Russians."[25] The idealization of the farmer as the honest son of toil, and as the good, patriotic, free citizen was a natural inference from the Physiocratic doctrine that the farmer, and he only, made possible the prosperity of the nation.

Condorcet was too independent a thinker to be a strict follower of any school of thought. As he was in advance of his age in his political liberalism, so, in some respects, he was in advance of his age in his economic liberalism. Unlike his fellow-Physiocrats he was interested in industry, especially in the function of machinery. This interest was perhaps due to his admiration for Adam Smith, to whose *Wealth of Nations* he frequently referred with approval. Condorcet had some interesting things to say concerning machinery, and his ideas and suggestions have quite a modern sound. He accepted Adam Smith's view of the advantages that accrued from a division of labor, due to machinery.[26] The substitution of machinery for handwork, he declared, caused unemployment, but only for a time. An equilibrium was soon established by the creation of new forms of employment, which came as a result of the establishment of new industries. Machinery made cheap articles, thereby increasing production by increasing sales.[27]

Even before the Industrial Revolution had made any visible advance, he foresaw the effect of machinery on the condition of the working class. At first, he declared, the substitution of machinery for hand labor will bring poverty to the worker. But, in time, machines will be so differentiated, so numerous, and so highly developed that manual labor will be considerably lessened. When that time comes there will be no violent fluctuations in industry; it will only be necessary to perfect the existing machines.[28] Condorcet clearly realized the deadening effect of machinery on the worker. "It stupefies the laborers, and narrows their ideas so greatly that they, themselves, become machines, incapable of anything except making certain movements." [29] But while the laborers remained tied to the machines, the upper classes derived benefit from the increased wealth produced by machinery, as a result of which they shared in the progress of civilization. Only in one way could the laborers also share in this progress, and that was through the establishment of a system of popular education; otherwise, industrial progress would act as a bar to the perfectibility of mankind.[30] Furthermore, the enlightenment even of the upper classes could not long exist if "the poor are condemned to eternal stupidity. When it spreads, not when it concentrates, does enlightenment increase." [31]

Of all the evils of the Old Régime its onerous system of taxation excited the most widespread opposition. Apart from the privileged orders, the clergy and the nobility, all elements of the nation suffered under this system, more or less: the lower classes more, and the middle classes less. In the opinion of the Physiocrats the great problem of reform was the unjust apportionment of the taxes, not the unjust distribution of wealth. They proposed, what they considered, a full and complete solution of this problem, namely, a single, direct tax (*Impôt unique*) on the Net Product, the only available source of wealth. All taxes, they argued, ultimately fell on the landowners, and on them alone, as only agriculture produced a surplus. Taxes, levied on other things, eventually fell on land, and with increased force. Wages and profits were reduced to a minimum by competition. Land only furnished a return above costs; therefore the wisest fiscal policy was to collect from those directly who must pay in the end, namely, the landowners. A direct tax, levied on the Net Product in proportion to its size, would be the simplest, the fairest, the least burdensome, the least expensive to levy, and the most productive of income to the state. It must be borne in mind that the single tax, advocated by the Physiocrats, was not at all the same as that advocated by Henry George. The single tax of the latter was a tax on *land values* with the object of abolishing private property in land. On the contrary, the Physiocrats were fervent champions of property in land, and they wished to strengthen it by abolishing the many restrictions placed upon land by the Old Régime. The portion of the Net Product that would go to the state, in the form of taxes, was figured by the Physiocrats as about one-third. For the state to demand more would be spoliation, not taxation. Curtailment of agriculture would follow, as there would not be sufficient capital with which to begin reproduction; and the nation would consequently sink into poverty.[32]

Although plausible and logical the *Impôt unique* was severely criticized and ridiculed by its opponents. Voltaire's famous satire, *Man of Forty Crowns* (*L'homme aux quarante écus*) ridiculed the single tax as absurd and unjust on the ground that it would put all the burden of taxation on landowners, and enable other rich men, especially the enormously wealthy financiers, to escape taxation. Curiously enough the notion that land alone should bear the brunt of taxation still has many adherents. How else can one explain the fact that American cities raise most of their revenues by taxing real estate.

Condorcet was intensely interested in the problems of

finance and taxation on which he wrote many pamphlets.[33] He was a merciless critic of the system of taxation under the Old Régime which he denounced as violating the principle of equality and the right of property.[34] Condorcet was especially opposed to indirect taxes which, he declared, entailed heavy expenses of collection and encouraged fraud. Indirect taxes, he declared, could be easily evaded by those who were in a position to do so, and those, who did not evade them, paid more than their share. Moreover, evasion of taxes encouraged the violation of law, and "from the desire to violate one law to that of violating all laws the transition is neither long nor difficult." [35]

Perhaps the most iniquitous form of taxation under the Old Régime was the corvée, a survival of serfdom, which fell exclusively on the peasants. It was a compulsory labor levy, either by the state or by the lord, that required the peasants to give a number of days' labor to the building or to the repairing of roads. Condorcet denounced the corvée as not only iniquitous but as uneconomical. "Roads built by well-paid laborers," he declared, "will cost less than those built by miserable, exhausted peasants who work badly because, receiving no wages, they are unable to nourish themselves properly." [36] The corvée was the most cruel of servitudes, "as it condemned men, who gain their livelihood by working for wages, to work for nothing. . . . The rigid requirements, the harsh discipline, the severe fines add desolation to misery, and humiliation to misfortune. This is a picture of the corvée." [37]

Condorcet subscribed fully to the Physiocratic doctrine of the single tax. A just tax, he declared, must be equal, and equality could be obtained only by a direct tax on the Net Product. A provision in his Declaration of Rights forbade the legislature to lay taxes on imports, on exports, and on the sale or transportation of foodstuffs, as not being applied to the Net Product.[38] However, the urgent necessity of raising money during the French Revolution caused Condorcet to break away from the Physiocratic doctrine of the single tax. In 1790 he urged the adoption of a personal tax based on the amount of rent paid for a dwelling, not for a place of business or workshop. The rate of the rent tax was to vary with the size of the family and with the size of the city in which the dwelling was situated.[39] As a member of the Convention, in 1793, Condorcet advocated a moderate progressive income tax on the ground that the rich should pay more taxes because they received more benefits from the government than did the poor.[40] When the Jacobins got control of the Convention, the attack on the aristocrats developed into an attack on the rich in general. Schemes for "soaking the rich" were proposed in the Convention which were opposed by Condorcet. "If the wealthy are prevented from increasing or from conserving their wealth," he declared, "they will be forced to use secret ways of enriching themselves . . . and the result will be a drying up of the sources of industry. . . . High taxes will compel the rich to reduce their expenditure and to conceal their wealth, which will result in ruining trades upon which poor laborers depend for their livelihood." [41]

If there was one right that the Physiocrats considered sacred, as well as natural, it was the right of property. In their view this right was at the very base of the *Ordre naturel* from which arose all the institutions essential to society. Property was the "tree of which all institutions are branches; they are nourished by it, and die if detached from it." [42] But property, like man in the eighteenth century, was bound and entangled by all sorts of restrictions. Feudal law dissipated the concept of ownership by the numberless rights, duties, privileges, and services connected with feudal landholding. Land, under feudalism, was held only as usufruct, not as private property in the full and exclusive sense of Roman law. The lord had privileges over his estate, which was not his property, either in the Roman or in the modern sense. He could not really sell it, divide it, or will it as he wished. Many large estates were indivisible through the system of primogeniture and entail that forbade the division of an estate which, by inheritance, was to go to the eldest son in its entirety. The succession to the land was, in a sense, like the succession to the crown; the heir inherited the sovereign powers over the estate. When the noble "sold" his estate, he really sold only his rights over it. To employ a modern analogy, the lord was a "trustee" of his estate, not its owner.[43]

In commerce and industry there were similar restrictions on property rights. Regulation of prices, of wages, of raw material, of methods of work, and of the quantity and composition of articles produced, imposed by the guilds and corporations, were limitations of property rights. "The restrictive laws," declared Condorcet, "the control of trade, and the indirect taxes were really attacks on the rights of property in that they limited the free exercise of it. One does not at all possess what one cannot freely dispose of." [44]

Finally, absolute monarchy constituted a constant danger to property rights through its unlimited power to tax. The king had need of a bureaucracy and of a royal army to maintain his authority, which necessitated the raising of large sums of money. He often resorted to arbitrary methods of taxation because there then existed neither well-regulated systems nor clearly articulated principles of taxation. Therefore, the power to tax was the power to destroy through confiscation.

With the free enterprise of the Commercial Revolution

came the doctrine of property as a natural right, a doctrine unknown to Roman law or to feudal custom. This view of property was inextricably bound up with the interests of the rapidly growing bourgeoisie who were engaged in economic enterprises that demanded a free and open market, in which buying and selling could be quickly consummated, and in which property could be easily translated into capital in order to finance their enterprises. Land, freed from feudal restrictions, would become a great source of capital by being used as collateral for loans; and industry, freed from the regulations of the guilds and from the restrictions of the monopolies, would liberate both capital and labor. The industrial property of the bourgeois, *la propriété mobilière,* was outside of the feudal system, and consequently had clear property rights. Bourgeois property, free to acquire and free to dispose of, was in hostile juxtaposition to feudal property, bound and fettered by restrictions. The "natural right" of property was, in the eighteenth century, a revolutionary doctrine, proclaimed as one of the rights of man which neither the decrees of monarchs nor the laws of legislative bodies could infringe.

The Physiocrats, more than any other group of writers in France, were the uncompromising champions of the doctrine of property as a natural right. A man's property was, to them, the measure of his freedom.[45] And they completely repudiated the "artificial" property rights that came from feudal privileges and monopolies which, they believed, originated in usurpation and violence which later became law and custom. They advocated the idea that everyone should have the freedom to will his property as he liked (*Droit de tester*), a logical application of the doctrine of the natural right of property. These views of the Physiocrats profoundly influenced the attacks on feudalism by the French Revolution. The abolition of dues and services, and the suppression of the guilds and corporations, during the Revolution, were not regarded as attacks on property, but as attacks on special privileges that were contrary to the rights of man. Property was vindicated by giving the peasants complete and undisputed rights to their lands; by giving the merchants and manufacturers full control over their goods; and by giving the workers complete freedom to labor. Primogeniture was abolished by the "law of partition" which required a father, in his will, to divide his real property equally among all his children. In the words of an historian of the French Revolution this wide distribution of property, and the clear title given to it, was "liberty made visible." [46]

Condorcet fully accepted the Physiocratic view of property as absolute, exclusive, and sacred. Of all the natural rights, he asserted, the greatest was that of property, and property owners "may justly be regarded as constituting what is essentially society." [47] Property should, therefore, be respected "to the point of superstition." [48] "The right of property," he declared, "is for every individual only the right of disposing freely what belongs to him. And the right to will property, which means the right which one freely exercises to dispose of his possessions at the moment of death, is a necessary outcome of the right of property." [49] Curiously enough Condorcet viewed the natural right of property as a protection of the poor, not of the rich. The less people possess, he asserted, the more do they desire to have the full protection of the laws of what property they do own, such as clothes, furniture, wages, savings, homes. "It is not only to defend the haves as against the havenots that laws are made for the protection of property. Even more it is to defend those who have little as against those who have much." [50] But it was difficult to teach the poor to respect the property of the rich because they "regard great wealth as a form of usurpation, as theft from themselves, which is unfortunately true in many instances." [51]

As a believer in the natural right of property, Condorcet was hostile to "communal property as contrary to nature," and to feudal property as based on privilege. However, he believed that there were some elements in the confused and intricate system of feudal landholding that could claim the rights due to property. How were these to be determined? Condorcet's test was, Did a given law or custom violate the rights of man, as, for example, serfdom? Then it should be suppressed without compensation. A distinction should be made, he contended, between those dues and services that arose from sovereign rights of the lord over the estate and those that were clearly property rights. The legislature had a right to suppress the former, but with compensation as determined by a judicial evaluation; it had no power whatsoever over the latter.[52]

In economic theory Condorcet was never the master, but always the disciple, sometimes of Quesnay, sometimes of Adam Smith, but generally of Turgot. He was interested in economics primarily as a social and political reformer, not as a student of the subject. As a believer in the open and free market, required by free enterprise that he advocated, Condorcet favored its concomitant, the price system. Prices, he declared, were determined by the law of supply and demand. Competition between buyers, which tended to raise prices, was, however, limited by their greater need of other commodities or by their resources. Competition between sellers, which tended to lower prices, was limited by their unwillingness to sell below a certain price.[53]

There was interesting speculation in France on the theory of value, not, however, by the Physiocrats who held no well-defined theory of value. The philosopher, Condillac, laid the foundation of the psychological theory of value in his work, *Le commerce et le gouvernement*, a theory developed in the nineteenth century by Jevons and by Böhm-Bawerk. It was that value was based upon utility which is relative, and which implied a measure of correspondence between a commodity and a given want. Quantity influenced value in that it intensified or weakened demand. Utility and quantity were, therefore, mental concepts, independent of the physical relation of things. Condorcet accepted Condillac's interpretation of value, without adding much to it.[54]

Condorcet's views on wages followed closely those of Turgot. It was Turgot who formulated a wage theory which, in essence, was similar to Lassalle's famous theory of the Iron Law of Wages. "In all sorts of work," declared Turgot, "it must happen, and in effect does happen, that wages are limited by the amount necessary to maintain the laborer," and it rises only when the cost of living rises.[55] However, Turgot contradicted himself when he asserted that a workman who does not make good wages does not do good work. Condorcet followed his master, even in his contradictions. Wages, he declared, could never be less than the amount necessary to sustain the laborer, otherwise he would not work; and they could never be more than the amount necessary to support the worker and his family in times of normal prices.[56] Elsewhere, however, he declared, that it was absurd to believe that a laborer could not get wages above his necessities because of competition of employers for labor.[57] This contradiction in both master and disciple was due to the discrepancy between the statement of an abstract principle and the observation of an everyday fact.

The Physiocrats, now so widely discredited, nevertheless, prepared the way for the classical economists. Their views concerning the distribution of wealth among those who co-operate to produce it, the laborers, the employers, and the landowners, profoundly influenced the views of Adam Smith.[58] Despite the fact that they limited productivity to agriculture the Physiocrats clearly saw the rôle that capital played in the production of wealth. According to Karl Marx the Physiocrats were the first economists to have a systematic conception of capitalist production in that they advocated that agriculture should be exploited capitalistically under the direction of capitalist farmers.[59] This view is well stated by the socialist historian, Jaurès. "The economists understood," he writes, "that agriculture should be promoted by the free circulation of its products and by a large investment of capital in land. These views were in harmony with the bourgeois ideas of free labor and free enterprise. Despite an apparent hostility to industry the Physiocrats are part and parcel of modern capitalism."[60]

CHAPTER NINE

RELIGIOUS LIBERALISM

NINETEENTH-CENTURY liberalism throughout western Europe showed marked hostility to revealed religion in general and to the Catholic church in particular. And nowhere more so than in France where anticlericalism, as this hostility became known, was the one bond that united all parties of the left, moderates, radicals, and socialists. Anticlericalism undoubtedly received its inspiration from the French Revolution that had waged uncompromising war against the church as it did against the other pillars of the Old Régime, the nobility and the monarchy. But the way was prepared by the philosophes who, though differing widely in other respects, were united in an aggressive war against the church. If undue virulence was shown by them in their attacks it was due to the conviction of the philosophes that the church, of all institutions, was the most powerful and most uncompromising enemy of human freedom.[1]

Like all the other philosophes, Condorcet was deeply hostile to revealed religion. He was even more vehemently antireligious than was his master, Voltaire, whose great renown as an enemy of the church has obscured the lesser freethinkers of his time. Although reared in a pious home and educated in Jesuit schools Condorcet was, as Sainte-Beuve truly states, "fanatically irreligious and smitten with a sort of hydrophobia on this subject." [2] Like Voltaire he regarded revealed religion as the result of man's "infirmity" during the primitive stage of his development. In Condorcet's opinion, the origin of nearly all known religions could be traced to this stage when, because of their credulity, men became the dupes of the priests, impostors who victimized mankind.[3] And all through the later stages of civilization, according to Condorcet, religion continued to be a gigantic system of hypocrisy, run by knaves who frightened their dupes by means of mysteries. Like Rousseau, Condorcet believed that primitive man had a religion of "pure deism mixed with some metaphysical notions," which was corrupted by the priests who "converted these beliefs into a vile mass of absurd superstitions calculated to advance the interests of the priesthood." [4]

Condorcet's antireligious bias crops out in nearly all of his works, especially in his famous *Sketch of the Intellectual Progress of Mankind,* in which religion is presented as the inveterate enemy of human progress. The Christian belief that man was naturally evil and could not be saved by his own efforts, unaided by divine grace, was opposed to Condorcet's fervent belief that man was naturally good, and that humanity could progress only through conscious and deliberate efforts toward improvement. To Condorcet, therefore, belief in progress was diametrically opposed to a belief in revealed religion.

From his writings it is difficult to tell whether Condorcet was an atheist or a deist. His hatred of revealed religion was so great that he exhausted himself in denouncing it, and, therefore, had no energy left to state his own position. He was too idealistic in temperament to be a follower of the creed of materialistic atheism, as preached by d'Holbach. At best, he was a vague deist, who believed that there existed a spiritual force among men that made for righteousness.[5] In his comment on Voltaire's article *Dieu* he gave the arguments of both deist and atheist, without, however, committing himself to either side. The only consolation was, he declared, that there was a universal agreement among philosophers as to the principles of morality, which proved that the best that man could do was to do his duty.[6]

Could morality exist without a belief in a Supreme Being? he asked. And his answer was that morality existed because ideas concerning good and evil arose as a result of reflection on human relations, which were neither arbitrary nor vague, but were determined by human nature; therefore, righteousness, justice, and duty had the same certainty and the same precision as all the other speculative sciences. "If we look into our hearts, we will find that good deeds attract us; that evil deeds repel us; and that remorse follows an evil deed; in a word, conscience is a necessary outcome of the human constitution."[7] Morality, therefore, had a "natural basis" in the very constitution of the human organism, which is shown in the sympathy that one feels for his fellows. "Man is naturally good because, although indifferent to good or evil when roused by selfish interests, the sentiments of pity and benevolence, arising from the nature of his moral constitution, lead him to goodness."[8] If Condorcet's attitude toward religion can be put into definite terms it was that of a present-day Ethical Culturist to whom right action, not belief or disbelief in God, is essential to the moral welfare of mankind. Condorcet's appeals to reason were invested with a moral fervor not to be found in the cool, satirical Voltaire nor in the sentimental, exuberant Diderot, both of whom made "reason" the battle cry of their crusade against revealed religion.

Condorcet saw little difference between one faith and another; all of them had, in one form or another, the original taint of intolerance. "National religions," he declared, "make men foolish and cruel to foreigners. Universal religions bring proselytism and intolerance. Religions, that are entirely practical, brutalize their followers. Religions, that are full of dogmas, make their followers foolish and cruel. What benefit do people derive by changing from one faith to another?" [9] Protestantism, in Condorcet's view, was somewhat better than Catholicism because it permitted a limited degree of free inquiry, in order to justify itself for separating from Catholicism. But this freedom of the Protestants extended to Christians only, and, therefore, did not affect mankind as a whole.[10] Many refused to become Protestants because, having merely a choice of chains, it was better to carry the one in which you were born. In both Catholic and Protestant countries anyone who wished to think for himself "had the choice of silence or the stake." [11]

Curiously enough, this uncompromising enemy of all revealed religions had a great admiration for Mohammedanism, and a favorable view of its founder. Of all religions, declared Condorcet, Mohammedanism was "the most simple in its dogmas, the least absurd in its practices, and the most tolerant in its principles." The Arabians cultivated the arts and sciences, and made contributions to poetry, chemistry, mathematics, and astronomy. Mohammed combined the talents of a statesman, poet, and warrior, which he employed *avec adresse, mais avec grandeur.*[12] Condorcet's admiration for Mohammedanism may be explained on the ground that it was far away, and its virtues could, therefore, be easily imagined by one who so intently saw the vices of the rival faith that was so near. The eighteenth-century philosophe saw deism and toleration everywhere: among primitive people, among Chinese, among Persians, everywhere, except among Christian Europeans. The myth of Mohammedanism, as a simple faith uniting many races and nations in a tolerant embrace, has persisted to this day. A modern instance is H. G. Wells' laudation of Mohammedanism in his *Outline of History*.

Condorcet's attacks on religion were dogmatic, hard, narrow, and humorless. Where the master, Voltaire, was sprightly and witty, the disciple was turgid, and even dull. Religion, he believed, was the chief cause of all of human ills; it corrupted morality, perverted human nature, prevented progress, and encouraged fanaticism, superstition, and hypocrisy. Denunciation succeeded denunciation, and the result was a tirade in monotone. Condorcet's views of religion were inspired by a hard rationalism that looked with disfavor upon anything that smacked of faith and mystery. Never did he show any critical understanding of the nature of religious experience, nor of the contributions of the church to Western civilization. To him Christianity was only a mass of *préjugés* which had stupefied and brutalized the masses, and always the deadly enemy of philosophers. "The great thinkers have never been believers." [13]

In his hatred of revealed religion Condorcet merely echoed the rationalistic views of his masters, Voltaire and Diderot. Militant freethinkers though they were, Voltaire and Diderot yet realized the utility of the church as an upholder of the social order. Therefore, they favored religious instruction for the masses whom they despised and feared. And, for the same reason, they favored union between church and state, but with toleration for those of other faiths and for those of no faith at all.[14] This attitude toward the church, disbelief in its doctrines and belief in its efficacy as a force for social conservatism, was generally characteristic of the freethinkers of the eighteenth century. They had no clear conception of a completely secular state, and, despite their bitter hostility to revealed religion, they generally favored the official recognition, by the state, of some faith which, in France, meant Catholicism.[15]

A complete liberal in his attitude toward the church, as he was in his attitude toward the state, Condorcet, alone among the philosophes, did have a clear conception of a completely secular state, a conception later realized by the Third French Republic. To favor a state church on the ground that it was a conservative influence in society was contrary to Condorcet's robust faith in progress and in the power of enlightenment, and to his staunch belief in democratic principles. In his scheme for establishing a national system of education he expressly forbade religious instruction in the public schools.[16] He openly advocated civil marriage and divorce.[17] Even more bold was his pronouncement in favor of complete religious freedom. He denounced the persecution of the Protestants by the government.[18] He severely condemned Rousseau's doctrine, proclaimed in the *Social Contract,* that there should be no toleration of those who hold intolerant views. *Cette maxime séduit par un faux air de justice.* Punishment should be meted out to those who persecute, and not to those who merely believe that persecution was commanded by God.[19] Condorcet denounced the system of maintaining an established church, with toleration for dissenters, as a form of insolence of a dominant faith toward those who did not adhere to it.[20] What he favored was religious freedom, not religious toleration.

Even before the French Revolution, the idea of separating church and state was clearly in his mind. "Of all the philosophers," writes Aulard, "Condorcet was the one who had most sense of the future, and he felt that separation of church and state meant the rule of liberty." [21] In his life of Turgot, published in 1786, Condorcet wrote that, as "public worship is necessarily the result of religious views of which one's conscience is the only legitimate judge, it is evident that the expense of maintaining such worship ought to be borne voluntarily by those who believe in it." [22] He also argued that an established church implied the right of revolution against a heretic prince. Therefore, the prince, to maintain his authority, should separate church and state, establish civil marriage and divorce, and civil registration of births and deaths.[23]

However, Condorcet was not ready, before 1789, to favor immediate separation of church and state. Some writers, he argued, were opposed to the payment of salaries by the state to clergymen because it was unjust to compel people to pay taxes for the support of a faith in which they did not believe. Even if this view was sound, separation of church and state should wait until public opinion was ready for it.[24] But the acceleration of public opinion, hostile to the church, by the French Revolution caused Condorcet to come out boldly in favor of the separation of church and state. To tax the people for the purpose of maintaining a church, he declared, was "against the rights of man, according to which anyone is as free not to pay for any faith as not to believe in any." [25]

During the French Revolution Condorcet's conduct was consistent with his theory, despite the swiftly changing panorama of dramatic events. His Declaration of Rights contained the following article: "Parliament is forbidden, under any pretext, to establish a tax to subsidize any faith or to permit any national property to be used for such purpose. A church should be supported by voluntary contributions only." [26] To establish an official religion, he argued, was to declare that religion was a human invention, founded on error, which could be maintained only by the aid of the state. In his pleas for separating church and state, Condorcet was inspired by the American example. The Americans, he declared, refused to establish a national church because they believed in religious freedom, and not in religious toleration.[27]

Like other anticlericals, Condorcet was especially hostile to the monasteries. The state, he argued, should not recognize perpetual associations, such as religious orders, because they reduced their members to a kind of slavery. Religious orders should not be permitted to exist without special authorization by the state, and the government should have the right to suppress them whenever necessary or advisable.[28] The lands of the monasteries, especially, roused the anticlericalism of the philosophe. In its very essence, declared Condorcet, a religious community was a violation of natural rights because the members were organized on the basis of perpetual vows. Property in the possession of religious communities, and of the church generally, he asserted, really belonged to the nation, which had the right freely to dispose of it as part of the public domain.[29] However, the usufruct had some claim to property rights, and should not be taken away without compensation. The wishes of the donors in regard to the property that they gave to the church should be respected only when these wishes were based on reason. The "absurd pretension" of donors that they can "divine the opinions, the principles, and the political and moral conditions of future ages" should be disregarded.[30]

However, Condorcet attacked the antireligious laws of the

French Revolution and the treatment of the priesthood on the ground that these laws violated natural rights. He warred against systems, not against men. When the religious orders were suppressed he demanded that pensions should be given to the monks and the nuns who were now left helpless. "When a corporation is destroyed," he declared, "what is left are the individuals who had composed it . . . having the same rights as other men, who should be treated according to the same principles of justice and humanity." [31]

As in other matters, Condorcet was far ahead of his contemporaries in his antireligious views. He did not limit himself to attacks on revealed religion, but he also advocated constructive policies leading to the establishment of a secular state. He was anticlerical as well as antireligious. Rigid in his adherence to abstract principles he applied the doctrine of natural rights as consistently in the religious as in the political sphere. And fervent in his democratic faith he, unlike his fellow philosophes, repudiated the notion that the masses should be held in check by supernatural beliefs that were flouted by the "enlightened." He was a forerunner of those anticlerical democratic statesmen and intellectuals, the Gambettas, the Ferrys, the Buissons, the Jaurès, the Waldeck-Rousseaus, and the Briands, whose labors succeeded in establishing France as a "lay state."

CHAPTER TEN

FEMINISM

IN the great ferment of revolutionary thought in France, during the eighteenth century, one institution generally escaped the merciless criticism, meted out to all others, and that one was the family. "In countries where good morals have even greater influence than good laws," says the Encyclopaedia, "the people cannot conceive a condition more happy than marriage."[1] And the explanation for accepting this most ancient of all institutions by the revolutionary philosophes was that they regarded the family as "natural"; whereas, the state, the church, and the economic order, they regarded as "artificial," the handiwork of the ages of ignorance and prejudice. As the family centered about woman, the attitude of the philosophes toward woman was, on the whole, a conventional one. They shared in the popular view that woman was naturally inferior to man.[2] The most revolutionary of the philosophes, Rousseau, had the most traditional views of woman. Rousseau restricted woman to position of wife and mother, whose education and public activity were to be severely limited.[3] Diderot wrote a severe condemnation of women, as an inferior sex, who were constantly conspiring to maintain their domination over men.[4]

Although marriage, as an institution, was seldom or never attacked, sex freedom was regarded with a degree of tolerance approaching indifference. In fashionable society the mistress had become an accepted convention, following the example of the court. Living in fashionable or in parvenu society, the philosophes took their manners and morals, if not their politics and economics, from the court. Nearly all the philosophes had mistresses, who constituted a sort of hetaerae in eighteenth-century France.

Sex freedom, however, did not imply the emancipation of woman. It was regarded, not as a principle of individual liberty, but as a form of normal indulgence. What is called today "free love" would have been considered wicked and sinful by fashionable France of that period. In other words, the French had a liberal attitude toward sex but not toward woman, an attitude which they have preserved to this day. This attitude was made possible by the suppression of the puritanic elements of the nation, the Huguenots and the Jansenists. The former lived in the obscurity of semioutlawry, and the latter were regarded with contempt by both court and salon. Eighteenth-century France was either Catholic or libertarian, and both were hostile to the puritan spirit.

Against this background of sex looseness, Condorcet presented an anomalous figure. He was a man of austere morals, and his relations with women were dictated by a sense of honor that was puritanic rather than chivalrous. So far as it is known Condorcet never indulged in a mistress. He was that rare man among the intellectuals of his day who was happily married, and entirely devoted to his wife. What is more significant, however, is that Condorcet severely criticized the institution of the family as it existed in his day, and became an ardent advocate of the rights of woman. He was the one

FEMINISM

philosophe who was a feminist, and in the most modern sense of that word, and he may be fairly described as the most outstanding pioneer in the movement for the emancipation of women, the forerunner of Mary Wollstonecraft and John Stuart Mill. In the society in which he lived Condorcet's feminist views were so unique that, had it not been for his high position and reputation, he would have been subjected to virulent criticism and ridicule. As it was, he was listened to respectfully, but not attentively.

Condorcet's temperament and experience may help to explain his liberal attitude toward woman. His shyness and sensitiveness, the result, according to some of his biographers, of his childhood experience in wearing girl's clothes, perhaps gave him a sympathetic understanding of the nature of women. His marriage to the brilliant Sophie de Grouchy undoubtedly influenced his feminist views throughout his married life. Condorcet was in constant intellectual communion with his wife, who stimulated his thoughts and who aided him in his writings. In Sophie he beheld the realization of the potential abilities of woman.

At a time when men did not have the vote, Condorcet was a strong and uncompromising champion of votes for women, as well as votes for men. The arguments in favor of woman suffrage and the replies of its champions to their opponents, made familiar by the woman suffrage movement of our time, can be found in Condorcet's two pamphlets, *Letters of a Citizen of New Haven* and *On the Admission of Women to the Suffrage*.[5] In these pamphlets Condorcet advocated complete legal and political equality of women with men. His views were so comprehensive and so advanced that they anticipated those of John Stuart Mill in his famous essay, *Subjection of Women*, written eight decades later. Today Condorcet's pleas in favor of woman suffrage have the familiar sound of well-worn platitudes, but when his pamphlets appeared they were regarded with bewilderment as expressing the most daring and the most unconventional of ideas.

Condorcet pleaded for woman suffrage on the basis of natural rights which, he declared, came solely from the fact that "men are impressionable beings, susceptible to moral ideas and of reasoning from these ideas. As women have the same qualities as men, they of necessity have the same rights. Either no one truly has any rights or all have the same ones. And he who is against the rights of another because of religion, color, or sex abjures his own rights." [6] To those who argued that women, being physically weaker than men, were inferior to them, and that menstruation and pregnancy incapacitated women mentally, as well as physically, Condorcet replied that the same objection applied to men who had the gout every winter and who caught cold easily.[7]

To the objection that women were influenced chiefly by sentiment, and not by reason—a weighty objection in the Age of Reason—Condorcet replied that this characteristic of women was not due to their nature but to their bad education and to their inferior social status.[8] Women, he asserted, were rational but not as men were rational because their interests and occupations differed from those of men. It naturally followed that the same things did not have the same importance to both sexes. "It is as reasonable for a woman to be concerned about her physical charms as it was for Demosthenes to be concerned with his voice and gestures." [9] Oppressive laws, enacted by men, established great inequalities between the sexes. These laws, declared Condorcet, whose origin was due to force and whose continuance was due to sophistry, created a social environment for women, different from that of men.[10] Receiving a different education and living under different laws, women naturally did not have the same sense of justice and fairness as did men.

To the stock argument that, if women were enfranchised, they would neglect the home, Condorcet replied that enfranchised women would no more abandon their children, their household, and their sewing than would an enfranchised farmer abandon his plow, and an enfranchised artisan, his shop.[11] He advanced the idea, which is not yet a platitude, that enfranchisement would bring women into a larger world; as a result of the greater knowledge and wider experience that they would acquire, women would be all the more fitted to be mothers and wives. "Gallantry may suffer as a result of such a reform but domestic virtues will be the gainer because of this equality." [12]

Condorcet advocated also that women be made eligible for all public offices. Naturally they would not be chosen to fill certain offices, such as military, because of natural disqualifications.[13] To those who feared giving the ballot to women on the ground that it would enable them to exercise a preponderating influence, Condorcet replied that enfranchisement would result in making women's influence public, which was far less to be feared than the secret influence that women exercised.

In respect to woman's mental capacity Condorcet held interesting views. The masses of women, he declared, had the same mental capacity as the masses of men; but in the highest forms of science and philosophy, requiring extraordinary brain power, women had shown no genius. However, they were fitted to do secondary scientific work which required chiefly exactitude and patience.[14] Most of the shortcomings of women, Condorcet believed, were due to their bad education, and he consequently favored giving women equal opportunities with men in all grades of education, from the highest to the lowest.[15] He acutely realized that women had been held back, not only by lack of education, but by a subtle yet powerful form of discouragement, induced by the conventions of society which treated them as mentally inferior to men. "The kind of constraint imposed on women by traditional views regarding manners and morals," he declared, "has influenced their mind and soul almost from infancy; and when talent begins to develop this constraint has the effect of destroying it." [16]

Condorcet's liberal views regarding the rights of women led him to liberal views regarding family and sex. The indissolubility of marriage, he believed, was a fertile source of all sorts of social evils, adultery, prostitution, and bastardy. Marriage, he claimed, should be a civil contract only. Divorce was to be granted on the recommendation of an advisory council, consisting of the relatives of both parties. This council was to decide on the custody and the education of the children, whose rights were to be scrupulously maintained. Alimony was to be granted to either husband or wife, depending upon circumstances. Unfaithfulness in marriage, Condorcet argued, came chiefly from bad laws that forbade divorce, and that upheld the tyrannical authority of parents to decide the marriage of their children. The evils of illegitimacy were due to the absurd laws that deprived illegitimate children of their natural rights. These laws had originated "in the class division of society, in the great inequality of wealth, in the system that prevents children from marrying without their parents' consent, and, above all, in the indissolubility of marriage." [17]

Condorcet favored the establishment of special hospitals and homes for unmarried pregnant women, to which they could go for confinement without incurring publicity. After confinement the mother was to be given an opportunity to make a livelihood. Institutions were to be established for illegitimate children, where they would be taught a trade.[18] Condorcet went so far as to advocate that illegitimate children should be given rights to the property of both their parents, which would result in the partial abolition of illegitimacy.[19] A woman who was unfaithful to her husband, he argued, did not necessarily lose all virtue. "She may still be a good friend and a useful companion to her husband, and even a good mother to her children." Public opinion and the laws severely condemned the frailty of women, because "men punish severely those evils of which they are the instigators and accomplices." [20]

A consistent feminist, Condorcet openly advocated birth control. Once reason kept pace with the progress of the sciences and the arts, he declared, men would realize that their obligation to their children was not only to give them birth, but to assure them well-being. Before bringing children into the world they would take into consideration the general welfare of humanity, the society in which they lived, and the family of which they were part.[21]

Although Condorcet condemned sexual looseness he did not regard it as a very great evil. "Of all the passions of kings, love is the least deplorable as it effects the people. It was not indeed Marie Touchet who counseled the Massacre of St. Bartholomew. Madame de Montespan did not contribute in the slightest degree to the revocation of the Edict of Nantes . . . the confessors of kings have done infinitely more harm to Europe than their mistresses." [22] Puritanism existed, Condorcet declared, in countries where people were brutal, and where laws were bad. In such countries sexual irregularities produced disturbances, and therefore had to be curbed. Moreover, the old, who ruled the community, wished to suppress the sexual irregularities of the young because they themselves were no longer capable of sex activity. Priests purposely exaggerated the evils of sex because it gave them great power over men, all of whom were either guilty or desired to be guilty of sexual irregularity; and over women, whose moral interests were mainly concerned with sex.[23]

Puritanism, maintained Condorcet, led straight to hypocrisy. "There is no virtue so easy to practice or appear to practice as chastity; it is compatible with the absence of real virtue and the presence of every vice. From the moment chastity is considered of great importance every scoundrel is sure of obtaining public esteem at little expense." In those countries that boasted of their high morality "every vice, every crime, and even debauchery were sure to be prevalent."[24] The evils of indecent books, Condorcet believed, were greatly exaggerated. "What can result from reading such books? Nothing except to encourage a disposition to be kind and indulgent. . . . The satellites of Cromwell did not carry indecent books in their saddle bags."[25] According to Condorcet the problem of sex will be solved only by the equality of men and women; when that finally takes place, there will no longer be a conflict between natural desire and the interests of society. Manners and morals will then become pure and kindly because they will not be the outcome of repression, inspired by fear and shame, but of relations freely entered into by men and women.[26]

Condorcet had a lenient attitude even toward sex depravities, such as prostitution and homosexuality. Police activity against prostitutes, he argued, was as little justified as against other people, as long as they did not create disturbances.

Prostitutes should not be sent to prison, but to an institution where they would be taught an occupation.[27] He denounced the cruel laws against homosexuals who, he believed, should not be molested unless they were guilty of violence. Their punishment should be public disapproval, as their evil influence is indirect like those of drunkards and gamblers. To punish homosexuals by burning them alive, as in France, was atrocious; or by exposing them to mob violence, as in England, was cruel and indecent.[28]

Condorcet's liberal views on sex were inspired more by his belief in the freedom of the individual than by a tolerance toward sexual indulgence. Women and men should be free to dispose of themselves in all ways not harmful to society. To destroy the conventions and laws that hampered sexual freedom was, to Condorcet, as right as to destroy the prohibitions of Mercantilism that hampered the activity of merchants, or the guild regulations that hampered the activity of artisans, or the censorship laws that hampered the activity of writers. Feminism was, therefore, an integral part of the complete pattern of liberalism that Condorcet so enthusiastically advocated. Abstract in his thinking and rigid in his logical deductions, Condorcet saw in woman no subtleties of feminine psychology, no primal depths of wife and mother, but an *être sensible,* capable of moral ideas, and a potential citizen of a free state. It is no small tribute to Condorcet that he regarded woman as a free human personality at a time, like the eighteenth century, which was saturated with sentiment toward the "fair sex," and in a country, like France, where cynicism was so frequently the overtone of gallantry.

CHAPTER ELEVEN

POPULAR EDUCATION

AN aspect of the Intellectual Revolution of the eighteenth century, that has been slighted by the writers of the movement, is popular education. The great fame of Rousseau's *Emile,* which deals with methods of teaching and educational psychology, has had the effect of obscuring the movement for universal, popular education. The philosophes realized, some of them dimly, others, clearly, that an ignorant people was a passive instrument in the hands of the rulers who used ignorance and superstition as a means of maintaining despotism in all its forms. Man was good but he was often deceived because of a lack of knowledge, hence popular education alone was the remedy, according to the more advanced of the philosophes. Profoundly influenced by Locke's sensational theory they were convinced that only through education could a new environment be created which would be free from prejudices and traditions.

It is difficult to get a correct idea of the state of illiteracy in eighteenth-century France, as there existed no system of statistics for the entire nation. There was no national system of education. In many of the towns elementary schools, called *petites écoles,* were established, which were supported, partly from the fees of the pupils and partly from church endowments. These schools taught religion and the three R's, and the teachers were priests or laymen under the control of priests. Secondary education was given in the "colleges" of which there were about six hundred in France. These institutions were exclusive private schools, in which the chief subjects of study were the classics and scholastic philosophy. There were also twenty-two universities, scattered about the country, that specialized chiefly in theology and in law. Illiteracy was so common, that, according to Aulard, fully eighty percent of the people of France could neither read nor write.[1]

Under the Old Régime there was no motive for popular education. The mass of people were peasants, living in isolated farms or hamlets, who had little need for education; illiteracy was no hindrance to them in their daily labor. Education, under the Old Régime, was regarded chiefly as a form of elegant accomplishment for the upper classes, and as an avenue to learning for the clergy.

Due to the advance of commerce and industry, during the eighteenth century, the urban population grew. Literacy was a necessity to the city dweller because his occupation, whether as artisan, clerk, or merchant, required a knowledge of reading and writing. A movement in favor of popular education began early in the eighteenth century. One of its pioneers was that tireless humanitarian, Abbé Saint-Pierre, who advocated public education for girls as well as for boys.[2] Réné de la Chalotais, in his *Essai d'éducation nationale,* published in 1763, advocated a national system of secular education as a means of opposing the educational influence of the Jesuits.[3] Turgot, in 1775, recommended the organization of a national council of public education, which was to establish schools in every parish to teach the three R's, science, and the duties of citizenship.[4] A year later appeared a more ambitious educational project, Diderot's *Plan of a University*, a memorial addressed to Catherine the Great.[5] Diderot made an eloquent appeal to the Russian Empress to establish schools, open to all the children of the nation, where teachers, paid by the state, would teach the elements of all the sciences. The Physiocrats were strong advocates of universal education in order to teach people the principles of the Natural Order. When the Constituent Assembly set about unifying France by establishing uniform administrative and legal systems, it sought also to establish a common educational system. In 1791 Talleyrand submitted a report to the Assembly recommending the establishment of a national system of education, primary, secondary, and professional.[6]

The movement for popular education in France during the eighteenth century, however, found its greatest champion in Condorcet. His famous Report on Education, presented to the Legislative Assembly April 20-21, 1792, constitutes a landmark in educational history.[7] In the opinion of the French statesman, Edouard Herriot, "there is no educational reformer in France who can afford to neglect this document in which is concentrated and epitomized the best in the experience and in the revolutionary thought of the eighteenth century."[8] This Report consists of (1) five memoirs, philosophic treatises on education; and (2) a detailed curriculum for schools of every grade, from the elementary to the university, and of every type, cultural, technical, and professional. "Probably no finer ideal of education in a national state has ever been set forth than that of Condorcet as given in his *Report*. Many of its provisions have been adopted in the national systems of education which have been developed since his time, while in large part it continues to represent an ideal

POPULAR EDUCATION 199

toward which the thoughtful leaders are striving." [9] Condorcet, unlike Rousseau, did not have the gift of a vibrant and eloquent style, hence his Report, original, profound, and amazingly forward-looking, did not receive the acclaim that was accorded to *Emile*.

"Public education is a duty that society owes to all citizens." [10] This opening sentence sounds the keynote of Condorcet's Report. A national system of education was to be established, the objects of which were "to assure to each one the opportunity of making himself more efficient in his work; of making himself more capable of performing his civic functions; and of developing, to the highest degree, the talents that one has received from nature, thereby establishing among the citizens actual equality in order to make real the political equality decreed by law." [11]

Throughout the Report Condorcet implies that education was essentially a public, not a private, function. The system of private schools, that catered to the rich under the Old Régime, went hand-in-hand with a caste system of society in which education was a sign of wealth and position. Consistent democrat that he was, Condorcet realized that the essential function of a free state was to open the door of opportunity to every citizen, the opportunity to lead a larger life in all respects, political, social, economic, and cultural. And the door of opportunity, in a democracy, was education, public, universal, and free in all grades. Otherwise, the mass of citizens, legally free and equal, would remain in a position of permanent inferiority. It was in the power of society, argued Condorcet, to diminish the effects of natural and social inequality by using its organized powers to give to the less fortunate individuals every opportunity for education. Ignorance not only led to poverty, but, according to Condorcet, it was in itself a form of poverty because it led to dependence, in this instance, on the learned. It was not necessary that everyone should have the same degree of education, but sufficient to guarantee to each one the enjoyment of his rights. In despotic states, Condorcet declared, the military power of the few was supported by the educated class on whose knowledge the masses depended. In free states, the man "who knows ordinary arithmetic, that he needs in daily life, is not dependent on the learned mathematician. The latter's talents could then be of the greatest use to him, without danger to the enjoyment of his rights." [12]

It was Condorcet's belief that an educated class, no matter how learned and talented, hindered the rapid progress of the race. Far greater would be the progress of mankind if the large amount of talent, of the first and second order, possessed by many gifted individuals among the masses were given the opportunity to develop through popular education. One of its special contributions would be to discover ability of the second rank, a type of ability which is especially useful in scientific research because discoveries are often the outcome of aid given by able assistants to great inventors.[13]

Of all the philosophes no one saw more clearly than did Condorcet the necessity of enlightening the masses. "One must not believe," he declared, "that the wealthy classes could continue for long to be enlightened if the masses were condemned to eternal stupidity. It is when it spreads, and not when it contracts, that enlightenment becomes really effective. The more that enlightenment is restricted to a few the greater is the danger that error will tarnish its brightness." [14] Only by means of education could a turbulent, unruly, superstitious populace be transformed into an orderly, enlightened, and self-contained people. Education was especially necessary in a democracy, otherwise the masses would not know their rights and would be unable to fulfill their political duties. "Diffusion of knowledge enables a people to establish good laws, a wise administration, and a truly free constitution." [15]

Education was essential in promoting the economic progress of the lower classes. Many would rise to the professional and commercial ranks, if they were not barred by lack of education and by the restrictions imposed on commerce and industry. Prosperity would become general, and it would then be of small consequence if some few were very wealthy. In an almost uncanny fashion did Condorcet, living as he did at the dawn of the Industrial Revolution, anticipate the present-day problem of educating for leisure. As industry advanced, he argued, the division of labor would become greater and greater, and each laborer would be limited to doing continuously only a few simple movements. The effect upon the laborer would be that his mind would almost cease to function. Such a situation would result in stupefying a portion of mankind, unless an extensive system of education was provided for this class of workers as a means of offsetting the effects of the monotony of their daily labor.[16]

As education, according to Condorcet, was a natural right it was a right that applied to women as well as to men. Women, too, were citizens, and needed education in order to know their rights and to perform their duties. A thoroughgoing feminist Condorcet was a stout advocate of equal educational opportunity for women. "One cannot see," he declared, "why one of the sexes reserves for itself certain subjects of knowledge, why matters that are generally useful to every human being should not be taught equally to both sexes." [17] Women's ignorance brought inequalities in the home, and poisoned the relations between the sexes. The ignorant wife was despised by her husband, and ridiculed by her sons. Only an educated wife could be a worthy companion to her husband, and be really interested in his work.[18] An ignorant mother was not a fit person to bring up her children.

Condorcet favored coeducation, in the primary grades, on the ground that it would lead to comradeship between the sexes. It would result, he argued, not in distracting the pupils from their studies, but in emulation in order to find preference in the eyes of the opposite sex. Men and women would associate freely, if boys and girls were prepared for their adult life by coeducation in school. Comradeship between the sexes would result in a higher morality by dissipating the illusions and excitements that are generally induced by separation. The real reason for separating the sexes in school, Condorcet clearly saw, was snobbishness. Aristocrats feared misalliances, which would come from association between boys and girls at school. Democracy should, therefore, favor coeducation as a means of destroying aristocratic exclusiveness, which is fostered by marriages inspired by family position.[19] "A constitution which establishes political equality will be neither durable nor desirable if it permits the existence of social institutions favorable to inequality." [20]

As a freethinker and anticlerical, Condorcet was strongly opposed to religious instruction in the public school. The church, not the school, was to be the place for religious instruction. Parents of all faiths and of all opinions would then send their children to secular public schools. He proposed to substitute moral and civic for religious instruction, a policy later followed by the Third French Republic. Moral instruction should be absolutely separated from religious dogmas and ceremonies because morality was everywhere the same;

but when morality was associated with religion, corruption was generally the result. In order to make sure that education would remain completely secular, priests were to be forbidden to teach in the public schools.[21]

Condorcet had the quite modern notion that vice was often the result of intellectual poverty rather than that of a lack of religious training. "Vice arises," he declared, "from the need of escaping from boredom in times of leisure and to make that escape through the sensations rather than through ideas."[22] He believed with all his soul in the moral influence of education, and he came to this view, partly as a result of discussions with Franklin.[23] Moral instruction, however, should be based strictly on scientific truth. The custom, Condorcet declared, of filling children's heads with unreal terrors, in order better to manage them, should be banished. Otherwise, when they grow to adolescence, a period when passion is strong and reason feeble, they will realize the contradiction between their desires and their views. On the first examination "the entire edifice of morality will collapse, and, henceforth, they will be convinced that everyone who speaks to them of duties is a liar and a hypocrite."[24]

Condorcet had an invincible repugnance to the teaching of dogmas of any kind, political as well as religious. According to him the aim of all education was to produce a type of mind, free, liberal, and critical, that would be able to carry on the progress of mankind without the hindrances of tradition and faith. To him, as to the other philosophes, the past was not the light of experience but the darkness of prejudices, from which the eighteenth century had succeeded in emancipating itself. He feared the creation of another past, equally vicious, unless every generation was taught to evaluate the existing ideas and institutions in the light of the latest scientific knowledge. Instruction should, therefore, be given in a critical, and not in a conforming spirit. There was altogether too great a tendency, he declared, on the part of the pupil to depend on the authority of the teacher or on that of a book. To counteract this tendency the teacher should encourage his pupils to study in a spirit of *libre examen* in order to avoid traditional ideas and consecrated attitudes that are generally favored by those who wish to perpetuate existing abuses.

The schools should not teach opinions as if they were true, especially in matters of politics and government. In a few notable passages, Condorcet clearly stated the danger of permitting the state to impose political dogmas through the medium of the public schools. "The aim of education," he declared, "is not to instill admiration for the existing political system but to create a critical attitude toward it. Each generation should not be compelled to submit to the opinions of its predecessors, but it should be enlightened so that it could govern itself by its own reason." [25] The constitution and the Declaration of Rights should be taught as facts, not as eternal truths. "It has been said," he declared, "that the teaching of the constitution of the country ought to form part of public instruction. That is doubtless true providing it is taught merely as a fact and as a system to be explained and analyzed. . . . But to teach the constitution as a dogma that is universally true or to arouse blind enthusiasm for it would result in making the citizens incapable of judging it. To say, 'Behold, this is what you should love and believe,' would be to create a kind of religion. It would result in chaining the mind, and in violating liberty in its most sacred aspect under the pretext of teaching to cherish it." [26] The false philosophers wished "to capture the imagination of the child in order to stamp on it images that time could not erase, so that the adult would be attached to the existing political system through blind sentiment." [27] The school should also avoid teaching nationalism, which would create "patriotic charlatans." On the contrary, children should be taught the history of foreign nations as well as that of their own in order to foster sympathy for all peoples. Especially should the schools teach loyalty to the rights of man. To Condorcet patriotism of ideas, not of country, was the chief aim of civic instruction.

Finally, Condorcet favored universal education on the ground that it was essential to the progress of mankind. An educated generation would not merely carry on, but would improve as a result of new discoveries. Education, therefore, constantly increased the social heritage, and became the supreme mechanism of progress. By means of education, nations could progress; and evils, incident to progress, could be avoided by preparing for changes in advance. A nation might be ruined by adhering to the very policies that had once brought prosperity.

Condorcet's approach to the problems of education was primarily that of a statesman and social philosopher. Only incidentally was he interested in child psychology and in methods of instruction. Education to him was a part of political science, and the supreme function of the school was to prepare citizens for a democratic state. As the teachers of his day saw in the child the future "gentleman," so did Condorcet see in him the future "citizen." All the subjects to be taught, all the methods to be followed, were designed to produce a "virtuous citizen," the sum of all known good, public and private. Condorcet was, in truth, the great theoretician of democratic national education, and his proposals constituted "a masterpiece of prophetic insight and true feeling for the instrumentalities of democratic education." [28]

The second part of the Report presents a complete plan of instruction in a national system of education, "a plan new, bold and of marvelous precision, yet containing nothing utopian, nothing extreme." [29] There were to be four grades, primary, secondary, institutes, and lycées all of which were to be free, and open to both men and women. An educated nation, not an educated class, was the aim of Condorcet's plan. The base of the entire system was to be the primary school, established in every district. It was to be a four-year course, and roughly corresponded to the *école primaire* of present-day France and to the primary school of present-day America. This school was to teach the three R's and the elements of geometry, geography, and agriculture. Moral instruction was to be given in the form of stories to arouse sympathy for all living things. There was also to be, what is now called, civic instruction in the rights and duties of citizens. The secondary school, also four years, roughly corresponded to the present French *école primaire supérieur* and to the American grammar school. A secondary school was to be established in the chief city in each district. It was to teach the elements of the pure and of the natural sciences, of commerce, of foreign languages, and of the social sciences. Attached to the secondary schools were to be libraries, laboratories, and botanical gardens. The institute roughly corresponded to the present French *lycée* and to the American high school. Institutes were to be established only in the chief cities in each department. They were to continue the work of the secondary schools, but with great emphasis on the teaching of science and on technical training. Here is seen the influence of the Encyclopaedia, which so greatly emphasized

POPULAR EDUCATION

the importance of the mechanical arts. As part of the work of the institute the students were to visit the workshops in order that their training might be along practical lines. Finally, came the lycée, roughly corresponding to the present university, which was to prepare primarily for the liberal professions. In a sense Condorcet's lycée anticipated the present university, for it was to comprehend the teaching of *toute connaissance,* and not limited, as were most of the universities of his day, to theology, law, and medicine. There were to be nine lycées, situated in the chief cities of France. Every profession was to be taught in these institutions, except the ministry which was restricted to seminaries.

Overtopping the four degrees of instruction there was to be organized a National Society of Arts and Sciences, composed of the learned men of the nation. Once established this body was to be self-perpetuating. Its seat was to be Paris, with branches in the departments. This body was to have complete supervision of the entire educational system of France.

There are several outstanding features in the curricula of the four grades, which included the teaching of midwifery as well as scientific agriculture, of military engineering as well as of arithmetic. One feature was the minimum time devoted to the classics and the great emphasis upon science. There was provision for only a few courses in Latin and Greek, on the ground that the ideas of the ancients were not in harmony with modern life, and that their literature was full of scientific errors.[30] Nearly all superstitions, Condorcet believed, were founded on ignorance of science, which should be taught in order to fortify mankind against false views and against charlatans.[31] "All errors in government and in society are based on philosophic errors which, in turn, are derived from errors in natural science." [32] Condorcet believed that the cultivation of fine literary taste, which he admitted came from an intensive study of the classics, was not essential in the fundamental education of the entire nation. His great emphasis on the teaching of science was due to the fact that he was far more influenced by the Scientific Revolution than by the classical Renaissance. In raising the issue of science *versus* the classics in education, Condorcet anticipated the educational views of Herbert Spencer, which had a great influence in giving science its present place in the schools. "He is the first who demanded forcefully that education, hitherto too exclusively literary, should also include serious instruction in science." [33]

Another aspect of Condorcet's plan is that the four grades constitute an open educational corridor, from the lowest to the highest. In order to abolish illiteracy everyone was to go to the primary school to receive the minimum of education. The grades, above the primary, were to be likewise open and free; but, obviously, only those parents who could do without the labor of their children, would be able to send them to the higher grades, which were to be public boarding schools, where only tuition, not maintenance, would be free. Condorcet fully realized that talented children of the poor would not, therefore, have the opportunity to develop their abilities. Despite early handicaps some talented but poor men would become educated through their own individual efforts. But Condorcet keenly realized the shortcomings of the "self-educated man" who has so often been held up as a model. "Those who have not received early education," he declared, "and who rise to enlightenment by their own efforts or by a happy chance never fully develop their powers." [34] In order to conserve all the abilities of the nation he provided for the establishment of scholarships, in the schools above the elementary, for the talented children of the poor, who were to be known as the *élèves de la patrie*.[35] These scholarships were to be given on the basis of competitive examinations, and the winners were to be boarded and lodged at public expense. According to Condorcet's plan, the state would say to all children: "Your parents have the means to give you only the knowledge that is most essential to you, but in this educational plan you are assured of easily getting and extending it. If nature has given you talent you can now develop it so that it will be lost neither to you nor to the nation." [36] The system of national scholarships, later established in France, owes its inspiration, in part, to Condorcet's fruitful suggestion of *élèves de la patrie*.

How about the mass of citizens who had gone through the primary schools and had no special talent? Were they to be left, with their three R's, ignorant of the intellectual progress that the world was making? What an intelligent man would do for himself the state should do for all, even for those who lack energy and ambition, was Condorcet's answer.[37] He made provision for a scheme of adult education which suggested the most modern experiments in this field. Sunday was to be the day of adult education for those whose schooling did not go beyond the primary grade. Condorcet did not visualize evening schools, living as he did before the short work-day came as a result of the invention of labor-saving machinery. Sunday, being given over to education, he argued, would be truly a day of rest because a healthy repose does not consist in doing nothing but in a change of activity. In these Sunday schools for adults, lectures and reading courses were to be given. There was to be civic instruction, based upon the Declaration of the Rights of Man. New laws were to be explained and discussed. Discoveries in science were to be explained.

In this way an intelligent public opinion would be formed, and the masses would no longer be, as they had always been, "docile instruments in adroit hands." [38] Farmers were to be instructed in scientific agriculture, as it was of the utmost importance to enlighten the tillers of the soil, who were generally opposed to new methods. Parents were to be instructed in the care and training of children, as "the ignorance and prejudices of parents are among the causes that degrade humanity and shorten the duration of human life." [39] These suggestions of Condorcet concerning adult education, bold and original for his day, are now almost universally applied. "All who are engaged in promoting the cause of adult education that we see developing on all sides, courses for adults, university extension, people's theaters, should salute him as one of their pioneers and masters. All that they need do is to take up his program and apply it." [40]

In teaching the moral and social sciences the most important thing to keep in mind, according to Condorcet, was that they were entirely new subjects of study, therefore free from political and religious traditions. The teaching of history was especially important. Condorcet severely criticized the historians who, because of their conservative bias, failed to enlighten their readers. According to these historians, the Roman Senate was a fountainhead of virtue; in fact it was a body composed of hypocritical and cruel tyrants.[41] In the teaching of history stress should be laid on biography. The lives of philosophers and scientists should be taught along with those of statesmen and soldiers; ideas, no less than public acts, constituted history.[42] Condorcet regarded Voltaire's famous universal history, *Essay on the Morals and Manners of Mankind*, as a model history because it was a record of civilization, with emphasis on the arts and sciences,

POPULAR EDUCATION

not a heroic tale of military and political exploits. He had little enthusiasm for popular heroes. "It is essential for all men to have the simple virtues of a sage, but very few find any use for heroic virtues; moreover, it is not beneficial that many should have such virtues or even desire to have them." [43] Because history should treat chiefly of arts and sciences it should be international, not national, in spirit. According to Condorcet a history should be so written that it "can be taught in England, in Russia, in Virginia, as well as in Berne or in Venice." [44]

It is surprising how Condorcet anticipated the modern problem of the intellectual independence of the teacher. If the aim of education was to produce a critical type of mind, teaching should not be authoritarian in spirit. "Generally all authority, of whatever nature and in whatever hands and in whatever way it was acquired, is a natural enemy of enlightenment. . . . Everyone who makes it his business to seek the truth is odious to those who exercise authority." [45] Hitherto, the teachers were mainly priests, who were unfitted to teach because there was an absolute incompatibility between the ecclesiastical functions and a system of national education. If a national system was to be under the control of the state, it would naturally follow that the teachers would be dependent upon the political power. How was the teacher to avoid jumping from the frying pan of church control into the fire of political control? Condorcet's solution of this problem was to organize the teachers as an autonomous body, really a teachers' guild. The National Society of Arts and Sciences was to appoint the teachers in the lycées. In each department the local branch of the Society was to draw up lists of candidates for teaching positions in the three lower grades. The teachers in the primary school would be selected, from the list, by the fathers in the district; and those in the secondary schools, by the local authorities; and those in the institutes, by committees of teachers in the lycées.[46] Teachers were to be paid by the state, and were to be provided with liberal pensions. They were to have permanent tenure; and dismissal was to be on charges and after a jury trial. Distinguished authors were to be selected to write some of the textbooks as their contribution to popular education. To make sure that the educational system kept step with progress, teachers, textbooks, and methods were to be subjected to periodic examination by the National Society.

All the schools were to be supported by the localities, aided by state subventions. There was no definite provision in the Report for a compulsory education law. Condorcet assumed that the desire for knowledge was itself compelling, hence there was no need of such a law. However, he was opposed to a state monopoly of education, a system inspired by Rousseau. He distinctly favored the maintenance of private schools as a means of correcting the evils of public education and of sustaining the zeal of the public teachers through competition. He believed that the rivalry of the private school would compel the public school to maintain a high level.[47]

It is the judgment of Brunetière that Condorcet's sole title to fame rests on his treatises on education. "What was as yet in the realm of Utopia for the Encyclopaedists and for Rousseau was made by him real and lasting."[48] Condorcet's Report included the educational reforms advocated in his day and anticipated those that triumphed in the nineteenth and twentieth centuries, such as the teaching of science, civic instruction, secular education, coeducation, and adult education. In France it was the inspiration of the educational reforms of the Convention, of Napoleon, of Guizot during the reign of Louis Philippe, of Duruy during the reign of Na-

POPULAR EDUCATION 213

poleon III, and of Ferry and Buisson during the Third French Republic.

In the history of popular education in France the first step was the law of 1833, fathered by Guizot, which established elementary schools throughout the nation. But these schools were neither entirely free nor entirely secular; and education was not made compulsory. The next great step was the Ferry Laws of 1881-86, fathered by Jules Ferry and Ferdinand Buisson, which made elementary education free, compulsory, and secular. However, the educational system, established by the Third French Republic, echoed the class divisions of the country. The masses went to the *écoles primaires,* elementary schools which did not prepare for secondary and higher education. The well-to-do went to the *lycées* which gave both elementary and secondary education; and the courses of study were so arranged that graduates could prepare for higher education in the universities or in professional schools. Both the *écoles primaires* and the *lycées* were public schools; the former were free, but fees were charged in the latter.

The World War gave a great impetus to democratic education in France. "The fathers fought in the same trenches, and their children should therefore sit on the same benches," was the cry of the new generation. A movement, known as the *Ecole unique,* was started by a group of young educators, who called themselves *les Compagnons.* They aimed to establish a unified system of national education, free to all, from the lowest to the highest grades. The movement found an enthusiastic supporter in Premier Herriot, whose ministry (1924-25) openly espoused the cause of the *Ecole unique.* It may be said that Condorcet's Report influenced this latest educational reform in France. Its power of conception and divination was so remarkable, declared Herriot, "that even today it seems infinitely more modern and more coherent than the existing system of education. . . . Not only did Condorcet foresee free education in all grades, but he constantly associated general culture with professional training, the education of the child with the education of the entire nation." [49] Important steps have since been taken to abolish the "two childhoods" in order to realize the ideal of a common education for the children of all classes. Since 1925 both the *écoles primaires* and the *lycées* have had the same curriculum, the same organization, and the same standards of teaching. In 1930 the government began the policy of gradually abolishing all fees in the secondary schools. The triumph of the *Ecole unique* would not mean the establishment of a state monopoly of education, a policy which is opposed by the reformers as it had been by Condorcet. Private schools, of any sort, would be freely permitted to exist alongside the national schools.[50]

Popular education has been the sustaining faith of liberals in all lands, and, especially, in America and France. Condorcet voiced this faith, so clearly and so ardently, that he might well be called the precursor of the contemporary movement for national education. This movement is no longer confined to the abolition of illiteracy, but aims to open the roads to all knowledge to anyone capable of traveling on them. A century and a half ago Condorcet conceived this great design in all its fullness.

CHAPTER TWELVE

THE REDISCOVERY OF AMERICA

ALWAYS has man dreamed of a better life than the one that he was living. If the evils of his existence seemed insurmountable he sought to find an escape either in a Heavenly City of future life or in an ideal commonwealth of his imagination. Plato's *Republic,* St. Augustine's *City of God,* and More's *Utopia* are the most famous examples of human striving for universal happiness.

With the discovery of America a new world swam within the ken of Europe. And it set the utopian imagination going in a new direction. Perhaps the ideal commonwealth was already in existence in the state of nature in the New World. And, if it was not, perhaps it could be established by those who sought to be free from the evils of the Old World. An ideal commonwealth was no longer an escape; it was now a prospect.

Of all those who, in the eighteenth century, were seeking for human betterment the French philosophes stand out preeminent. These humanity-intoxicated writers were convinced that a perfect society was not only possible but might even be in existence. History which, in the words of Voltaire, was a "mass of crimes, of follies, and of misfortunes," surely could show no instance of such a society. Could their own age, the Age of Reason, furnish an example of a country wherein reigned liberty and equality? At first the hopes of the philosophes of finding such a country centered on England. Due to the great admiration for English institutions, expressed by Voltaire in his *Letters on the English* and by Montesquieu in his *Spirit of Laws,* a veritable Anglomania raged in France.[1] England, in French liberal opinion, was that happy land wherein a representative parliament, not a despotic monarch, governed the people; wherein dissenters from the established faith were tolerated; and wherein there was no system of censorship.

But England, as a Heavenly City, evaporated toward the end of the eighteenth century, largely as a result of the hostile feeling between the French and the English, who fought on three continents during the Seven Years' War. The search for the Heavenly City began anew, and, this time, the philosophes were more fortunate. French travelers returned from the New World bearing marvelous tales of having found the only true and ideal state. A literature about America appeared in France in which the former was pictured with rapturous enthusiasm as a land wherein the rights of man were universally recognized, and wherein lived a liberty-loving people whose rulers were philosophers. America alone seemed to have all the necessary conditions for the realization of the ideals of the philosophes. She was a primitive land, and, therefore, in the "state of nature." The inhabitants had come to America in search of liberty, and had established free governments on the basis of compacts. Having no traditions and no prejudices, America was a *tabula rasa* on which the philosopher and statesman were free to write. At last the great dream of the philosophes and the actual situation in America

REDISCOVERY OF AMERICA 217

coincided. "For half a century the philosophes had demanded a new order, and their dreams were realized in another land. What had been for them only words and paper had, in America, become flesh and blood; words had become things. The Golden Age had returned, and they were thrilled with longing to read news of it. They were feverish with admiration, desires, and hopes." [2]

So widespread was the interest, roused by the French writers, in colonial America that it constituted a veritable rediscovery of the New World. Foremost among these literary discoverers was Abbé Raynal whose famous book, *Philosophic and Political History of European Settlements and Commerce in the Two Indies*, appeared in 1770. It contained eloquent descriptions of life in the American colonies, where the people were shown to be simple in their manners, virtuous in their life, and tolerant in religion. The book can hardly be described as a history; it is rather a tract for the times, being filled with attacks on despotism and superstition. It had an enormous vogue in its day, and became the model for many books on America. Almost as famous as the book of Raynal was Crèvecoeur's *Letters of an American Farmer*, published in 1784, an idyll of colonial America, with sentimental descriptions of nature and of the simple virtues of the Americans. Another well-known volume was *Voyages of Marquis de Chastellux in North America* which appeared in 1786. The author, the Marquis de Chastellux, gave a picturesque and entertaining account of his visit to America. The journalist, Brissot, who became the leader of the Girondins during the French Revolution, came to America, and wrote several volumes, which outdid even Raynal's book in its rhapsodic admiration of the free and simple life in the New World.[3] Of all the books on America in the eighteenth century, the most critical was Mazzei's *A Historical and Political Study of the United States* which appeared in 1788. It exposed the errors of Raynal and Chastellux, and gave a fairly reliable history of each colony.[4]

The idealization of colonial America found expression in an extravagant admiration of the Quaker. Voltaire, in his *Letters on the English,* had discovered the Quaker, as a hero, and had praised him as that unusual Christian who was both religious and tolerant. But the Quaker in sophisticated England was out of place; he needed the background of primitive America to be exhibited in all his virtues. In the Quaker settlement of Pennsylvania, the French admirers of America found a veritable *Age d'Or,* a Utopia "without masters and without priests" where reigned peace, tolerance, justice, and virtue. Raynal, Crèvecoeur, and Brissot outdid each other in their admiration of the Quaker. Pennsylvania became synonymous with America, and the broad mantle of the Quaker covered all the colonials.[5]

The second phase of the rediscovery of America, in the eighteenth century, was concerned with the American Revolution. In this phase the most prominent figure was Condorcet, who became an ardent protagonist of American political ideas. Condorcet's contact was with Americans, not with America, as he never visited this country. He came to know Americans who were visiting France, and was especially attracted by Paine and Franklin. The Masonic "Lodge of the Nine Sisters," of which Condorcet was an active member, was a common meeting place of French and American liberals.[6] There Condorcet came into contact with Franklin, and he shared, fully and ardently, in the enthusiastic admiration of his fellow countrymen for the American philosopher. The immense popularity of Franklin in France was due, to a large

REDISCOVERY OF AMERICA 219

extent, to the belief that that highly sophisticated and shrewd gentleman was the reincarnation of the primitive man, with all his virtues intact, but made agreeable in the familiar form of an eighteenth-century philosopher. Paine became Condorcet's intimate friend and co-worker, from whom he learned much of America. Condorcet's knowledge of American political ideas came chiefly from the writings of Paine, of Franklin, and of Jefferson and from the Federalist. He studied assiduously the *Collection of the Constitutions of the English Colonies* (*Recueil des lois constitutives des colonies Anglaises*), a compilation of American state constitutions, translated into French and published in 1778, which had a wide circulation in France. Throughout the twelve volumes of Condorcet's collected works there are frequent references to America. He, too, indulged in the eighteenth-century habit of writing imaginary letters in criticism of his country. In his *Letters of a Citizen of New Haven* and *Letters of a Citizen of the United States*, Condorcet praised America as the inspiration of the ideas and policies that he advocated for France.[7]

The America that Condorcet discovered was not the colonial America, so much praised by the literary travelers; it was the America that came into existence as a result of the American Revolution. Unlike Raynal and Crèvecoeur he was not in search of a Utopia in some far-off primitive land. His great search was to discover the laws of social progress, as revealed by history, and to apply them to the great problems of his day. Such a method would lead to continuous progress, and, finally, to the perfectibility of mankind. In Condorcet's opinion the Americans of the Revolution were the first people that had sufficient vision and courage to adopt this method. The corrupt nations of Europe "could not believe," he declared, "that in the forests of the New World there lived a race of men who had a profound understanding of the principles of human society, and whose first experiments were lessons to Europe." [8]

Curiously enough Condorcet did not see in the American Revolution a violent uprising against constituted authority, similar to the Puritan Revolution in England which he detested. To him the American Revolution was a vindication of the rights of man, against usurping despotism, by a strong, self-confident people who were led by the philosophers, Franklin, Jefferson, and Paine. The war that followed the assertion by the Americans of their natural rights took place, as he believed, because it could not be expected that the public order would be left undisturbed in the midst of a struggle between a people, bent on reëstablishing its rights, and the tyrants who had usurped them.[9] Condorcet failed to see that the American Revolution was the culmination of struggles, during the colonial period, between England and the Thirteen Colonies, concerning all sorts of interests, political, social, and economic. To him it was a bold experiment in the application of the doctrine of the rights of man to actual conditions. In the American triumph, he beheld, as, later, Goethe beheld in the triumph of the French revolutionary soldiers at the battle of Valmy, the beginning of a new era in history. In his *Sketch of the Intellectual Progress of Mankind* Condorcet especially emphasized the importance, in world history, of the American Revolution. The American cause "was pleaded before the tribunal of opinion in the presence of all Europe. The rights of man were firmly sustained and developed, without restrictions or reservations, in writings that circulated from the shores of the Neva to those of the Guadalquiver. This discussion penetrated the most enslaved countries, the most remote villages, whose inhabitants were astonished to learn that they had rights. They learned to value these rights, now that they knew that other men had dared to assert and to defend them." [10] Typically and completely the ideologue, Condorcet, saw in all national and class struggles a conflict of ideas, not of interests. And his interpretation of the American Revolution was, in consequence, vitiated by this limitation, which was also the limitation of his age.

Once started on the road to political freedom by the Revolution the Americans, in Condorcet's view, created systems and methods of attaining it, which finally solved the problem that had confronted the liberal thinkers of the eighteenth century of how an evil system was to be abolished, and a good one, established. Every step in the process of creating a free state, taken by America, harmonized with Condorcet's scheme of political liberalism.[11] In other words, America was the one country, according to Condorcet, where liberalism, in all its manifestations, was adopted both in theory and in practice.

Of primal importance, in his opinion, were the Declaration of Independence and the Declaration of Rights in the new state constitutions, which definitely formulated the doctrines of natural rights and popular sovereignty. These philosophic Declarations were novel in public law. Their predecessor, the English Bill of Rights, was not philosophic in tone; it merely demanded the specific rights of subjects and of members of parliament. The abstract political philosophy that European thinkers had been discussing, for two centuries, was at last made practical by the political movement in America. Condorcet sang paeans of praise to the Virginia Declaration of Rights and to the American Declaration of Independence. "The first Declaration of Rights that is entitled to be called such is that of Virginia, adopted June 1, 1776; its author is entitled to the eternal gratitude of mankind." [12] The Declaration of Independence, he declared, was a concrete illustration of the "restoration of humanity's title deeds," the comment of Voltaire on Montesquieu's *Spirit of Laws*. It was not sufficient that natural rights "should be written in the books of philosophers and in the hearts of virtuous men; it is essential that the ignorant and the weak should read them in the example of a great people. America has given us this example. The act by which she declared her independence is an exposition, simple and sublime, of rights that have been sacred, though long forgotten." [13]

From America, too, according to Condorcet, came the second step in the process whereby a people passed from despotism to freedom, namely, the creation of a new government through the adoption of a written constitution, drawn up by a constitutional convention. To Condorcet a constitutional convention was a great innovation in political science. It assumed confidence in natural reason and in the knowledge and love of natural rights.[14] After the adoption of the Declaration of Independence the states in America adopted constitutions, generally through the machinery of conventions. In 1780 Massachusetts inaugurated the method of having a constitution, drawn up by a convention chosen for that purpose; the constitution was then submitted for ratification to the voters. Then came the famous federal convention of 1787. These events greatly impressed Condorcet. "Then was observed," he declared, "for the first time, the example of a great people throwing off all their chains at once, and peaceably establishing a system of government which, it believed, would be most conducive to its happiness. Their geographical situation and political history obliged the Americans to establish a federal republic; and thirteen republican constitutions appeared, about the same time, all based on a solemn recognition of the rights of man, the preservation of which was their chief object." [15]

The adoption of state and federal constitutions in the United States, by constitutional conventions, showed the influence of the theory of "contract." A written constitution was an actual illustration of the vast assumption of the social contract, so widespread in the eighteenth century, which even Rousseau, its most fervent advocate, really did not believe had ever taken place. To Condorcet the proceeding was marvelous, as indeed it was marvelous. "There is something arresting and majestic in this spectacle of a new structure, framed deliberately in the full light of modern record . . . achieving that sacramental, intangible air of immemorial things. Here is something which had not grown, but was planned; which took no force from the weight of centuries, but was put together, mechanically in a few years; which had no foundation in sanctifying legend and the appeal to some vastly distant heroic time, but reposed on the known debates, arguments, and votes of recent men." [16]

A written constitution is unquestionably America's original contribution to the science of government. It was widely adopted, during the nineteenth century, by the European nations when they overthrew absolutism and established parliamentary government. The purpose of a written constitution was: (1) to stabilize conditions after a revolution had taken place; and (2) to guarantee, for the future, the fundamental rights gained by the revolution.

To Condorcet the great opportunity that came to the Americans, as a result of their Revolution, was that of initiating a constitution. In breaking away from England the Americans "were compelled to destroy, at one blow, all the bonds of government, and to create new ones in the midst of the distractions of war. The wisdom that they showed in creating new laws astonished the most enlightened nations of the world." [17] When the federal constitution appeared Condorcet translated it into French, adding critical comments on each article.[18] His most important criticism concerned the Senate. He considered the six-year term too long, and he advocated the popular election of Senators, as being nearest to a unicameral system which he preferred to a bicameral system. He was also opposed to the equal representation of the states in the Senate, and he favored a system of representation proportional to the population of the states.

Condorcet leveled a severe criticism at the American system of separating the three powers of government, the validity of which is recognized in our day. "Why, for instance," he asked, "is the simplicity of these constitutions (federal and state) disfigured by the system of the balance (separation) of powers; and why is identity of interests rather than equality of rights adopted as the principle"? [19] There was a difference, he remarked, between seeking the best means to combine three powers of government that already existed, as in England, and seeking to establish similar powers in a country where they did not exist "in order to have the pleasure of setting them against one another." [20] Separation of powers, Condorcet believed, would lead to the establishment of a government, unknown to the constitution, which would effectively unite the separated powers by means of corruption. What Condorcet would call the "constitutional" but "unreal" government of America is largely the outcome of the system of checks and balances, aptly described by Woodrow Wilson as the "literary theory" of our constitution.[21] Real government had to assert itself, and it did so through nonconstitutional machinery, the political boss and the political machine which are peculiarly American in origin. However evil their influence they have, nevertheless, performed a necessary function, otherwise they would not persist in the face of the many crusades that have been led against them. Their function has been to bring harmony into the American system of government, divided into separate compartments by the impractical system of separation of powers, through the pressure of a unified, thoroughly integrated party machine.

The final step in the process of passing from despotism to freedom was a regular method of amending the constitution, also of American origin. Condorcet beheld in the amendment clauses of the American state and federal constitutions the creation of a mechanism for peaceful progress which, in his opinion, was the only alternative to violent revolution. "Until now," he wrote in 1789, "several of the American states have been the only ones to realize the utility of providing, in advance, for methods to revise existing constitutions, and to submit these revisions—and even entirely new constitutions—to the representatives of the nation, chosen for this special task." [22] These peaceful methods of political change were original with America. They were not borrowed from England where, "despite the fact that every enlightened man recognizes the evils of the existing system of representation, parliamentary reform will be long deferred. Those who profit from the abuses will seek to maintain them." [23] Despotism was as impossible in America as was violent revolution, and for another reason: both houses of the legislature represented the people, and bad laws could, therefore, be easily changed.[24]

When Condorcet was appointed chairman of the committee to draw up a constitution for the French Republic, the American example was ever before his eyes. "America appeared to them (Condorcet and Paine) the model of good government," remarked a contemporary.[25] Of all the American constitutions, that of Pennsylvania, drawn up in 1776, filled Condorcet with overflowing enthusiasm. In his view this document was the very mirror of political wisdom, and he "just doted" on it. "It was distinguished from most of the other state constitutions," he declared, "by a greater equality, and from all of them in that the legislative power was confined to one house." [26] The Pennsylvania constitution had been drawn up by a constitutional convention, presided over by Franklin. Its democratic character, as well as its association with the Quaker colony and with Franklin, gave that document immense prestige in France, where it was hailed as the very embodiment of the rights of man.[27] The provisions in the Pennsylvania constitution that especially appealed to Condorcet were a popularly elected unicameral legislature; a popularly elected executive committee; and a popularly elected Council of Censors with power "to enquire whether the constitution had been preserved inviolate in every part." [28] Following the example set by the constitutions of the American states, Condorcet prefaced his project of a constitution for the French Republic by a Declaration of Rights. It also followed the example of some of the American states by providing for constitutional conventions specifically elected for that purpose, with a popular referendum on the result.[29]

Condorcet's discussions of American constitutional history and practice were abstract in character. He said little or nothing of the historic, the political, and the economic conditions, which gave rise to the state and federal constitutions. In his view they were the outcome of speculation in political science by enlightened philosophers and statesmen. There is,

REDISCOVERY OF AMERICA 227

in the Boston Public Library, John Adams' copy of Condorcet's *Sketch of the Intellectual Progress of Mankind.* Nearly every page in it contains caustic, and even violent, criticisms of the author's philosophy of history. On the margin of the following sentence, "If we examine the nature of these constitutions (American) we shall discover in what respect they were indebted to the progress of the political sciences," Adams writes. "Fool! Fool!" It was the impatient exclamation of one who knew the realities of American politics.[30]

America, having established a political system based upon the rights of man, was now, according to Condorcet, in a position to create institutions and to formulate policies in harmony with her free constitution. Because of this unique circumstance, America was destined to have a profound influence in the world. In 1786 he wrote a pamphlet, *The Influence of the American Revolution on Europe* in which he diagnosed American ideas and foretold their rôle in the world.[31] According to Condorcet, America was the pioneer of religious freedom, as Europe had been, of religious toleration. The enlightened statesmen of Europe had adopted the policy of toleration, he declared, because this policy was the only way to bring peace to countries distracted by religious wars. With toleration, however, went a privileged state church, as well as liberty of worship to dissenters. But Americans, said Condorcet, regarded toleration as an "outrage against human nature"; what they desired was complete religious equality through separation of church and state.[32] In the Virginia law of 1785, separating church and state, and in the provision of the American constitution forbidding Congress to establish a national church, America proclaimed the new ideal of religious freedom. This ideal was not inspired by a hatred of Christianity; on the contrary, declared Condorcet, the Americans were the most religious people in the world. Religious peace was most assured in America because everyone was free to follow his conscience in the choice of his faith.[33] Condorcet's explanation remains true to this day. There has never been in America the widespread hostility to revealed religion and the bitter hatred of Christianity, so characteristic of France since the eighteenth century.

America, too, according to Condorcet, was antimilitaristic and peace loving. It was the one nation that had laid the foundations of permanent peace: (1) by establishing a militia, instead of a standing army, which made impossible the existence of a military class with military traditions; and (2) by uniting the states into a confederation, which created a model for a league of nations. "In the Old World," he declared, "a few eloquent philosophers, especially Voltaire, cried out against the injustice and the absurdity of war. . . . But in America love of peace is the attitude of a great and brave people who well know how to defend their firesides and how to fight for their freedom. Wars of ambition and of conquest are condemned in America by the calm judgment of a humane and peaceful nation." [34]

Condorcet suggested a way in which America could be an influence for universal peace. For long, he declared, the European powers had waged war for the control of the West Indies; but, after the American Revolution, America was in a position to dominate the Caribbean because she could conquer and hold the islands more easily than could Europe. Due to America's advantageous geographical position no European power would dare to wage war, in that region, against her wishes. Would America herself embark on an imperialistic career in the Caribbean? To the ideologue, Condorcet, ever seeing abstract principles as the motive power of national policies, there was no likelihood of such an event because America was inspired by the libertarian principles of the American Revolution, which precluded the idea of having subject peoples. Only by the imprudent conduct of Europe would America be driven to a policy of conquest in the Caribbean.[35] The advent of America, therefore, meant the creation of a peace zone in the New World, which would eliminate a cause for war among the European powers. Condorcet's analysis of the future policy of the United States regarding European intervention in the New World, in a sense, foreshadowed the Monroe Doctrine.

External peace was, then, America's policy in harmony with her free constitution. So, according to Condorcet, was internal peace. A people like the Americans, he reasoned, who made their own laws, obeyed them. In America "the respect for law is the prime inspiration of the public and private conduct of the citizens." [36] Opposition found peaceful expression in a free press which was regarded by Americans "as the most sacred of the rights of man." [37] Only a European, as optimistic and as abstract as was Condorcet, could make these observations on the law-abiding habits of Americans, observations that came from a naïve faith in political logic. The uprising in Massachusetts, in 1786, known as Shay's Rebellion, rather disturbed Condorcet's optimistic views regarding the peaceable character of Americans. He gave a description of this uprising, but minimized its importance by saying that there were more serious disturbances in despotic countries, and that America was relatively tranquil. He instanced the Gordon riots against the Catholics in England, in 1780, as a far more serious public disturbance than was Shay's Rebellion.[38]

Freedom of trade was another policy favored by America. She was opposed to the restrictions on commerce and industry, imposed by the Mercantilist system. And because of this free trade policy, Condorcet prophesied a great increase of commerce between America and Europe.[39] For a long time, he declared, America will export only foodstuffs and raw materials because of her immense, fertile lands. She will of necessity import manufactured articles from Europe, as most of her capital will be tied up in agriculture. In the trade with America, England's advantage, Condorcet argued, consisted in that the English and Americans had a common language; but this advantage was counterbalanced by a dislike of England, felt by the Americans, due to the American Revolution. A knowledge of the French language, by Americans, would facilitate commerce between France and America; and Condorcet suggested that France should establish schools, to which Americans would send their children. However, the Americans being Protestants, the Catholic religion was not to be taught in these schools.[40]

But there was one blot on the American escutcheon that, otherwise, was so fair in Condorcet's eyes. It was slavery. That ancient institution, so long dead in Europe, was, in the opinion of Condorcet, an evil result of the discovery of America. The inhabitants of Africa were enslaved to labor on the plantations of America, he declared, because it was believed that the products of the New World, tobacco and sugar, could not be grown without Negro labor. The existence of slavery in the land that produced the Declaration of Independence puzzled him. He naïvely admonished his beloved Americans to liberate their slaves, otherwise the world would get the impression that they had fought for liberty, not as a human right, but as a selfish advantage over other people.[41] But he comforted himself by remarking that enlightened Americans felt the shame as well as the danger of slavery, hence "this blemish will not for long soil the purity of American laws." [42] He gave instances to show that slavery was being gradually abolished: the provision in the federal constitution making possible the abolition of the slave trade after 1808; the forbidding of slavery by Massachusetts; and the emancipation law of Pennsylvania. There were few Negroes in the eight Northern states, and, before long, Condorcet believed, all America would be free of Negro slavery.[43] His view regarding the gradual disappearance of slavery in America did not show a lack of understanding of the situation. It was the view commonly held in his day. What kept the Negro a slave in the eighteenth century was chiefly the cultivation of sugar, to which his labor was deemed essential. And the United States was not, at that time, a producer of sugar. The great development of the cotton culture, which encouraged the extension of slavery, was unforeseen before the invention of the cotton gin.

The future of America was a theme that greatly fascinated Condorcet. By establishing political and religious liberty, he declared, America will become the asylum for the oppressed of all nations. He advised the persecuted French Protestants to go to America, "where there was liberty of conscience and political freedom; where all were equal; where all laborers may hope for work, and even, for wealth; where no monopolistic guilds condemned poor artisans to servitude and misery; and where vast lands awaited the hand of the cultivator." [44] Freedom in America, Condorcet believed, would result in bringing freedom to Europe; those who fled from despotism in Europe would hold their oppressors up to public scorn, which would have the effect of causing the European rulers to moderate their tyranny. Poverty will be abolished in America, as the poor man will easily be able to gain a livelihood in a land with so varied a climate. There being no class distinctions in America, the masses were not doomed to misery and stupidity. Widespread education will advance human knowledge, and, in several generations, America will produce as many men interested in the advancement of knowledge as all of Europe. Thus America would accelerate the progress of mankind. By becoming an independent nation America was destined to create a new culture. Had they remained colonials "the desire to shine in the eyes of the English would have destroyed all other sentiments in the souls of talented Americans." [45]

What Condorcet beheld in America was a figure reflected in the shining mirror of the generous principles of eighteenth-century philosophy. And no one in France saw this figure more clearly and gazed at it more rapturously than did this devoted lover of America. It was a figure drawn by Franklin, Paine, and Jefferson who so deeply influenced the views of the French intellectuals regarding America. Condorcet visualized the New World as the first opportunity that came to mankind to create society anew, not beginning with savagery, as did the old society, but with civilization, and that of the most advanced type. All the evils from which the old society in Europe suffered, he believed, were a heritage from its evil past. America, of all the countries, had no such past. She began her national life with freedom, equality, and enlightenment; and, therefore, America's mission was to be a beacon light of progress for all mankind.

Condorcet's splendid vision of the future in America was stimulated by his ardent hopes for reform in France. The

American Revolution gave great encouragement to the philosophes in their century-old struggle against the Old Régime. It was the success of the Americans that gave them the first assurance that the stars in their courses were fighting for them. Especially did their hopes run high when the French joined the Americans in their struggle against England. During the critical period that followed in France the American Revolution was an important element among the influences that led to the outbreak of the French Revolution.

CHAPTER THIRTEEN

THE IDEA OF PROGRESS

POLITICAL and social conditions in the eighteenth century were ripe for the popularization of the idea of progress. The feudal political order had collapsed with the establishment of dynastic national states. The feudal social order was disintegrating with the advent of modern capitalism. The great increase in international trade, due to the Commercial Revolution, had given a stimulus to production, and the Industrial Revolution was beginning in France as well as in England. To the new capitalist class that was emerging, change was welcomed because it meant an increase of wealth through a better system of production. The capitalist mentality, which was taking definite form during the eighteenth century, was, therefore, hospitable to a dynamic idea, such as progress.

Progress is a modern, even a recent, idea.[1] Among the ancient Greeks and Romans the tradition of a Golden Age was prevalent, of a period long in the past, when man lived in an earthly paradise. Man's history was a story of degeneration, beginning with the Golden Age, through the Silver Age, through the Brass Age, and finally to the Iron Age. This view was well described by Hesiod in his *Works and Days*. The eternal and fundamental were always present, and man merely veered around a never changing universe; it was his fate, and that of human society, to degenerate and to decay as they grew older.[2] Today the belief is general that man rose from the lower animals; in ancient times, it was commonly believed that man fell from his high estate and degenerated from the god-like to the purely human. In other words, time was the enemy. The dread that haunted the ancient imagination was the dread of the future. They were miserable today, and would be more miserable tomorrow, hence the hearkening back to the "good old days" of the Golden Age.

There was another theory, held by the ancients, the theory of cycles, espoused by the Pythagoreans, by Plato, and by Aristotle. By cycles was meant a number of years containing good and evil; each cycle would repeat the events of a former cycle. In other words, the Trojan War would be fought in each recurring cycle for all eternity. There was as little concept of progress in the theory of eternal recurrence of cycles as there was in that of progressive deterioration from a Golden Age.[3]

During the Middle Ages, the Golden Age was shifted from the past to the future; but the future was to be in the next world. On earth man was a pawn of Providence, and history consisted of a series of epochs, beginning with the creation of the world, which came as a result of the intervention of the Deity. This view was well stated by Bossuet in his *Universal History*. As the very essence of the idea of progress is that it is the outcome of man's psychical and social nature and of his own deliberate efforts, the idea of divine intervention, even when it was for the good of mankind, was no contribution to the theory of progress.[4]

Both in ancient and in medieval times, change was looked

upon with dread because it was identified with calamity. Social progress had been so slow that it had been imperceptible, and man came to conceive society as stable and permanent. The changes that were seen were associated with death and destruction, the results of depredations by invading armies, or of the eruption of volcanoes, or of the ravages of plagues. Therefore, it was quite natural to regard change, not as beneficent, but as destructive.

The origin of the modern idea of progress may be traced to the sixteenth and seventeenth centuries. The Scientific Revolution gave new views of the world and of man's relations to it, which produced an "intellectual climate" favorable to the idea of progress. These new views were based on the belief in the stability of the laws of nature and in the solidarity of the natural sciences, hitherto regarded as separate and detached. It was now possible to have a notion of the continuity of the world, unbroken by the interventions of the Deity and safe from the ravages of time.[5]

The discovery of America revealed a primitive world, the inhabitants of which were savages, living a life "according to nature." At first the American aborigines were viewed as curiosities, but, as more became known of their manner of life and of their views, the idea began to spread that they were in a *stage* of development. In other words, all civilized people had progressed from savagery which had been their former state. This notion implied that no people could be permanently barbarous or inferior; existing differences in the degree of civilization among peoples were due to circumstances which could be changed by enlightened laws.[6] That progress had taken place among the civilized European nations was revealed by the new history, which appeared in the eighteenth century. The histories of Europe, written by Vol-

THE IDEA OF PROGRESS 237

taire, Gibbon, and Hume, emphasized the idea that great changes for the better had taken place in human affairs from ancient to modern times.[7]

The Commercial Revolution, which resulted from the discovery of America, brought about social changes in Europe through the rapid expansion of commerce. Changes in society were noticed that led, not to decay or to destruction, but to prosperity due to an increase in wealth. And these changes for the better created an atmosphere favorable to the spread of the idea of progress.

The new intellectual and social situation in Europe, during the sixteenth and seventeenth centuries, was likewise favorable to the reception of the idea of progress. And in the writings of the period, especially in those of Francis Bacon, Descartes, Leibnitz, and Fontenelle, the idea of progress was boldly visualized, though not completely and thoroughly developed.

During the second half of the seventeenth century a famous quarrel arose, in France, between two groups, the "ancients" and the "moderns." It centered around the question whether the ancient peoples were superior to the modern peoples; if they were superior, the best that the moderns could do was to imitate the ancients. Indirectly it came as a result of the publication, in 1688, by Charles Perrault of *Parallèle des anciens et des modernes* which, according to Brunetière, marked "the true beginning of the literary history of the eighteenth century as Condorcet's *Esquisse* marked its end."[8] Natural laws, everywhere and at all times, argued those who championed the moderns against the ancients, were universal and invariable; they controlled both ancients and moderns. But the moderns inherit the contributions of the ancients, to which was added their own contributions, and that clearly made the moderns superior to the ancients. Many joined the side of the moderns, and argued that it was they who were truly the ancients because they represented a more mature world. One famous champion of the moderns was Fontenelle, whose *Digression sur les anciens et les modernes* popularized their views. Nature, he reasoned, made both ancients and moderns of the same "paste," but experience, due to time, and larger knowledge, due to improved institutions, gave the advantage to the moderns.[9]

It was in the eighteenth century, and in France, that the idea of progress became an intellectual passion. "One could justly say," writes Brunetière, "if one so wished, that the whole literary history of the eighteenth century is dominated by the idea of progress which, beginning with the limited views expressed by Perrault in his *Dialogues*, broadens slowly, and, finally, ends in the limitless vista of Condorcet's dream." [10] The attack upon authority and tradition, and especially upon religion, by the philosophes produced an attitude favorable to the idea of progress. Tradition became synonymous with superstition; it was identified with the dead and with the past. Unlike the idea of evolution, which is regarded as a blind force that works automatically through nature, without a beginning and without a purpose, the idea of progress was regarded as having a beginning, which came as a result of the spread of knowledge and of enlightenment, and as having a purpose, the perfectibility of mankind. In the eighteenth century, nature itself was believed to have a purpose, the happiness of mankind, which could be discerned only through reason. Therefore, reason could not be dissociated from the idea of progress, which the rationalists of the eighteenth century used as a weapon against revealed religion. Progress, in their view, was rational and capable of proof, but revelation was arbitrary, personal, and supernatural. It was a situation similar to that in the nineteenth century, when the rationalists used evolution as a weapon against the orthodox conception of God as the creator of the world and of all its inhabitants.

During the first half of the eighteenth century, the leading protagonists of the idea of progress were Abbé Saint-Pierre and Turgot. The former was an uncompromising pacifist who regarded universal peace as the touchstone of all human progress. In his *Projet pour perfectionner,* Saint-Pierre traced the history of progress from its beginning in the Iron Age, when men were savage and violent, to the Silver Age which comprised the many centuries until the eighteenth when wars were no longer normal but only occasional; and, finally, he foresaw the Golden Age of the future when universal and perpetual peace would reign. He made a rather interesting and acute observation that, whereas the sciences and the arts had progressed, morals and politics had remained largely the same as they always had been.[11]

It was Turgot, in two addresses, delivered before the Sorbonne in 1749 and 1750, who sounded the keynote of continuous social progress as being the organic principle of history. "All epochs," he declared, "are connected by a sequence of causes and effects, linking the conditions of the world to all conditions that have gone before it . . . the human race, from its origin, appears to the eye of a philosopher one vast whole which, like the individuals composing it, has had its infancy and development." [12] History was the life of mankind, and was ever progressing toward perfection. "None before Turgot, and few after him, have described so well how age is bound to age, how generation transmits to generation what it has inherited from the past and won by its own exertions." [13]

Important as was Turgot's contribution to the idea of progress, it was only a suggestion. Nowhere did he develop it either in a system of social philosophy or in a history of mankind. It was left to his friend and disciple, Condorcet, to do both in his most famous work, *Sketch of the Intellectual Progress of Mankind* (*Esquisse d'un Tableau historique des progrès de l'esprit humain*), published in 1795, after his death. This book "first treated with explicit fullness the idea to which a leading rôle was to fall in the ideology of the nineteenth century." [14]

The *Esquisse* is a sketch of the history of mankind from primitive times to the French Revolution. It is divided into nine Epochs dealing with the progress of humanity through various stages. There is an additional chapter, the tenth Epoch, which deals, not with the past, but with the future development of mankind. It must be kept in mind that the *Esquisse* is only a prospectus for a universal history. The circumstances under which it was written, the author in hiding from the Terror, precluded the possibility of Condorcet's undertaking so vast an enterprise as writing a universal history. He did manage, however, to write fragments of such a history, which are elaborations of the first, fourth, fifth, and tenth Epochs of the *Esquisse*.[15]

Throughout the *Esquisse* the idea of progress is presented as the determining factor in all history. It is the key to all human development in the past and to human perfectibility in the future. Unlike most of the other philosophes, Condorcet did not regard history as "a mass of crimes, of follies, and of misfortunes" which mankind would do well to disregard. "He recognized," says Bury, "the interpretation of history as the key to human development, and this principle controlled subsequent speculations on Progress in France."[16] In Condorcet's view history should concern itself chiefly with the condition of the masses of mankind. "It is this part of history," he declared, "the most obscure and the most neglected, of which few sources of knowledge exist, that a historian should treat, when he describes a discovery, an important theory, a new system of laws, a political revolution. He should try to determine what effect these changes had on the masses of the people."[17] Condorcet severely criticized the historians for neglecting the life of the masses, as revealed by laws, institutions, and ideas, and concentrating on the deeds of great men who, to such historians, *forment veritablement l'espèce humaine*. But, he acutely observed, it is fairly easy to write a history describing the deeds of individuals, as the facts were ready at hand. To write a history of the life of the people was, however, difficult because it required great philosophic insight to select the essential facts that illustrated it. This type of historian must, therefore, be a social philosopher who should do for humanity what the scientist did for nature.[18] Condorcet's views of history and of the function of the historian, enunciated at the end of the eighteenth century, would even now be considered quite "advanced."

The *Esquisse*, then, is a history dominated by a social philosophy. In his Introduction, Condorcet maintained that history had two uses: (1) to establish the facts of progress; and (2) to discover its laws in order to determine the future development of mankind. The progress of mankind was "subject to the same general laws that are observed in the development of the faculties in each individual; it is the result of a similar development, at the same time, of many individuals united in society. But the situation disclosed at each instant depends on what preceded it which, in turn, influences future development." [19] History should, therefore, present the *changes* that have taken place, and the influence of each event upon the succeeding event. In this way would be established the fact of progress, or the unlimited perfectibility of mankind, which "has no limit other than the duration of the globe in which nature has placed us." Progress may be more or less rapid, but it will never retrograde "as long as the earth occupies the same place in the universe, and as long as the universal laws neither destroy our globe nor produce such changes in it that man will no longer be able to exist.[20]

The obstacles to progress are *préjugés*. In each epoch of history certain prejudices arose that continued to have an influence, long after they had been discredited, because men clung to the prejudices of their childhood, of their nation, and of their age. Most of our prejudices were, therefore, not really ours, but a heritage of our ancestors; and history should expose their origin and influence in order to prevent the evils that arise from them.[21] According to Condorcet, history was to unveil the past in order to be an inspiration to future progress. "I know well how the past gives prestige to customs, established in those centuries, which would be little regarded if one were to consider the absurd opinions that dominated those centuries, and the profound ignorance of all sciences, of all rights, and all duties in which they were plunged." [22] Voltaire, according to Condorcet, was the historian who wrote history in order to expose the past. Research could not be dull to a man like Voltaire who, having a sense of humor and quick at sensing the ridiculous, "could find an inexhaustible source of amusement in the absurdities, both theoretical and practical, of our ancestors." [23] Progress always had determined enemies; the conservative philosophers who opposed new truths; the masses who retarded the truths already known; and the powerful vested interests who profited by the existing systems.

History had another and an even more important aim, according to Condorcet, and that was to discover the laws of human behavior in order to foretell the future. "If there exists a science of foretelling the future progress of mankind, of directing it, and of accelerating it, the first foundation of that science must be the history of progress already achieved."[24] But man's history was not an isolated phenomenon because man was no longer regarded as a special creation, apart from the rest of the universe; he was part of nature and subject to its laws. The assimilation of man to nature was a cardinal doctrine of Condorcet, whose belief in human progress was a reflection of his belief in the uniform and harmonious working of natural laws. "The only ground for belief in the truth of the natural sciences," Condorcet declared, "is that universal laws, known or unknown, which regulate the phenomena of the universe are necessary and constant; and why is this principle any the less true for the development of the intellectual and moral faculties of man than for other operations of nature?"[25] If natural phenomena, whose laws are known, can be predicted, why should it be regarded "as chimerical to trace a fairly plausible picture of the future of mankind based upon a knowledge of history."[26] In other words, civilization has been a steady climb onward and upward. In the past progress had been fitful, blind, and accidental; but in the future it was to be consciously and deliberately guided according to certain principles. And these principles could be discovered only through the study of history.

Having stated his philosophy of history, Condorcet then

begins his story of mankind. The first Epoch he devotes to a description of primitive life which, he declared, could only be conjectured from the physical and moral nature of man, as there existed no definite information regarding that period. The earliest human society was the family, due to the long infancy of the offspring, which necessitated prolonged care by the parents. From this situation arose the institution of marriage and the sentiment of morality. Condorcet's view of the origin of morality was similar to that of Rousseau before him and of Adam Smith after him. It was that morality originated in sympathy, a physical feeling of uneasiness at the sight of suffering and a consequent impulse to allay it.[27] It is significant that Condorcet begins his history with man already in existence. Of his origin he says nothing, but he does clearly state that man is an animal, and that the only difference between man and the beasts is that the former uses tools. Animals, he believed, reasoned like men but in a far more rudimentary fashion. There are insensible gradations in the power to reason "from the brute to the savage and from the savage to Euler and Newton."[28] Elsewhere, Condorcet argued, that man was a separate species because all men naturally learned how to talk and how to walk on two feet. The difference between man and monkey was greater than that between horse and ass, but less than that between horse and bull. How man originated, he declared, was a problem insoluble at present and for a long time to come, but it was not a problem that the human mind was incapable of solving.[29]

Progress began with primitive man who laid the foundation of morality, of the arts, and of the sciences. And it came as a result of the natural development of the human faculties, not from a divine revelation by a deity which was handed

THE IDEA OF PROGRESS 245

down by tradition to succeeding generations. Already, in this earliest period, man encountered his inveterate and uncompromising enemy, religion. Every epoch in man's history, as depicted by the *Esquisse,* has been the scene of an epic struggle between the god of darkness, religion, and the god of light, philosophy, each striving for man's soul. Primitive man, Condorcet declared, originated two superstitions which have inflicted untold calamities on humanity. These were (1) a belief in the survival of the soul after death; and (2) a belief in gods, created by the savage imagination in man's own image. A priestly class arose whose interest it was to keep the people in ignorance in order to control them through superstition. In the "credulity of the first dupes and in the vulgar cunning of the first impostors" a division of mankind arose which persisted, according to Condorcet, through all the ages down to the French Revolution.[30]

During the second Epoch man took his first step of progress toward civilization. In contrast to Rousseau's views in his *Discourse on the Sciences and Arts,* Condorcet maintained that the advance of the arts and sciences made for the amelioration and not for the degeneration of mankind. Increase of knowledge produced virtue and happiness, and the decay of knowledge among a civilized people produced corruption. The passage from "a rude society to a civilized state of enlightened and free people, is by no means a degeneration of mankind, but a necessary crisis in its gradual advance toward perfectibility."[31] The new period was characterized by the domestication of animals in order to answer the need for larger quantities of food and clothing. Slavery appeared as a result of using prisoners of war as laborers. Agriculture arose, due to the discovery that some plants gave better subsistence to flocks. Because of the difference in the size of flocks classes began to make their appearance. Institutions and ideas arose, based on authority, and with them came "the art of deceiving men in order to despoil them." [32]

The third Epoch deals with the period from the agricultural stage to the invention of the alphabet. The development of agriculture marked the true beginning of civilization. Property rights now became definite because each parcel of land had its owner. In his view that the origin of civilization was due to the establishment of property in land, Condorcet accepted Rousseau's interpretation in his famous essay, *Discourse on Inequality*. Society was now divided into rich and poor: those who had land and those who did not. Manufactures were established, and with them came the organization of trade guilds. Commerce grew with the appearance of a merchant class. The third Epoch was the period when social, religious, and political institutions were definitely established. The prevailing social system was feudalism, the existence of which Condorcet did not believe was "an evil peculiar to our part of the world, but one that could be found almost everywhere during similar periods of civilization." [33]

The fourth Epoch is devoted entirely to the Greeks, the first people to appear in the *Esquisse*. Of the Jews, to whom Bossuet devoted so much space in his *Universal History*, Condorcet did not devote a single line. In all probability he, like Voltaire, regarded the religious contribution of the Jews as inimical to the progress of mankind. Condorcet was greatly enamored of the Greeks, "whose genius opened all the avenues to truth, and whom nature had prepared and whom fate had destined to be the benefactors and guides of all nations and of all ages." [34] Among the Greeks the function of the priest was limited to religion, and consequently there was freedom of thought. The leaders of the Greeks were not priests but philosophers, of whom Condorcet writes at great length and with rapturous enthusiasm. He was convinced that Democritus inspired the philosophy of Descartes, and that Pythagoras inspired the universal system of Newton. A conflict arose between the priests and the philosophers, which led to the death of Socrates, "an important event in the history of mankind." [35] According to Condorcet, the Greeks did have ideas of political liberty, but these ideas were not based upon the rights of man but upon the rights of each class. Therefore, they sought to establish political systems in which the existing classes could preserve their liberties. The Greek political system was based upon the existence of slavery and on the assembly of all citizens as lawgivers, therefore it could not be a model for modern nations.

The fifth Epoch continues with the ancient period down to the beginning of the early Middle Ages. It describes the great advance of the sciences, especially of mathematics and of medicine, in the Alexandrian period of Greek civilization. But when the Alexandrian period began to decline, philosophers and scientists gave place to grammarians and critics. It was a time of decadence when views were based upon authority and tradition, not upon reason, and when the judgment of a book "depended on its age, or on the difficulty of understanding or of finding it." [36] During the decline of the Alexandrian period an idea prevailed regarding the degeneracy of mankind and of the superiority of ancient over modern times, an idea "so false and so pernicious." [37] The latter part of the fifth Epoch is devoted to the Romans, of whom Condorcet entertained opinions that were not at all complimentary to the conquerors of the world. He seems to imply that, from the cultural point of view, Rome was unimportant; and that Latin culture was merely a variation of Greek decadence. Science, philosophy, and the arts, he declared, were "foreign to the soil of Rome." Neither did Condorcet have a high opinion of the political ability of the Romans who, he declared, were "the sport, in turn of their tyrants and their defenders." They attempted the impossible task of applying a system of government, originally designed for a single city, to the whole world. Rome was unable to maintain herself except by continual wars, and was finally destroyed by her own armies. The only contribution that Rome gave to the world, according to Condorcet, was a system of jurisprudence.

Curiously enough Rome was important, in Condorcet's opinion, because of Christianity. The conquered peoples in the Empire, he declared, readily espoused doctrines renouncing worldly happiness; such doctrines consoled these "children of misfortune." He describes with bitter sarcasm the spread of Christianity in the Empire. "Twenty sects, Egyptian and Jewish, united to attack the religion of the Empire. But they fought one another with equal fury, and the outcome was the triumph of the religion of Jesus, and the ruin of all the others. From their débris was formed a history, a dogma, a ritual, a morality which gradually drew the mob of visionaries." The spirit of the new faith was "in harmony with the period of decadence and misfortune"; oppressed humanity welcomed a religion in which all were equal in slavery. Contempt for human knowledge was a leading characteristic of Christianity, and its triumph signalized "the complete breakdown of science and philosophy." [38]

The sixth and seventh Epochs deal with the early Middle Ages, which are painted in the colors of the darkest hue. A "disastrous period" was the early Middle Ages, when the human mind rapidly descended from the heights to which it had raised itself. "Barely did a glimmer of the light of talent or of human goodness and greatness pierce its profound darkness. Theological moonshine and superstitious delusions were then the only characteristics of human genius, and religious intolerance was then the only morality." [39] It was the golden age of the dupe and the knave, when the folly of the former and the trickeries of the latter became the basis of a great system of oppression, the Catholic church. Under paganism, argued Condorcet, religion had been an instrument of the governments, but in medieval times the government became an instrument of the church. During the early Middle Ages, a new religion appeared, Mohammedanism, of which Condorcet entertained surprisingly favorable views.[40] He hated Christianity so intensely that he was all too ready to see good in any of its opponents, even in an opposing religion. Politically the period was one of feudal anarchy, and the people suffered under the triple tyranny of the king, the warrior, and the priest. Despite the constant struggles that went on between kings and nobles, between popes and emperors, between nobles and cities, there was great respect for the principle of authority and for precedent, which were exalted in books, both sacred and profane. "A proposition was not adopted because it was true, but because it was written in this or that book, and had been applied in this or that country for many centuries." [41]

At best, according to Condorcet, the Middle Ages contributed, not something positively good, but something relatively bad from which good things followed. These were: (1) scholasticism, whose subtleties, used as a means of embarrassing and ensnaring an opponent, sharpened the wits of its practitioners and made possible philosophic analysis; (2) serfdom which made the common man a member of the lower class, not an article of merchandise, as he had been under slavery; and (3) gunpowder "which seemed, at first, to threaten the destruction of the human race," but which, by revolutionizing the art of warfare, created equality between the knight in armor and the common soldier that resulted in destroying the superiority of the feudal nobles over the common people.[42]

The eighth Epoch covers the period from the invention of printing to the eighteenth century. Its leading theme is the invention of printing, as a result of which "knowledge became the object of an active and universal commerce." In the opinion of Condorcet this discovery was the most revolutionary event in all intellectual history. It made possible the formation of public opinion, and the bringing together, by means of the printed page, vast numbers of people scattered in different places. Progress in the past had been slow and halting, and, at times, there had even been retrogression; but, with the advent of printing, it could be rapid, certain, and easy. Fortunately for mankind the kings and priests did not realize that printing would have such effects, otherwise they surely would have suppressed the invention. In the days before printing it was easy to destroy a book by destroying a few manuscripts, but printing has made the destruction of books impossible as long as there existed "a single corner in the world in which there is freedom of the press." [43] Progress was now safe at last.

Another outstanding event in this Epoch was the discovery of America. The importance of this event was that it made possible the study of humanity in all lands and in all stages of civilization. Clear ideas could now be had of the influence of nature and of institutions upon mankind. Unfortunately, however, the discovery of America resulted in reviving the ancient institution of slavery through the African slave trade.

Condorcet devotes considerable space, in this Epoch, to the Scientific Revolution of the sixteenth and seventeenth centuries. He pays glowing tribute to the work of Copernicus, Galileo, Kepler, Bacon, and Descartes, through whose labors, tradition and authority "gave way to universal and natural law and to human reason." Condorcet's emphasis upon the scientific aspects of the Renaissance, instead of upon the revival of Greek and Latin, is in harmony with the latest interpretation of the Renaissance. Preserved Smith, in his recent study of the intellectual history of Europe during the sixteenth and seventeenth centuries, gives little space to the classical revival which, he declares, "was soon outgrown and thereafter acted as an oppression rather than as an emancipation." To the sciences he devotes almost one-third of his volume, because "the scientific rebirth is the most distinguishing trait of the period." [44] Another intellectual contribution of the Epoch, according to Condorcet, was the growth of modern languages. Latin, as the language of the educated, was an "eternal obstacle to true equality" as it perpetuated errors and prejudices by dividing mankind into learned and unlearned. This obstacle was removed when the modern tongues became the languages of learning and culture.

These great steps of progress occurred during the period of the Protestant Revolution, when "the monster, fanaticism, maddened by the wounds that it had received, redoubled its fury and hastened to destroy its victims because it feared reason which was approaching to rescue them." [45] Luther, declared Condorcet, announced to an astonished world that Catholicism was a corruption of Christianity, and that, in order to be a good Christian, one must abjure the authority of the priest. Condorcet, however, had little enthusiasm for Protestantism, except as an exposure of Catholicism. Freethinking people, he declared, found restraints in both Protestant and Catholic countries. Nevertheless, Protestantism made a contribution to freedom of thought by seceding from Catholicism. The Protestants could not then, "without the grossest contradiction, restrict the right of examination too greatly, since it was upon this right that they founded the legitimacy of their separation." Protestantism gave freedom of thought "not to men but to Christians," hence "the chain was not broken but it was less heavy and more extended." [46]

The ninth Epoch treats of the period from Descartes to the French Revolution, and is the longest chapter in the book. It is the period, according to Condorcet, when Newton established the true system of the universe; when Locke analyzed human nature; when Rousseau analyzed human society; and when Turgot, Price, and Priestley gave to the world the idea of progress. It was Locke's sensational theory that suggested to the philosophes a method of finding truth in the social sciences as certain as that in the natural sciences.[47] To Condorcet, the eighteenth was the greatest of centuries. Before this period, man's life and thought were dominated by prejudices, and all history might be said to have been in the Dark Ages, pierced now and then by a fitful gleam of enlightenment, as in Greece. Elsewhere, Condorcet paid rhapsodical tribute to the enlightenment of the eighteenth century, as the period when "enlightened men in all lands exchange their knowledge, have the same ideas, have common interests, and speak the same language." [48] Man's halting steps from primitive times toward the Heavenly City of perfectibility were quickened during the Age of Reason, and he now strode forward, boldly and rapidly, on the sure road of progress. "Living in this happy age," exclaims Condorcet, "and being witnesses of the last efforts of ignorance and of error, we have seen reason emerge victorious from this struggle, so long and so difficult, and we can at last cry out, 'Truth has conquered and mankind is saved.' " [49]

Enlightenment spread in all countries of western Europe, chiefly through the work of the philosophes who influenced both rulers and people. Governments followed enlightened public opinion, though at a distance. Religious intolerance abated its fury, and customs and manners became milder. The natural sciences advanced rapidly, which resulted in destroying erroneous views in politics, in morals, and in religion. "The progress of the natural sciences is very destructive to such errors because it frequently destroys them, without seeming to do so, by exposing their obstinate defenders to ridicule." [50] Condorcet goes into a lengthy discussion of the leading idea of the Age of Reason, the rights of man. He praises Rousseau as the man who "merits the glory of putting the rights of man among those truths which one can no longer forget or oppose." [51] Toward the end of the eighteenth century, enlightenment became so widespread that it was no longer slow and intangible, as formerly. It directly "influenced the masses," and the outcome was the American and French Revolutions. Condorcet laid great stress on the influence of the American Revolution upon France, "a country which was, at the same time, most enlightened and least free." The Americans, for the first time, gave the example of a great people that asserted their natural rights, threw off their chains, and established a government based upon these rights. In their quarrel with England they insisted that "man born on the American side of the Atlantic had received from nature the same rights as those born under the meridian of Greenwich." [52] Strangely enough, the Americans were aided in their struggle for freedom by the despotic monarchies of Europe. Condorcet's explanation was that the Americans, having no feudal system, no hereditary caste, and no system of religious intolerance, limited themselves merely to the establishment of a new government in place of the British. His interpretation of the American Revolution is that it was purely a political movement, and, therefore, made no attack on the then existing social structure.[53] And that was the reason why it was not opposed by the European monarchies whose chief interest was to maintain their feudal social system.

As the outstanding example of a philosophe who was also an active revolutionist, Condorcet proclaimed the French Revolution as the great event which gave an immense acceleration to human hopes. To Condorcet, declared Jaurès, the French Revolution was only an episode of a world revolution that was destined to transform all nations, the second part of the prologue, of which the American Revolution was the first, to a universal drama.[54] In comparison with the American Revolution the French Revolution was more complete and more thorough, as it "had to embrace the whole economy of society and to change every social relation." It attacked, at the same time, royal despotism, political inequality, religious intolerance, the feudal system, and aristocratic privilege, abuses which covered all Europe. Therefore, all the powers combined against France in order to crush the Revolution. On her side were only *la voix de quelques sages, et le vœu timide des peuples opprimés.*[55]

The last chapter of the *Esquisse* deals with the future of mankind. It is the most original chapter of all, and has been the subject of widespread comment, far more so than the book itself. In this chapter, Condorcet laid down the general principles of social development and gave an outline of future society. What he foretold, however, did not arise from his imagination but from what he conceived to be the laws of progress derived from a study of history. Condorcet was an altruist, not an utopian, and in his work "the historic approach makes a *scientific junction* with the utopist." [56] The *Esquisse* was written during the most vivid period of the French Revolution, when the enlightenment of the eighteenth century was being rapidly translated into new institutions and laws. Progress, at last, became visible, and Condorcet could well have believed that the future happiness of mankind was no longer a dream but a reality.

Unlike the past, the future, according to Condorcet, will be based upon: (1) the equality of the nations; (2) the equality of individuals within a nation; and (3) the perfectibility of mankind. Inequality, which had been the condition of humanity from the earliest times until now, will, in the future, give place to equality, "the chief aim of the social arts." Are differences in civilization, noticeable in the various races, due to their nature or to defects in their social systems? History, which alone can answer that question, gives the strongest reasons for believing that "nature has put no limits on our hopes," and has condemned no race to remain permanently backward. There will be equality of all races and nations because the egalitarian principles of the French Revolution are accepted by enlightened people everywhere. Equality between Europeans and the inhabitants of the colonies will come as a result of the abolition of slavery and of the trading monopolies. Hitherto, the colonies had served for the enrichment of the monopolistic trading companies. Now that the colonies have become independent, a great emigration will set in from

Europe, and they will become "the homes of industrious people who will come to these happy climes to seek prosperity which is denied to them in the land of their birth." [57] The aborigines in the New World will either be reduced to a few, or become assimilated with the colonists, or disappear entirely as a result of the competition of the whites. In Asia and Africa, the inhabitants will adopt the civilization of the West, and will free themselves by using their European masters "either as useful tools or as generous liberators." And "the day will arrive when the sun will shine upon free men only, who will regard reason alone as their master; and when tyrants and slaves, priests and their treacherous tools will exist only in the pages of history and in the scenes of the theater." [58]

As a result of the equality of nations, war will be regarded "as the greatest of plagues and as the greatest of crimes." Nations, Condorcet reasoned, could not become conquerors without losing their own freedom. A permanent league of nations was the only means of maintaining universal peace and the independence of every nation, whose chief object should be "security, not power." In order to achieve universal peace it was necessary to establish free institutions and a universal language, which would bind nations together and so hasten the progress of fraternity.[59]

The inequality of individuals, according to Condorcet, was due to differences in wealth, in inheritance, and in education. The natural order, he argued, tended toward economic equality but it would be absurd, and even dangerous, to establish economic equality by law, as natural inequalities existed among individuals. Hitherto, laws and institutions had tended to encourage inequalities which exist in society as a result of the system of privilege. But a just system of government and society will have for its object the diminishing of inequalities in wealth; and only those differences will remain that are based upon natural abilities.[60] Inequalities of wealth could be diminished by laws favoring, not the concentration, but the distribution of wealth, through the establishment of freedom of commerce and industry, through the abolition of the system of marriage for money, and through equal inheritance. Coöperative credit associations were to be established to loan money to poor young men, with which to establish themselves in business. The old, who had no resources, were to be aided by a system of old age pensions.[61]

Another great inequality was that between the sexes. The most important factor in future progress, declared Condorcet, will be the "complete destruction of those prejudices which establish between the sexes the inequalities of rights that are bad even for the favored male sex. In vain does one try to justify this discrimination against women by asserting the physical, moral, and intellectual differences between men and women. These inequalities originated in force, and cannot be justified by sophistry." [62]

Inequalities in education will be diminished by a system of universal education. As an enthusiastic advocate of universal education, Condorcet believed that it would be the most important factor in abolishing all inequalities.[63] Great differences in fortune, argued Condorcet, would be impossible when universal education made possible the utilization of the abilities that lie dormant among the masses. Even in the most enlightened countries "not one-fiftieth of those that nature has endowed with talent receive the instruction necessary to develop it." [64] The future will no longer see the masses wretched, ignorant, and depraved. "Folly and misery will be accidents, occurring only now and then, and not the habitual lot of a considerable portion of mankind." As a result of the high degree of civilization attained by the people, morality itself will become natural, and all acts contrary to the rights of another will become "as physically impossible as, at present, it is impossible for most people to commit a barbaric act in cold blood." [65]

Before the appearance of Malthus' famous *Essay on Population,* Condorcet considered the problem of the increase of population in relation to subsistence.[66] Population would increase as a result of these beneficent reforms, he declared, but would it increase beyond subsistence, and therefore cause humanity once more to retrograde? Condorcet's answer to this question anticipated the arguments of those who opposed the Malthusian doctrine that the masses were doomed to eternal poverty because population would always outrun the means of subsistence. He asserted that the food supply would increase as a result of the progress of science; machinery will multiply the force and abilities of men by increasing production and by diminishing the time of labor necessary to produce them.[67] The same piece of land will nourish more individuals, and each individual will produce more food. If the problem of subsistence was not solved in this way, then Condorcet had another solution, and that was to limit population by practicing birth control. If ridiculous prejudices, he declared, did not give to morality an aspect of austerity "that is corrupting and degrading instead of purifying and elevating, people would know that their obligations to those not yet born consist not merely in bringing them into the world but also in assuring them well-being. The purpose of such obligations is the welfare of humanity, of existing society, and of the family, not the puerile idea of encumbering the earth with useless and unhappy beings." [68]

Finally, the *Esquisse* contains a prophecy which has been ridiculed by its critics as the most chimerical part of the most fatuous of books. It is the perfectibility of the human organism. Condorcet believed that the duration of human life had no assignable limit, and that the span of life could be increased indefinitely by perfecting the human body. It could be done "by preventive medicine, by proper diet and housing, by a manner of living which would develop bodily strength through moderate exercise, and, finally, by the abolition of the two most active causes of deterioration, poverty and wretchedness on one hand, and enormous wealth on the other." Preventive medicine will abolish contagious and hereditary diseases, as well as those due to climate, to food, and to the nature of employment. And the abolition of all disease is not a vain hope. Doubtless, "men will not become immortal," but a time will come "when death will be nothing more than the result either of an unexpected accident or of the slow destruction of the vital forces." [69]

The *Esquisse* may be characterized as a typical product of philosophe mentality. No other volume, produced in eighteenth-century France, presents so faithfully the views of man and of the world held by the philosophes. Its attitude toward human society was inspired by the physics of Newton, in which the conception of uniform, universal, natural laws, that governed the universe, was made to apply to social organization. The law of progress was essential in Condorcet's social machine as was the law of gravitation in Newton's World Machine. Condorcet's attitude toward human nature was inspired by Locke's sensational theory that all knowledge comes as a result of experience received through the senses from the natural and social world. "Man is born with the faculty of receiving sensations," he declared.[70] And from this faculty arise moral ideas which determine the immutable laws of truth and justice. The method, applied by the *Esquisse* to the solution of human problems, was that inspired by Descartes's method of logical deduction from assumed principles. It was from Cartesianism that Condorcet derived the idea of the independence and supremacy of reason, which he applied in his judgment of human history and institutions and in his prognostication of the future of mankind. However, Condorcet's mind, abstract, logical, rigid, was yet charged with ethical passions that came from his ardent, sympathetic temperament. It broke through the intellectual grooves, fashioned by the Cartesianism of his day, and caused him to behold vistas of human progress far beyond the vision of his contemporaries.

The "last will and testament" of the eighteenth century, as Croce characterizes the *Esquisse*,[71] is also an almost perfect expression of the ideals and hopes of that age: its humanitarianism; its cosmopolitanism; its belief in the power of reason and in the innate goodness of human nature; and, above all, its faith in progress. In a sense, the idea of progress became the central doctrine of a social religion of which Condorcet was both the theologian and the apostle. Having renounced revealed religion, and with it the hope of immortality, he dreamed of a secular immortality of which his unbounded faith in progress was perhaps a rationalization. "If the unlimited perfectibility of mankind," he declared, "is, as I believe, a universal law of nature, man should not regard himself as a being, circumscribed by a fleeting and isolated existence and destined to disappear after a succession of good and evil fortune for him and for those whom chance

THE IDEA OF PROGRESS 261

has placed in his way. He is an active part of the great whole and a participant in an eternal work. Existing for only a brief moment on a point in space, he can, through his labor, embrace all places, unite himself to all ages, and be effective long after his memory has disappeared from the earth." [72]

Like Montesquieu's *Spirit of Laws,* Condorcet's *Sketch of the Intellectual Progress of Mankind* was a new kind of a book. It was not really a history, or even a plan of a history, as Condorcet gave but little indication of being a scientific historian. Even in the pre-Rankian period of the eighteenth century, histories were produced that rank high in scholarly attainment: Gibbon's *Decline and Fall of the Roman Empire,* Voltaire's *Essay on the Morals and Manners of Mankind,* and Hume's *History of England.*[73] But Condorcet had only a meager knowledge of historical sources, and lacked sympathy with historical methods. He did not fully realize the importance of historical documents, even false ones, as true expressions of historic conditions, though not always of the sincere views of those who wrote them. "Only meditation," he declared, "can, by a happy combination of ideas, lead us to general truths regarding the science of man." [74] The *Esquisse* deals, not with this country or with that, but with "man in general." It is a history about an abstraction, humanity, which undergoes changes as a result of the working of an impersonal natural law, that of progress. Seldom do great personalities appear on the scenes depicted by this history; it is all about causes, ideas, movements, and stages of development. In reading the *Esquisse* one gets a curious impression that Condorcet is writing the history of an uninhabited world. It is true that it describes how the torch of civilization was passed on by various peoples: by the Greeks of ancient times, by the Italians of the Renaissance, by the

Americans and the French of the eighteenth century, but these peoples merely emerged to pass on the torch and then vanished from history. This "happy artifice" of Condorcet, according to Auguste Comte, enabled him to write a history of a single race, humanity. It resulted in producing, in very crude form it is true, a history of ideas rather than that of nations.

The *Esquisse* is an outstanding work in the literature of the social sciences. Its influence was so great that it became, in the opinion of an historian of the idea of progress, "a point of departure for the social philosophy of the nineteenth century." [75] In England, as already noted, the classic work of Malthus, *An Essay on the Principle of Population, as it affects the future improvement of Society: with remarks on the speculations of Mr. Godwin, M. Condorcet, and other writers*, which appeared in 1798, was written in part as an answer to the *Esquisse*. The social philosophies of James Mill and John Stuart Mill were clearly inspired by Condorcet's ideas. According to Elie Halévy, Condorcet's views of social progress profoundly influenced the views of the Utilitarians in England.[76]

In France Condorcet's concept of social progress, and, especially, this emphasis on the Golden Age of the future suggested the speculations of the school of Utopian socialists, Fourier and Saint-Simon. "It was Condorcet," declared Saint-Simon, "who was first to conceive the idea of writing a history of the past and future of general intelligence. His project was sublime, but his execution was worthless." Saint-Simon condemned the *Esquisse* on three counts: (1) It gave an impression that man possessed language from the very beginning, whereas, language came only after a long process of development. (2) It presented religion as an obstacle to human welfare. History teaches, declared Saint-Simon, that "men of genius civilized mankind" by the means of religions, which were nothing else than "philosophic systems materialized." Religious institutions, like others, have their periods of infancy, maturity and decadence. (3) The idea of the unlimited perfectibility of mankind was erroneous. The capacity of the human mind does not increase; it can merely replace what it loses. The ancients were superior to the moderns in literature and in the science of war, though the moderns are superior to them in scientific achievements.[77] In his last criticism Saint-Simon shows that he misunderstood Condorcet's idea of perfectibility. Nowhere does Condorcet imply that progress means an increase in the capacity of the human mind. Throughout he makes it clear that it is the increase of knowledge, and its spread among the masses, that is responsible for social progress. It is understandable that Saint-Simon should have ascribed to the ancients superiority in literature; the classics were still models, even to advanced modern thinkers, in the early part of the nineteenth century. But that he should have ascribed superiority in warfare to the ancients, considering the modern use of gunpowder in warfare, is quite astonishing.[78]

A far greater admirer of the *Esquisse* than Saint-Simon was Auguste Comte who enthusiastically proclaimed Condorcet as his "spiritual father." "After Montesquieu," he declared, "the most important advance in the fundamental conception of sociology was made by the unfortunate Condorcet in his memorable work, the *Esquisse*. . . . For the first time the scientific idea of the social progress of mankind, an idea of universal significance, was at last clearly and definitely proclaimed." The "immortal few pages" of the Introduction and the last chapter on the future of mankind were, in Comte's opinion, the basis of all subsequent developments of sociology. They clearly showed, for the first time, that civilization was the "outcome of a progressive development, all the steps of which are closely related to one another through the working of natural laws, which can be revealed by a philosophic study of history, and which determine for each epoch, in a manner entirely positive, the degree of civilization that society experiences, either as a whole or in its parts." But Comte severely criticized the body of the *Esquisse* as contradicting the aim and purpose announced in the Introduction. The Epochs, he declared, show no connection with one another, and, as a consequence, the book becomes "a long and tiresome declamation." Condorcet's treatment of the Middle Ages was the "insensate outcome of eighteenth-century philosophy." It presented a contradiction between "the immense improvement attained by humanity at the end of the eighteenth century and the retrograde influences that Condorcet constantly attributes to the entire past, to all its ideas, to all its institutions, and to all its dominating forces." There is, then, a hiatus between the theologic, autocratic past and the free-thinking, democratic present; and history is "a perpetual miracle, and the progressive march of civilization becomes an effect without a cause." Although Condorcet did have a concept of social progress he did not, according to Comte, discover its true laws, and, therefore, his vision of the future is defective.[79]

The fundamental weakness of the *Esquisse*, as Comte has so well explained, is due to the fact that although Condorcet had an idea of social progress, he did not have a clear idea of social evolution. He explains, clearly enough, how a given stage in human history is higher than that which preceded it, but he does not explain how one develops from the other, which is social evolution. According to Croce this was "progress without development" because Condorcet regarded the past as a horror from which man has escaped into the enlightened eighteenth century.[80] The *Esquisse* is consequently not a study of the evolution of civilization, but a succession of epochs that are held together by the author's passionate belief in the unity of mankind. In discussing political, social, and economic changes Condorcet did not explain their relation to the new ideas that came with these changes. How then did new ideas originate and how did they influence mankind? Condorcet's answer was typical of the eighteenth-century ideologue. They originated, he believed, in the minds of the *éclairés*, the great scientists and philosophers, and influenced mankind through propaganda unless hindered by prejudices. Ever increasing enlightenment, due to fuller knowledge and clearer reason, would expose the inadequacies of existing institutions and accepted ideas. Therefore it was one's bounden duty to favor the discovery of new abstract truths as the only means of advancing continuously the progress of mankind. The store of truths, contributed by the great thinkers, became a social heritage; the larger it grew the greater was the intellectual ability of mankind. Behind the entire process was universal nature that comprehended all, from the fall of a sparrow to the birth of a new social order.

What then did Condorcet contribute to the idea of progress? In the first place, he clearly formulated the notion that progress was a natural law, based upon the nature of man, and that this natural law can be discovered only through a study of history. The *Esquisse* endeavors to give historic confirmation of this law by its great emphasis on the steps taken by mankind toward liberty and equality. In the second place,

Condorcet, along with Turgot, emphasized the social aspect of human progress, the advance of mankind through changing institutions and conditions. Hitherto, the purely intellectual aspect had been emphasized, notably in the quarrel between the "ancients" and the "moderns." In the third place, Condorcet contributed the idea of future determinism. It is his great emphasis on the future which gives the *Esquisse* a unique place in the intellectual movement of the eighteenth century. The idea of the unlimited perfectibility of mankind was never before so clearly stated and so fully developed as in this book. Condorcet's interest in the theory of probability gave him a sense for the future which was scientific and not utopian. His outline of the future development of mankind is in fairly definite terms; and what he prognosticates seems a reasonable deduction from the intellectual movement in the eighteenth century and from the French Revolution. The *Esquisse* is, therefore, a product of the hopes of the former and of the fulfillment of the latter. It is no wonder that the reactionaries in France, who hated both movements, turned with fury on the book. In his biting essay on Condorcet, Sainte-Beuve stigmatized the *Esquisse* as "the last and most fastidious dream of pure reason infatuated with itself; it is the Encyclopaedist ideal in all its opaque beauty." [81] Another hostile critic of Condorcet declared that "awaiting the blow of the guillotine he dreamed of the infinite prolongation of human life, of the perfection of human reason in the future, in a word, of the Golden Age. He should rather have died twice than to die for a chimera." [82]

In one respect the *Esquisse* is a work of intellectual propaganda against the Old Régime. It is, therefore, according to Flint, disfigured by a "passionate and prejudiced spirit of sectarian fanaticism." [83] The propagandist spirit of the Ency-

THE IDEA OF PROGRESS 267

clopaedist in Condorcet was not equal to the task of maintaining a scientific attitude toward historic institutions. He could not see the contributions to civilizations that the church and the monarchy had made in past ages, therefore they stood condemned at all times and in all places as evil influences on the life of mankind. It might be explained, however, that Condorcet, being a revolutionist, was too much concerned with the weight of the dead past on the living present to view it calmly as a heritage instead of a burden. This extreme antitraditionalism of Condorcet, so characteristic of the philosophes, undoubtedly influenced the ideology of the French Revolution. That movement sought emancipation from the past, and avoided historical justification for its acts as deliberately as the English and American Revolutions had sought it.

Despite all its faults of omission and commission, the *Esquisse* suggests methods of approach to the study of history that are distinctively novel and enlightening. Condorcet looks at the past with the eyes of the present, and he, therefore, has a consciously critical attitude. He makes no vain efforts to transport himself into the past in order to write of the period as if he were living in it. Scientific as he may be in his method of gathering data, and fair as he may be in judging persons and events, the historian is not a disembodied spirit who hovers over historic documents and records *wie es eigentlich gewesen ist*. He is part and parcel of the life of the age in which he lives, and his work cannot be really understood without reference to its ideas and prejudices.[84]

The *Esquisse* is frankly a "liberal" history. Condorcet denounced the historians of his day who, he declared, were opposed to human rights, and "seem to favor the party which, under the pretext of establishing a more stable, a wiser, and a more peaceful government, really aimed to concentrate authority in the hands of the rich. Such historians denounced those who defended the equality and independence of the people as 'factions' and 'rebels.' " [85] To Condorcet the history of civilization is the history of enlightenment, hence the *Esquisse* consistently applauds those elements that were the protagonists of progress and emphasizes those events that led to changes for the better. It is truly cosmopolitan in spirit; neither racial nor national sympathies or antipathies intrude whatsoever. It is a remarkable tribute to Condorcet that, although he wrote the book at a time when France was experiencing a tremendous outburst of nationalism, not a single chauvinistic word escaped his pen.

Finally, the *Esquisse* is a pioneer work in what is now called intellectual history. As a historian, Condorcet was undoubtedly influenced by Voltaire's *Essay on the Morals and Manners of Mankind* which set a new fashion of interpreting history in the light of intellectual and social progress. The *Esquisse* is primarily a history of ideas, the "mind in the making," in James Harvey Robinson's expressive phrase, and of their influence in the march of human progress. Condorcet's assumption is that the mind alone is the creative element in human life, and it alone is capable of determining the fate of mankind. This intellectual determinism visualizes progress as the conscious and deliberate effort of man to better himself and the conditions under which he lives. Therefore, the *Esquisse* is a forerunner of such intellectual histories, written in the nineteenth century, as Buckle's *History of Civilization in England*, Lecky's *History of European Morals* and *Rise and Influence of the Spirit of Rationalism in Europe*, Draper's *History of Intellectual*

Development of Europe, and White's *History of the Warfare of Science with Theology in Christendom.*

The idea of progress stood out in bold relief in the ideology of the eighteenth century. Being taken for granted as a fundamental law of nature and of society it was a subject for abstract speculation rather than for social research. During the first half of the nineteenth century its vast significance was realized, and a search began for the definite laws of social progress, which found expression in the work of the Utopian socialists, and, especially, in the work of Auguste Comte. In this way came into existence the "science of society," or sociology.

During the second half of the nineteenth century the idea of progress received powerful reënforcement in the field of biology through the theory of organic evolution, associated with the work of Darwin. This theory destroyed definitely the notion of the fixity of species, in which most of the philosophes believed, and gave a cogent explanation of the ascent of man from the lower animals.[86]

Progress became an article of faith. Its great popularity, even among the masses of the people, may be explained as being the result of the rapid advance of the Industrial Revolution. During the nineteenth century progress came to mean the exploitation of natural resources and of human labor by the means of constantly improving technological methods. Accumulation of wealth, through free enterprise, became the very touchstone of the progress of a nation.

But poverty dogged the heels of progress. Despite the fact that capitalism had succeeded in creating a world in which there was a surplus of goods, instead of as in the precapitalistic era, a deficiency of goods, poverty was the portion of the lower classes. This situation brought forth the socialist criticism, associated with the work of Karl Marx, which asserted that progress, under a capitalistic economy, results in the ever-increasing impoverishment of the masses of mankind. And the future would see their complete ruin unless the capitalist system was overthrown.

The socialist criticism has, in our day, caused many to question their faith in progress. No longer is it believed to be natural and inevitable, as it was believed in the eighteenth and nineteenth centuries. The limitless vista of Condorcet's dream of the perfectibility of mankind was of the very essence of liberalism at its rosy dawn. Into that eighteenth-century dream went a belief in the essential goodness of human nature, a love of mankind, and a faith in reason that never faltered. After the experience of the nineteenth century, with its revolutions, its nationalist wars, and its aggressive imperialism, perfectibility no longer dominates the ideology of liberalism. Belief in progress persists, but as a process of a definite achievement, the result of a conscious and deliberate solution of problems, limited in scope, that arise in a constantly changing social order.

CHAPTER FOURTEEN

CONDORCET AND LIBERALISM, AN EVALUATION

IT was Condorcet's misfortune to be a lesser luminary at a time when the great lights of the philosophe movement dazzled the intellectual skies of France. In each field to which he contributed he was outshone by some major luminary in that field: by d'Alembert in mathematics; by Voltaire in anticlericalism; by Turgot in political economy; by Montesquieu in political science; and by Rousseau in education. Therefore, despite Condorcet's real importance, he has suffered oblivion; he is but a name, except to a few, even in France.

It would be unjust to the philosophe, however, to say, as did Sainte-Beuve, in his hostile estimate of Condorcet, that his system of ideas came entirely from Turgot, and that he "merely developed it, extended it, and devoted himself more and more to the task of applying and of propagating it." As we have seen, Condorcet added something which was original with him, and which opened up wider vistas of progress in almost every field to which he contributed. This was especially true of his contributions to popular education, to feminism, and to the idea of progress.

Aristocrat by tradition and descent, reserved and diffident in manner, Condorcet was yet a complete and thorough democrat, as tested by his political and social views. As Spinoza is said to have had an intellectual love of God, Condorcet may be said to have had an intellectual love of the people. To the philosophe, the people were the primal source of the inspiration to create a free society, and the ultimate repository of the wisdom of the philosophers and of the discoveries of the scientists. It was his devotion to the cause of the people that caused the shy, retiring Condorcet to become an active reformer.

Unfortunately for Condorcet he had neither the wit of Voltaire, nor the eloquence of Rousseau, nor the elegant suavity of Montesquieu. His lack of style seriously hampered his popularity as a writer. At best, Condorcet's style is forceful and logical; at worst, stilted and declamatory. Even when his writing is clear it lacks relief, and the result is a sort of literary monotone. Condorcet is at his best in the *Esquisse*. In his last hours, alone and proscribed, the philosophe's ardent temperament and passionate love of humanity broke through all his reserves and found expression in pages of lofty eloquence.

Condorcet's personal qualities complete his portrait as the perfect ideologue that he has so often been depicted. He was a "man of principle," grave, impersonal, naïve. Like the other philosophes, and even more than they, his method was the *a priori* one of assuming the absolute truth of abstract principles to guide him in his thinking and in his actions. Condorcet's early training as a mathematician reënforced his tendency to abstract thinking, and he endeavored to solve social and political problems in the spirit of a mathematician proving a theorem. He accepted certain axioms: the natural goodness of man, the evil effects of inherited institutions and of prejudices, and the inevitability of progress. To declare a self-evident political truth, clearly and authoritatively, meant to create it. Steeped in this secular mysticism of the eighteenth century, Condorcet evolved a system of political scholasticism as tenuous and as unreal as the theology which he so greatly abhorred. Among the philosophes he was the theologian of political rationalism.

However, by the very dint of his preoccupation with social and political ideas, by his coherent body of doctrines, and by his rigid method of logical exposition, Condorcet succeeded in creating a complete pattern of liberalism. A criticism of Condorcet's ideas and methods, therefore, constitutes a criticism of modern liberalism.

Both as a political system and as a social philosophy liberalism came into prominence with the expanding economy of the Industrial Revolution. Individual enterprise, urged on by the profit motive, was considered the best means of promoting national prosperity. Eighteenth-century liberalism created an abstraction, the "individual," who was given unfettered freedom of enterprise, provided he did not entrench on the freedom of enterprise of other individuals by establishing monopolies. Later, in the nineteenth century, the "individual" made his appearance as the "economic man" whose charter of freedom was "enlightened self-interest." The eighteenth-century dreamers of equality, the Condorcets in France and the Jeffersons in America, envisaged a future society composed mainly of small individual proprietors, independent farmers in the country and mechanics and merchants in the city, who would establish a government founded on "equal rights to all and special privileges to none."

But the Industrial Revolution, as it developed during the nineteenth century, turned to naught this great dream of human equality. It created a new society in which there was even greater inequality than under the Old Régime. The eighteenth-century liberals did not foresee that the economic opportunities, offered by industrialism, would open up careers to those who possessed acquisitive talents, which would result in the coming into existence of a new class of property owners, the industrial capitalists, whose wealth would far outstrip that of the privileged aristocrats. By establishing the freedom of the market the capitalists discerned unlimited possibilities of wealth expansion through the exploitation of natural resources, new inventions, and new markets. And their success was due to the acceptance of laissez faire, a liberal principle which became the very breath of life of the new acquisitive society. The vast fortunes amassed by capitalists were protected, not by legal privileges, as were the lands of the aristocrats, but by the liberal principle of the natural right of property. Neither did the eighteenth-century liberals foresee that the mass of people in the new industrial society would consist of nonpropertied workers, equal before the law and having an equal voice in the government, who, nevertheless, were in a dire state of poverty and insecurity. By insisting on laissez faire liberalism succeeded in creating an "agnostic state" which refused to intervene on behalf of the workers or on behalf of the consumers lest it violate the consecrated doctrine of natural rights.

In the sphere of government, liberalism likewise had unexpected results. In order to function politically it created another abstraction, the "citizen," whose lineage was traced back to the ancient Roman Republic. In their ignorance of Roman history, the liberal philosophes conceived Roman citizenship as a badge of freedom and of equality, not as it really was, a special privilege conferred by the Republic on a small portion of the population. In the autocratic states of

LIBERALISM, AN EVALUATION

the eighteenth century, there were no "citizens," only subjects divided into castes who enjoyed privileges or suffered discrimination in accordance with their rank. Against the special interests of the guild, the corporation, the church, the nobility, the liberals opposed the general interests of "the public," a collective abstraction composed of individual citizens. They assumed that the ordinary man, who was primarily concerned with his individual welfare, would, when performing his duties as a citizen, suddenly undergo a process of political transubstantiation and concern himself solely with the public weal. All that was necessary to perform this miracle was enlightenment, which a free government would be ever ready to supply. Liberalism refused to identify the citizen as a farmer, a workingman, a merchant, a professional, lest class interest emerge to confuse and to confound the public-spirited citizen upon whom they based their political ideology.

But reality broke through these abstractions created by liberalism. Legislation in things that mattered was seldom the outcome of the "general will" but of the special interests of class, of section, and of party. Vested economic interests obtained privileges. Organizations of all sorts of groups sought favors through pressure politics. Real political power was wielded by the political machine, the boss, and the lobby. Political corruption and patronage often determined important policies. These are a few illustrations of the conflicts that raged behind the façade of self-government. To manipulate the political machinery and to confuse the mind of the "citizen" was the way to political success.

Today the problem of liberalism is how to preserve its precious heritage, civil rights and responsible government, a problem that confronts the great nations that have remained faithful to the liberal tradition, England, France, and the

United States. Liberalism is not synonymous with laissez faire, which was merely a phase of its historical development during the nineteenth century. New economic problems have appeared in the twentieth century: (1) the concentration of vast amounts of capital in the hands of great corporations; and (2) the concentration of armies of unskilled laborers in gigantic plants due to mass production. The vast increase in production has made the industrial system continually more unstable; periodic crises bring ever greater depressions in business, which entail unemployment on a vast scale. Security for both capital and labor is essential if freedom of enterprise is to survive. And security, if at all possible, can come only with social legislation and state regulation of business enterprise through economic planning. It is the task of liberalism in the twentieth century to transform the political and economic order which had suited a society, newly born industrially, but which no longer suits the mature industrial society of our time.

In the political field the new liberalism must repudiate the myth of the citizen on which is based our absurd system of elections which has made a farce of representative government. It must create new political machinery, based frankly on occupational representation and on concentration of power. As competition in the old economic order found a political counterpart in the multiplicity of competing parties, frequent elections, and frequent cabinet changes, so today consolidation in industry must find a political counterpart in concentration of power. Responsibility in government can be more efficiently maintained by giving more authority to the executive, who would wield power, not as an irresponsible dictator, but as a democratically chosen official responsible to a legislature whose essential function would be to act as the nation's monitor.

Progress has been the peculiar heritage of liberalism to which it must be ever faithful in order to survive. That is why the libertarians of the eighteenth century so passionately insisted on the necessity of every generation revising the existing system of government and society. And nothing was so much to their credit as their fear lest the generous principles, which they so eloquently proclaimed, should become hardened into new traditions, and serve as a bar to the future progress of the race.

NOTES

CHAPTER TWO: THE SOCIAL AND ECONOMIC TRANSFORMATION OF FRANCE DURING THE EIGHTEENTH CENTURY

1. The economic transformation of France has been well described by a number of French historians. See especially the standard works in this field of E. Levasseur, *La France industrielle en 1789* (Paris, 1865), *Histoire des classes ouvrières et de l'industrie en France avant 1789*, 2 vols. (Paris, 1901) and *Histoire du commerce de la France*, 2 vols. (Paris, 1911), vol. I; H. Sée, *L'Evolution commercial et industrielle de la France sous l'ancien régime* (Paris, 1925); C. Bloch, *Etudes d'histoire économique de la France (1760-1789)*, (Paris, 1900); M. Kovalewsky, *La France économique et sociale à la veille de la Révolution*, 2 vols. (Paris, 1909-1911); and G. Martin, *La grande industrie sous le règne de Louis XIV* (Paris, 1913).
2. Levasseur, *Histoire des classes ouvrières*, II, 523-534.
3. G. Martin, *La grande industrie en France sous le règne de Louis XV* (Paris, 1900), 185-195.
4. Levasseur, *La France industrielle en 1789* (Paris, 1865), 99.
5. Levasseur, *Histoire des classes ouvrières*, II, 537.
6. Levasseur, *La France industrielle en 1789*, 18.
7. Charles Ballot, *L'Introduction du machinisme dans l'industrie française* (Paris, 1923).
8. Ballot, *op. cit.*, Avant-Propos, VII.
9. Levasseur, *La France industrielle en 1789*, 21.
10. For further details concerning the Industrial Revolution in France see Ballot, *op. cit.*, 43-45, 436 ff.; Martin, *La grande industrie en France sous le règne de Louis XV*, 134-136; H. Carré et al., *Le règne de Louis XVI*, 203-229 in E. Lavisse (ed.) *Histoire de France* (Paris, 1910), IX; G. F. Renard and G. Weulersse, *Life and Work in Modern Europe*, trans. by M. Richards (London, 1926), 184-185; and Sée, *op. cit.*, 296.
11. Levasseur, *Histoire*, II, 541.

12. Ballot, *op. cit.*, Introduction, 1.
13. For a comprehensive description of French commerce during the eighteenth century consult Levasseur, *Histoire*, II, 512-566, and by the same author, *Histoire du commerce de la France*, I.
14. E. Lavisse and A. Rambaud, *Histoire générale* (Paris, 1896), VII, 661.
15. Sée, *L'Evolution*, 179-201; E. Martin Saint-Leon, *Histoire des corporations de métiers* (Paris, 1922), 519; G. Renard, *Syndicats, Trade Unions et Corporations* (Paris, 1909), 125-126; P. Boissonnade, *Essai sur l'organisation du travail en Poitou* (Paris, 1900), II, 79.
16. Renard, *op. cit.*, 89.
17. Levasseur, *Histoire*, II, 509-511; Renard and Weulersse, *op. cit.*, 189.
18. Sée, *L'Evolution*, 272.
19. H. Sée, *Modern Capitalism*, trans. by H. B. Vanderblue and G. F. Doriot (New York, 1928), 123.
20. Renard, *op. cit.*, 143.
21. Renard and Weulersse, *op. cit.*, 162.
22. H. Carré et al., *op. cit.*, 227-229.
23. De Tocqueville's view (*The State of Society in France Before the Revolution of 1789*, trans. by Henry Reeve (London, 1888), 19-28) was upheld by a Russian historian, I. Loutchisky, whose book, *L'Etat des classes agricoles en France à la veille de la Révolution* (Paris, 1911), is a notable study of peasant landholding under the Old Régime. Loutchisky considers those peasants as "proprietors" who held land in hereditary tenure. These proprietors, he proves, were growing in number, though their farms were too small and too poorly cultivated to maintain a family. G. Lefebvre, "Les recherches relatives à la répartition de la propriété et de l'exploitation foncière à la fin de l'ancien régime," *Revue d'Histoire Moderne* (March-April, 1928), upholds the view of Loutchisky, but with modifications. The French Revolution, according to these historians, did not create peasant proprietorship through the suppression of feudalism and through the sale of the confiscated estates; it merely confirmed and extended it. Those peasants who already had land increased their holdings; as a rule the landless peasants, having no money, were not in a position to acquire land. It was largely the bourgeois who bought the confiscated lands of the nobles and the church.
24. Loutchisky, *op. cit.*, ch. IV. In England the landlord had become a proprietor in the modern sense, leasing farms to tenants and employing laborers.
25. H. Sée, *Esquisse d'une histoire du régime agraire en Europe aux XVIIIe et XIXe siècles* (Paris, 1921), ch. 1; L. Gottschalk, "The

Peasant in the French Revolution," *Political Science Quarterly* (December, 1933).
26. L. Ducros, *French Society in the Eighteenth Century*, trans. by W. de Geijer (London, 1926), 248.
27. D. Ogg, *Europe in the Seventeenth Century* (London, 1925), 307; H. Carré, *La Noblesse de France* (Paris, 1920), ch. 1, gives good description of the various categories of nobles.
28. J. Brissaud, *A History of French Public Law*, trans. by J. W. Garner (Boston, 1915), 299; "Noblesse" in M. Marion (ed.), *Dictionnaire des institutions de la France au XVII^c et XVIII^c siècles* (Paris, 1923); Necker, *De l'Administration des Finances de la France* (Paris, 1784), III, 145.
29. G. Roupnel, *La ville et la campagne au XVIIe siècle* (Paris, 1922), 158.
30. Carré, *La Noblesse de France*, 38; A. L. Guérard, *The Life and Death of an Ideal* (New York, 1928), 237-238. For a description of the new nobility see de Tocqueville, *op. cit.*, 77-80; Renard and Weulersse, *op. cit.*, 236 ff.; and L. Ducros, *op. cit.*, 48-95, 242-265.
31. See excellent characterization of Louis XV in Guérard, *op. cit.*, 227-231.
32. A. Aulard, *Christianity and the French Revolution*, trans. by Lady Frazer (Boston, 1927), 32.
33. L. Ducros, *op. cit.*, 224.
34. M. Léonce de Lavergne, *Les Assemblées provinciales sous Louis XVI* (Paris, 1879), Préface, XIII.

CHAPTER THREE: THE RISE OF THE PHILOSOPHES

1. K. Martin, *French Liberal Thought in the Eighteenth Century* (London, 1929), 12.
2. On the philosophes treated collectively: E. Caro, *La fin de dix-huitième siècle*, 2 vols. (Paris, 1880); E. Faguet, *Dix-huitième siècle* (Paris, 1890); F. J. Picavet, *Les Idéologues* (Paris, 1891); A. V. Espinas, *La Philosophie sociale du XVIIIe siècle et la Révolution* (Paris, 1898); L. Ducros, *Les Encyclopédistes* (Paris, 1900); J. Fabre, *Les Pères de la Révolution* (Paris, 1910); J. P. Belin, *Le mouvement philosophiques de 1748 à 1789* (Paris, 1913); H. Sée, *L'Evolution de la pensée politique en France au XVIII^a siècle* (Paris, 1925); M. Roustan, *The Pioneers of the French Revolution*, trans. by Frederic Whyte with an Introduction by Harold J. Laski (London, 1926); D. Mornet, *La pensée française au XVIIIe siècle* (Paris, 1926); Eva Elizabeth Hoffman-Linke, *Zwischen Nationalismus und Democratie* (Muenchen und Berlin, 1927); L. Brunel, *Les philosophes et l'Académie française au dix-huitième*

siècle (Paris, 1884); K. Martin, *French Liberal Thought in the Eighteenth Century* (London, 1929); F. J. C. Hearnshaw (ed.), *The Social and Political Ideas of Some Great French Thinkers of the Age of Reason* (London, 1930); C. Becker, *The Heavenly City of the Eighteenth-Century Philosophers* (New Haven, 1932); D. Mornet, *Les origines intellectuelles de la Révolution française* (Paris, 1933); and A. Le Flamanc, *Les Utopies pré-révolutionnaire et la philosophie du XVIIIe siècle* (Paris, 1933).

3. A. de Tocqueville, *The State of Society in France Before the Revolution*, trans. by Henry Reeve (London, 1888), 120.
4. Roustan, *op. cit.*, 216.
5. D. Mornet, *Les origines intellectuelles de la Révolution française*, 419-431; E. Allain, *L'Instruction primaire en France avant la Révolution* (Paris, 1881); A. Rambaud, "Petites écoles," *Dictionnaire de pédagogie et d'instruction primaire*, Pt. I, vol. I.
6. A. Aulard, *Histoire politique de la Révolution française* (Paris, 1901), 25.
7. Quoted in D. Mornet, *Les origines intellectuelles*, 426.
8. Necker, *Œuvres complètes* (Paris, 1820-21), XV, 257.
9. Grimm, *Correspondance littéraire* (Paris, 1877-82), XV, 84; d'Alembert "Essai sur la société des gens de lettres et des grands," *Œuvres* (Paris, 1805), III.
10. *Correspondance littéraire, philosophique et critique*, by Grimm, Diderot, Raynal, Meister, 16 volumes (Paris, 1877-82).
11. H. Taine, *The Ancient Régime*, trans. by J. Durand (New York, 1931), 170.
12. Ch. Aubertin, *L'Esprit public au XVIIIe siècle* (Paris, 1889).
13. F. Rocquain, *L'Esprit révolutionnaire avant la Révolution* (Paris, 1878).
14. E. Champion, *La France d'après les cahiers de 1789* (Paris, 1897).
15. A. Aulard, *op. cit.*, 24-28. Aulard is of the opinion that all of the philosophes, before 1789, were opposed to both republicanism and democracy.
16. E. Faguet, *Questions politiques* (Paris, 1899), 3.
17. A. Sorel, *L'Europe et la Révolution française* (Paris, 1903), I, 234.
18. Roustan, *op. cit.*, 22-24.
19. Martin, *op. cit.*, 69.
20. Belin, *op. cit.*, 366.
21. Quoted by Mornet, *La pensée française au XVIIIe siècle*, 200.
22. Mornet, *Les origines intellectuelles*, 472.
23. A. de Tocqueville, *op. cit.*, 120.
24. Fréron was a literary critic with a sharp pen who attacked the views of the philosophes and especially those of Voltaire. See F. C. Green, *Eighteenth-Century France* (New York, 1931), 111-155.

CHAPTER THREE   283

25. A suggestive treatment of this theme is to be found in F. Barry, *The Scientific Habit of Thought* (New York, 1927), ch. 1.
26. Taine, *op. cit.*, 177.
27. L. Strachey, *Landmarks in French Literature* (New York, 1923), 145-146.
28. On the subject of censorship in France during the eighteenth century see J. P. Belin, *Le mouvement philosophique de 1748 à 1789* (Paris, 1913) and *Le commerce des livres prohibité à Paris de 1750 à 1789* (Paris, 1913); F. C. Green, *op. cit.*, 194-221; F. Brunetière, *Etudes critiques sur l'histoire de la littérature française*, Deuxième Série (Paris, 1893), 160-252. A list of condemned books may be found in the appendix of F. Rocquain. *L'Esprit révolutionnaire avant la Révolution, 1715-1789* (Paris, 1878).
29. F. Brunetière, *Etudes sur le XVIIIe siècle* (Paris, 1911), 207.
30. D'Alembert, *Œuvres* (Paris, 1805), XV, 305-306.
31. Condorcet, "Esquisse d'un Tableau historique des progrès de l'esprit humain," *Œuvres* (1847-1849), VI, 12. This justification of the methods of the philosophes caused John Adams to burst into moral indignation. In a letter to Jefferson he wrote that this "new philosophy was, by his own account, as insidious, fraudulent, hypocritical and cruel as the old policy of the priests, nobles and kings." P. Wilstach (ed.), *Correspondence of John Adams and Thomas Jefferson* (Indianapolis, 1925), 113.
32. J. Morley, *Rousseau* (London, 1886), II, 56.
33. See article "Presse" in the *Encyclopédie* wherein the argument is presented that a free press is advantageous to the existing order because the reader sits quietly at home by himself, and is, therefore, not part of a mob listening to inflammatory speeches.
34. Brunetière, *Etudes sur le XVIIIe siècle*, 201-202.
35. Mme. de Staël, *De la Littérature* (Paris, 1842), 414.
36. From the Memoires of Count de Ségur quoted in L. Ducros, *French Society in the Eighteenth Century*, trans. by W. de Geijer (London, 1926), 329-330.
37. J. Ortega y Gasset, *The Revolt of the Masses*, trans. from the Spanish (New York, 1932), 25.
38. B. Croce, *History*, trans. by D. Ainslee (New York, 1921), 244.
39. Brunetière, *Histoire de la littérature française classique*, III. Le Dix-huitième siècle (Paris, 1912), 350.
40. H. Laski, *Studies in Law and Politics* (New Haven, 1932), 20.
41. A. W. Benn, *The History of English Rationalism in the Nineteenth Century* (London, 1906), I, 4.
42. L. Brunel, *op. cit.*, Préface, X.
43. D'Holbach, *Système de la nature* (Paris, 1821), I, chapters VI-VII.

44. Voltaire, *Letters Concerning the English Nation*, with an Introduction by Charles Whibley (London, 1926), Letter VI.
45. J. Morley, *Diderot and the Encyclopaedists* (London, 1886), I, 5.
46. I. Babbit, *Democracy and Leadership* (Boston, 1924), chapter on "Rousseau and Idyllic Imagination."
47. C. Becker, *The Declaration of Independence* (New York, 1922), 51.
48. Article "Homme" in the *Encyclopédie*.
49. See interesting analysis of the legend of primitive virtue in H. N. Fairchild, *The Noble Savage* (New York, 1928) and in C. B. Tinker, *Nature's Simple Plan* (Princeton, 1922).
50. J. B. Bury, *The Idea of Progress*, new edition (New York, 1932), 5. For further discussion of the idea of progress see *infra* chapter XIII.
51. Montesquieu, *Spirit of Laws*, The Author's Preface.
52. G. M. Trevelyan, *The Recreations of an Historian* (London, 1919), 44.
53. Strachey, *op. cit.*, 142.
54. D'Holbach, *Système sociale* (London, 1773), II, 36-37.
55. Condorcet, *Sur le sens du mot révolutionnaire*, XII, 618.
56. Mably, Des droits et des devoirs du citoyen, *Œuvres* (Paris, 1794-1795), XI, 364.
57. Quoted in Sée, *op. cit.*, 222.
58. For Condorcet's attitude on government see *infra* chapter VI. For Diderot's attitude see M. Tourneaux, *Diderot et Catherine II* (Paris, 1899) and articles "Représentant," "Autorité" and "Législateur" in the *Encyclopédie*.
59. D'Alembert, *Œuvres* (Paris, 1805), XV, 294.
60. Morley, *Critical Miscellanies* (London, 1886), II, 233-234.
61. *Ibid.*, II, 218-219.
62. Diderot, "Plan d'une université pour le gouvernment de Russie," *Œuvres* (Paris, 1875-1879), III, 493.
63. Strachey, *op. cit.*, 145.
64. H. Hoeffding, *A History of Modern Philosophy* (London, 1900), I, 457.

CHAPTER FOUR: CONDORCET BEFORE THE FRENCH REVOLUTION

1. The first edition of Condorcet's works appeared in 1804, and consisted of 21 volumes. But this edition was incomplete and not carefully edited. The best edition of his works, to which the citations in this book refer, is Condorcet, *Œuvres*, 12 volumes (Paris, 1847-1849), edited by A. Condorcet O'Connor and M. F. Arago. This edition is not entirely complete. In addition, see Condorcet, *Essai sur l'application de l'analyse à la probabilité des décisions rendues à*

CHAPTER FOUR 285

la pluralité des voix (Paris, 1785); Ch. Henry, *Correspondance inédite de Condorcet avec Turgot* (Paris, 1883); and L. Cahen (ed.) "Un fragment inédit de Condorcet," *Revue de Metaphysique et de Morale* (September, 1914). Extracts from the writings of Condorcet are to be found in J. B. Severac (ed.) *Condorcet*; F. Buisson (ed.), *Condorcet* (Paris, 1929), and F. de la Fontainerie (ed.), *French Liberalism and Education in the Eighteenth Century* (New York, 1932). The first biography of Condorcet was that by M. F. Arago "Biographie de Jean-Antoine-Nicolas Caritat de Condorcet" in Condorcet *Œuvres*, I, I-CLXXI, a sketch of the philosophe's life based on information supplied by his daughter Mme. O'Connor, incomplete and not entirely correct; A. Charma, *Condorcet* (Caen, 1863) of little historical value; J. F. E. Robinet, *Condorcet: sa vie, son œuvres* (Paris, 1893), a fairly scholarly work; L. Cahen, *Condorcet et la Révolution française* (Paris, 1904), the standard work on Condorcet based on published and unpublished sources devoted chiefly to his activities during the Revolution; F. Alengry, *Condorcet, Guide de la Révolution française* (Paris, 1904), considers Condorcet "the political educator of his contemporaries," scholarly in treatment, but uncritical in its judgment of Condorcet's importance; A. E. Burlingame, *Condorcet, the Torch Bearer of the French Revolution* (Boston, 1930), the first biography in English by an enthusiastic admirer; Hélène Delsaux, *Condorcet journaliste* (Paris, 1931), a scholarly study of an important phase of Condorcet's career. Good sketches of Condorcet are to be found in *Grande Encyclopédie*; *Dictionnaire Pédagogique*; J. Morley, *Critical Miscellanies*, 3 vols. (London, 1888-1892), II; A. Guillois, *La Marquise de Condorcet* (Paris, 1897); F. Picavet, *Les Idéologues* (Paris, 1891); J. Fabre, *Les Pères de la Révolution* (Paris, 1910); H. Sée, *L'Evolution de la Pensée politique en France au XVIIIe siècle* (Paris, 1925) and "Condorcet, ses idées et son rôle politique," *Revue de Synthèse Historique*, 1905, X, 22-33; R. Doumic, *Etudes sur le littérature française*, 5e série (Paris, 1906); Sainte-Beuve, *Causeries du Lundi*; A. Dide, "Condorcet," *La Révolution Française*, 1882, II, 695-709, 745-754, 947-958; F. Brunetière, *Histoire de la littérature française classique* (Paris, 1912), III, 582-592. The histories of the French Revolution by Aulard, Sorel, Jaurès, and Mathiez contain accounts of Condorcet's activities during the Revolution. On various aspects of Condorcet's life and work: R. Doumic, "Lettres d'un philosophe et d'une femme sensible," *Revue de deux Mondes*, 6e période, V, 302-325, 835-860, VII, 57-81; A. Aulard, *Les Orateurs de la Législative et de la Convention* (Paris, 1885), I, 265-281, and "Les Origines du parti républicain," *Revue de Paris* (May, 1898); M. Frayssinet, *La Ré-*

publique des Girondins (Toulouse, 1903); P. Sakman, "Condorcet und der demokratische Gedanke," *Preussische Jahrbücher* (Jan.-March, 1903); E. Hoffman-Linke, *Zwischen Nationalismus und Demokratie* (Muenchen, 1927); A. Stern, "Condorcet und der Girondistische Verfassungsentwurf von 1793," *Historische Zeitschrift*, 1930, CXLI, 479-496; A. Mathiez, "La Constitution de 1793," *Revue de Paris* (July, 1928); L. M. Gidney, *L'Influence des Etats-Unis d'Amérique sur Brissot, Condorcet et Mme. Roland* (Paris, 1930); L. Cahen, "La Société des Amis des Noirs et Condorcet," *La Révolution Française*, 1906, L, 481-511; Ph. Sagnac, "Condorcet et son 'Moniteur' de 1788," *Revue d'Histoire moderne et Contemporaine*, 1911, XV, 348-351; A. Aulard, "Le feminism pendant la Révolution française," *Revue Bleu* (March 19, 1898); A. Duruy, *L'Instruction publique et la Révolution* (Paris, 1882); G. Compayré, *Histoire critique des doctrines de l'éducation en France*, 2 vols., 5 éd. (Paris, 1885), II, 273-290; F. Vial, *Condorcet et l'éducation démocratique* (Paris, 1903); L. Amiable, *Une loge maçonnique d'avant 1789* (Paris, 1897); E. Caillaud, *Les Idées économiques de Condorcet* (Poitiers, 1908); L. Brunschvicg, *Le progrès de la conscience dans la philosophie occidentale* (Paris, 1927); R. Flint, *Historical Philosophy in France* (New York, 1894); J. Delvaille, *Essai sur l'histoire de l'idée de Progrès jusqu'à la fin du XVIIIe siècle* (Paris, 1910); M. Defourny, "La philosophie de l'histoire chez Condorcet," *Revue Néo-Scolastique* (May-June, 1904); S. Krynska, *Entwicklung und Fortschritt nach Condorcet und A. Comte* (Bern, 1908); F. Alengry, *Essai historique et critique sur la sociologie chez Auguste Comte* (Paris, 1900); J. K. Niedlich, *Condorcet's "Esquisse d'un Tableau historique" und seine Stellung in der Geschichtsphilosophie* (Erlangen, 1907); E. Kohn-Bramstedt, "Condorcet und das Geschichtsbild der späten Aufklärung," *Archiv für Kulturgeschichte*, 1929, XX, 52-82; and Sir James G. Frazer, "Condorcet on the Progress of the Human Mind," *The Zaharoff Lecture for 1933*.
2. F. Arago, "Biographie de Condorcet" in *Œuvres*, I, VII.
3. L. Cahen, *Condorcet et la Révolution française* (Paris, 1904), 5.
4. *Ibid.*, 7.
5. Arago, *op. cit.*, I, XVI.
6. These Eloges are to be found in *Œuvres*, II-III.
7. *Correspondance entre Voltaire et Condorcet*, I, 30.
8. Arago, *op. cit.*, I, XVI.
9. Arago, *op. cit.*, I, X; see Ch. Henry, *Correspondance inédite de Condorcet et de Turgot* (Paris, 1883).
10. *Correspondance entre Voltaire et Condorcet*, I, 151-155; Arago, *op. cit.*, I, XLI.
11. *Vie de M. Turgot*, V, 1-233; *Vie de Voltaire*, IV, 1-186.

CHAPTER FOUR

12. *Notes sur Voltaire*, IV, 623.
13. *Lettres d'un théologien*, V, 273-341.
14. For an inimitable description of this curious *ménage à trois* see R. Doumic, "Lettres d'un philosophe et d'une femme sensible," *Revue des deux Mondes*, 6ᵉ pèriode, V, 302-325, 835-860; VII, 57-81.
15. Arago, *op. cit.*, I, XCIV.
16. Doumic, *op. cit.*, V, 322.
17. *Infra* chapter VIII.
18. *Correspondance entre Voltaire et Condorcet*, I, 115.
19. *Réflexions sur l'esclavage des nègres*, VII, 61-140.
20. *L'état des Protestants en France*, V, 391-573.
21. *Correspondance entre Voltaire et Condorcet*, I, 3, 100-101; see L. Brunel, *Les philosophes et l'Académie française au dix-huitième siècle*.
22. E. Seligman, *La justice en France pendant la Révolution (1789-1792)*, (Paris, 1913), I, 99-102.
23. After the death of Condorcet his widow lived in retirement until her death in 1823. The daughter, Elisa, married an Irish refugee, General O'Connor, who served under Napoleon. On the home life of the Condorcets see A. Guillois, *La marquise de Condorcet*.
24. *Portrait de M. le Mis de Condorcet, par M$^{lle.}$ de l'Espinasse*, I, 626; cf. Guillois, *op. cit.*, 62.
25. *Conseils de Condorcet à sa fille*, I, 617.
26. *Portrait de M. le Mis de Condorcet*, I, 633-634.
27. Quoted in Aulard, *Les Orateurs de la Législative et de la Convention* (Paris, 1885), I, 272 footnote.
28. *Essai sur la constitution et les fonctions des assemblées provinciales*, VIII, 123.
29. On this famous society see L. Amiable, *Une loge maçonnique d'avant 1789* (Paris, 1897); D. J. Hill, "A Missing Chapter of Franco-American History," *American Historical Review*, XXI, 709-719; G. Martin, *La Franc-Maçonnerie française et la préparation de la Révolution* (Paris, 1926), and *Manuel d'histoire de la Franc-Maçonnerie française* (Paris, 1929); and G. Huard, *L'Art Royal; essai sur l'histoire de la franc-maçonnerie* (Paris, 1930).
30. *Eloge de M. le comte de Milly*, III, 185.
31. L. Cahen, "Société des amis des Noirs et Condorcet," *La Révolution française*, L, 481-511.
32. *Infra* chapter VII.
33. *Réflexions sur les pouvoirs*, IX, 266. Even before the Revolution Condorcet showed republican leanings, as a result probably of his admiration for America. "A republican constitution is the best of all," he had declared (*Vie de M. Turgot*, V, 209). In the opinion of Cahen he was a republican in principle, but he did not consider

France before 1789 ripe for republicanism (L. Cahen, *Condorcet*, 26). In the opinion of Sée Condorcet was not a revolutionist but an advanced liberal who wished to prepare France for republicanism by abolishing the Old Régime. See H. Sée, "Condorcet, ses idées et son rôle politique," *Revue de Synthèse Historique*, X.
34. *Essai sur la constitution et les fonctions des assemblées provinciales*, VIII, 129.
35. *Lettres d'un bourgeois de New-Haven*, IX, 11.
36. *Ibid.*, IX, 12; *cf. Essai sur la constitution et les fonctions des assemblées provinciales*, VIII, 127-142.
37. *Lettres d'un bourgeois de New-Haven*, IX, 1-93. See *infra* chapter X.
38. P. Boiteau, *L'Etat de la France en 1789* (Paris, 1889), 103 ff.; L. de Lavergne, *Les assemblées provinciales sous Louis XVI* (Paris, 1879).
39. *Essai sur la constitution et les fonctions des assemblées provinciales*, VIII, 115-659.
40. *Sur la formation des communautés de campagne*, IX, 433-435.
41. Ph. Sagnac, "Condorcet et son 'Moniteur' de 1788," *Revue d'histoire moderne et contemporaine*, XV, 348-351.
42. M. P. Paganel, *Essai historique et critique sur la Révolution française* (Paris, 1815), II, 219.

CHAPTER FIVE: CONDORCET DURING THE FRENCH REVOLUTION

1. A. Aulard, *Histoire politique de la Révolution française*; and J. Jaurès, *Histoire socialiste de la Révolution française*, 8 vols. (Paris, 1922-24).
2. F. Alengry, *Condorcet, Guide de la Révolution française* (Paris, 1904).
3. *Lettres d'un citoyen des Etats-Unis, à un français*, IX, 120-121.
4. *Déclaration des Droits*, IX, 175-211.
5. L. Cahen, *Condorcet et la Révolution française* (Paris, 1904), 138 ff.
6. On Condorcet as a journalist, see Delsaux, *Condorcet journaliste*.
7. Cahen, *op. cit.*, 176 ff.
8. *Infra* chapter IX.
9. *Sur les opérations nécessaire pour rétablir les finances*, XI, 363-386; *Mémoires sur la fixation de l'impôt*, XI, 405-470; *Sur la proposition d'acquitter la dette exigible en assignats*, XI, 485-515; *Des causes de la disette du numéraire*, XI, 529-540; *Mémoires sur les monnaies*, XI, 581-673; and *Sur la distribution des assignats*, X, 303-316.
10. *Mémoires sur les monnaies*, XI, 606-607.
11. *Des causes de la disette du numéraire*, XI, 532.
12. Delsaux, *op. cit.*, 172.

CHAPTER FIVE 289

13. *Moniteur,* Nov. 3, 1791.
14. *Sur l'admission des femmes au droit de Cité,* X, 119-130.
15. *Infra* chapter X.
16. Aulard, *op. cit.,* 73.
17. *Ce que les citoyens ont droit d'attendre de leurs représentants,* XII, 558.
18. *Adresse à l'Assemblée Nationale, sur les conditions d'éligibilité,* X, 85.
19. *Lettres d'un gentilhomme,* IX, 223.
20. *Infra* chapter XII.
21. A. Aulard, "Les origines du parti républicain," *Revue de Paris* (May, 1898).
22. Delsaux, *op. cit.,* 17.
23. J. Michelet, *Les femmes de la Révolution* (Paris, 1855), 86.
24. *De la République,* XII, 227-237.
25. F. Buisson (ed.), *Condorcet* (Paris, 1929), 45.
26. *Lettres d'un jeune mécanicien,* XII, 239-241.
27. Aulard, *Histoire politique,* 138-139.
28. *Ibid.,* 140.
29. *Ce que les citoyens ont droit d'attendre de leurs représentants,* XII, 566-567.
30. XII, 107-166; X, 317-344.
31. Cahen, *op. cit.,* 174.
32. Aulard, *Les orateurs de la Législative et de la Convention,* I, 281.
33. *Sur l'Instruction publique,* VII, 167-573; see Jaurès, *op. cit.,* III, 431-452; for discussion of this Report see *infra* chapter XI.
34. *Sur l'Instruction publique,* VII, 434.
35. *Projet d'une exposition des motifs,* X, 445-455.
36. *Projet de constitution française,* XII, 499.
37. *Opinion sur les émigrants,* X, 223-242.
38. *Rapport,* X, 521-530.
39. *Instruction sur l'exercice du droit de souveraineté,* X, 531-540.
40. Alengry, *op. cit.,* 157.
41. *Fragment de justification,* I, 602.
42. *Le véritable et le faux ami du peuple,* I, 530.
43. *Aux citoyens français. Sur la nouvelle constitution,* XII, 663; *cf. Fragment de justification,* I, 603-604.
44. *Réflexions sur la Révolution de 1688, et sur celle du 10 Août, 1792,* XII, 195-213.
45. Robinet, *Condorcet,* 124.
46. *Mémoires de Madame Roland* (Paris, 1884), II, 297.
47. *Moniteur,* May 8, 1794.
48. Quoted in Aulard, *Les Orateurs,* I, 269.
49. *Opinion sur le jugement de Louis XVI,* XII, 267-303.

50. Buchez et Roux, *Histoire parlementaire*, XXI, 162-163.
51. Quoted in Cahen, *op. cit.*, 459.
52. Alengry, *op. cit.*, 180.
53. *Opinion de Condorcet*, XII, 305-311.
54. *Réponse à l'adresse aux provinces*, IX, 489.
55. *Projet de Déclaration des Droits*, and *Projet de constitution française*, XII, 417-501.
56. M. Deslandres, *Histoire constitutionnelle de la France* (Paris, 1932), I, 258.
57. For a detailed analysis of *la Girondine*, see *infra* chapter VI.
58. *Archives parlementaires*, Première Série, LVIII, 583 ff.
59. *Moniteur*, April 25, 1793.
60. *Ibid.*, April 27, 1793.
61. A. Mathiez, "La constitution de 1793," *Revue de Paris* (July-Aug., 1928), 300.
62. *Sur la nécessité d'établir en France une constitution nouvelle*, XII, 529-542.
63. *Discours prononcé à la convention, sur la convocation d'une nouvelle convention nationale*, XII, 581-597.
64. The text of the constitution of 1793 is to be found in F. M. Anderson (ed.), *The Constitutions and Other Select Documents Illustrative of the History of France* (Minneapolis, 1908); see discussion in Aulard, *Histoire Politique*, 296-313, and in A. Mathiez, "La constitution de 1793," *Revue de Paris* (July-Aug., 1928).
65. C. D. Hazen, *The French Revolution* (New York, 1932), II, 652.
66. *Aux citoyens français. Sur la nouvelle constitution*, XII, 651-675.
67. *Extrait du Moniteur du 10 Juillet, 1793*, XII, 678.
68. *Fragment de justification*, I, 574-605.
69. *Esquisse d'un Tableau historique des progrès de l'esprit humain*, VI; see *infra* chapter XIII.
70. *Esquisse*, VI, 286-287.
71. J. Morley, *Critical Miscellanies*, II, 196.
72. The last days of Condorcet are well described in A. Guillois, *La Marquise de Condorcet*, 133-173.
73. Arago, *Biographie de Condorcet*, I, CLI-CLVII.
74. Cahen, *op. cit.*, 547.
75. Sainte-Beuve, "Condorcet," *Causeries du Lundi*.

CHAPTER SIX: POLITICAL LIBERALISM

1. M. Frayssinet, *La République des Girondins* (Toulouse, 1903), 138.
2. His most important writings on government are: *Lettres d'un bourgeois de New-Haven*, IX, 1-93; *Lettres d'un citoyen des Etats-Unis*, IX, 95-123; *Essai sur la constitution et les fonctions des assemblées*

CHAPTER SIX

provinciales, VIII, 115-659; *Idées sur le despotisme*, IX, 145-173; *Déclaration des Droits*, IX, 175-211; *Lettres d'un gentilhomme à Messieurs du Tiers Etat*, IX, 213-259; *Sur la forme des élections*, IX, 285-330; *Examen sur cette question: est-il utile de diviser une assemblée nationale en plusieurs chambres?* IX, 331-364; *Lettres à M. le comte Mathieu de Montmorency*, IX, 365-391; and *Plan de constitution*, XII, 333-501.
3. *De l'influence de la Révolution d'Amérique sur l'Europe*, VIII, 5-6; cf. *Vie de M. Turgot*, V, 178-179; *Recueil de pièces sur l'Etat des Protestants en France*, V, 495; *Déclaration des Droits*, XII, 417-422.
4. *Lettres d'un bourgeois de New-Haven*, IX, 14.
5. *Sur le sens du mot révolutionnaire*, XII, 618.
6. F. Alengry, *Condorcet*, 679.
7. L. Cahen, "Un fragment inédit de Condorcet," *Revue de Métaphysique et de Morale*, XXII, 586.
8. *Tableau général de la science*, I, 543.
9. *Déclaration des Droits*, IX, 179.
10. *Esquisse d'un Tableau historique*, VI, 72.
11. See his essay, *Idées sur le despotisme*, IX, 145-173.
12. For Condorcet's indebtedness to America, see *infra* chapter XII.
13. *Essai sur la constitution et les fonctions des assemblées provinciales*, VIII, 230.
14. *Essai sur l'application de l'analyse à la probabilité des décisions rendues à la pluralité des voix* (Paris, 1785), XLII.
15. *Sur la forme des élections*, IX, 310-314; *Lettres d'un bourgeois de New-Haven*, IX, 24-28; *Plan de constitution*, XII, 396-399; *Essai sur l'application de l'analyse*, CLXXVII.
16. *Essai sur la constitution et les fonctions des assemblées provinciales*, VIII, 193.
17. *Esquisse d'un Tableau historique*, VI, 263.
18. *Discours prononcé dans l'Académie française*, I, 392.
19. Ch. Henry, *Correspondance inédite de Condorcet et de Turgot*, 132.
20. *Essai sur l'application*, CLXXXV.
21. On the subject of probability consult J. M. Keynes, *A Treatise on Probability* (London, 1921); J. Bertrand, *Calcul des Probabilités* (Paris, 1889); and I. Todhunter, *History of the Mathematical Theory of Probability from the Time of Pascal to that of Laplace* (Cambridge, 1865).
22. *Tableau général de la science*, I, 539-573.
23. *Essai sur l'application*, CLXXXIX.
24. *Ibid.*, XI; Todhunter, *op. cit.*, chapter XVII contains a complete analysis of Condorcet's system of probability.
25. *Essai sur l'application*, CLXXXIII.
26. *Ibid.*, CXL.

27. J. Bertrand, *op. cit.*, Introduction, XLV.
28. *Tableau général de la science*, I, 552.
29. *Observations de Condorcet sur le vingt-neuvième livre de l'Esprit des Lois*, I, 378.
30. *Exposition des principes et des motifs du plan de constitution*, XII, 337.
31. *Projet de Déclaration des Droits*, XII, 422.
32. *Essai sur la constitution et les fonctions des assemblées provinciales*, VIII, 276.
33. *Examen sur cette question: est-il utile de diviser une assemblée nationale en plusieurs chambres?* IX, 331-364.
34. *Ibid.*, IX, 352.
35. *Ibid.*, IX, 355-356.
36. *Idées sur le despotisme*, IX, 150.
37. *Lettres d'un bourgeois de New-Haven*, IX, 75.
38. *Exposition des principes et des motifs du plan de constitution*, XII, 355.
39. See excellent discussion of this interpretation in A. Esmein, *Eléments de droit constitutionnel* (Paris, 1921), I, 468.
40. *Idées sur le despotisme*, IX, 149.
41. *Essai sur la constitution et les fonctions des assemblées provinciales*, VIII, 557.
42. *Que toutes les classes de la société n'ont qu'un même intérêt*, XII, 646.
43. *Sur l'instruction publique*, VII, 214-215.
44. *Vie de Voltaire*, IV, 115.
45. *Idées sur le despotisme*, IX, 154-155.
46. *Ibid.*, IX, 155.
47. *Ibid.*, IX, 156.
48. *Lettres d'un citoyen des Etats-Unis à un français*, IX, 98.
49. See R. Bickart, *Les parlements et la notion de souveraineté nationale au XVIIIe siècle* (Paris, 1932).
50. *Posthumous Works of Frederick II, King of Prussia*, trans. from the French (London, 1789), XI, 49-50.
51. *Esquisse d'un Tableau historique*, VI, 177.
52. *Lettres à M. le comte Mathieu de Montmorency*, IX, 375.
53. *Essai sur la constitution et les fonctions des assemblées provinciales*, VIII, 224.
54. Arago, *Biographie de Condorcet*, I, CIII.
55. *Fragment de justification*, I, 575-576.
56. On this subject see the interesting essay of L. Cahen, "Un fragment de Condorcet," in *Revue de Métaphysique et de Morale*, XXII.
57. Condorcet "like Montesquieu, and even more than he, was the founder of constitutional law," Alengry, *Condorcet*, 679.

CHAPTER SIX

58. *Projet de Déclaration des Droits*, XII, 417-422; and *Projet de constitution française*, XII, 423-501.
59. A. Aulard, *Histoire politique de la Révolution française*, 280-296.
60. *Projet de constitution française*, XII, 421-422.
61. *Ibid.*, XII, 425-426.
62. *Assemblées provinciales*, VIII, 247.
63. Quoted in Delsaux, *Condorcet journaliste*, 166.
64. Condorcet's idea of a popular censure by means of the Initiative and Referendum was adopted in modified form by the Constitution of 1793 (F. Anderson, *The Constitutions and Other Select Documents* (1908), 179). Later it was adopted in Switzerland where it became the distinctive feature of its system of government. A. Esmein, *Eléments de Droit constitutionnel* (Paris, 1921), I, 417-421.
65. *Projet de constitution française*, XII, 476-479.
66. *Ibid.*, XII, 480.
67. *Vie de M. Turgot*, V, 212.

CHAPTER SEVEN: INTELLECTUAL AND SOCIAL LIBERALISM

1. *Assemblées provinciales*, VIII, 189.
2. *Journal d'instruction sociale*, XII, 612.
3. *Essai sur l'application de l'analyse*, CLXXXIV.
4. *Philosophie générale*, IV, 290.
5. *Vie de Voltaire*, IV, 182.
6. *Dissertation philosophique et politique*, V, 378.
7. *Eloge de Franklin*, III, 422-423.
8. *Vie de M. Turgot*, V, 212.
9. *Dissertation philosophique et politique*, V, 373.
10. *Discours sur les Conventions nationales*, X, 214.
11. *Correspondance générale*, I, 333.
12. *Dissertation philosophique et politique*, V, 380.
13. *Fragment sur la liberté de la presse*, XI, 307.
14. *Ibid.*, XI, 290.
15. *Vie de Voltaire*, IV, 34.
16. *Fragments sur la liberté de la presse*, XI, 262-270.
17. *Ibid.*, XI, 292-293.
18. T. Hobbes, *Leviathan*, ch. XI.
19. Montesquieu, *Spirit of Laws*, Book VI; C. B. Beccaria, *An Essay on Crimes and Punishments*, trans. from the Italian (Albany, 1872).
20. *Vie de M. Turgot*, V, 190.
21. *Réflexions sur la jurisprudence criminelle*, VII, 24.
22. *Vie de M. Turgot*, V, 191.
23. *Réflexions sur la jurisprudence criminelle*, VII, 22.
24. Arago, *Biographie de Condorcet*, I, CXXI-CXXII.

NOTES

25. *Dissertation philosophique et politique*, V, 372.
26. *Ibid.*, V, 369.
27. R. Doumic, "Lettres d'un philosophe et d'une femme sensible," *Revue de deux Mondes*, Sixième période, V, 856.
28. *Lettres d'un bourgeois de New-Haven*, IX, 46.
29. *Ibid.*, IX, 71-72.
30. *Vie de M. Turgot*, V, 201.
31. *Esquisse d'un Tableau historique*, VI, 265.
32. *Notes sur Voltaire*, IV, 508.
33. *De l'influence de la Révolution d'Amérique sur l'Europe*, VIII, 22; *Notes sur Voltaire*, IV, 508.
34. *Fragment de justification*, I, 591.
35. *Réflexions sur l'esclavage des Nègres*, VII, 61-140.
36. *Au corps électoral, contre l'esclavage des Noirs*, IX, 469-475.
37. *Sur l'admission des Députés des planteurs de Saint-Domingue, dans l'Assemblée Nationale*, IX, 479-485.
38. Quoted by Alengry, *Condorcet*, 451.
39. *Réflexions sur l'esclavage des Nègres*, VII, 69-90.
40. *Ibid.*, VII, 85.
41. *Ibid.*, VII, 86.
42. *Ibid.*, VII, 95-105.
43. The anti-slavery agitation in France resulted in the emancipation of the Negroes. In 1794 the Convention abolished slavery in the French colonies, and the freedmen were given rights of citizenship. But slavery was restored, in 1802, by Napoleon. It was finally abolished, in 1848, by the Second French Republic which gave compensation to the masters.
44. *Assemblées provinciales*, VIII, 455-462.
45. Quesnay, "Droit naturel" in E. Daire (ed.), *Physiocrates* (Paris, 1846), 46.
46. Quoted in Delsaux, *Condorcet journaliste*, 170.
47. *Examen sur cette question: est-il utile de diviser une assemblée nationale en plusieurs chambres?* IX, 351.
48. *Que toutes les classes de la société n'ont qu'un même intérêt*, XII, 650.
49. *Sur l'impôt progressif*, XII, 633.
50. *Vie de M. Turgot*, V, 196.
51. *Ibid.*, V, 187.
52. *Déclaration des Droits*, IX, 208.
53. *L'Assemblée nationale aux Français*, X, 330.
54. *Esquisse d'un Tableau historique*, VI, 248. Malthus, who was moved to write his famous book on population as a reply to Condorcet's *Esquisse*, objects to Condorcet's scheme on the ground that the popularization of credit would discourage business enterprise and

encourage the increase of population by removing the fear of poverty from the lower classes. *Essay on Population*, Bk. III, ch. 1.
55. *Esquisse*, VI, 247; *Sur les caisses d'accumulation*, XI, 392-393.

CHAPTER EIGHT: ECONOMIC LIBERALISM

1. *Supra* chapter I.
2. Voltaire, Art. "Blé," *Dictionnaire philosophique*.
3. G. Weulersse, *Le mouvement physiocratique en France de 1756 à 1770* (Paris, 1910), I, 316-333.
4. On the physiocrats: E. Daire (ed.), *Physiocrates* (Paris, 1846), contains the chief writings of the leading Physiocrats; Adam Smith, *Wealth of Nations*, Book IV, chapter 9; G. Weulersse, *Le mouvement physiocratique en France de 1756 à 1770*, 2 vols. (Paris, 1910); H. Higgs, *The Physiocrats* (London, 1897); H. Denis, *Histoire des systèmes économiques et socialistes*, 2 vols. (Paris, 1904-1907); L. de Lavergne, *Les économistes français du XVIIIe siècles* (Paris, 1870); Y. Guyot, *Quesnay et la physiocratie* (Paris, 1896); C. Gide and C. Rist, *Histoire des doctrines économiques* (Paris, 1926); J. Bonar, *Philosophy and Political Economy in Some of Their Historical Relations* (London, 1922); and N. J. Ware, "The Physiocrats," *American Economic Review*, XXI, 607-619.
5. E. Caillaud, *Les Idées économiques de Condorcet* (Poitiers, 1908), 21.
6. Weulersse, *op. cit.*, II, 17.
7. *Eloge de M. Trudaine*, II, 218.
8. *Monopole et Monopoleur*, XI, 37-58.
9. *Vie de M. Turgot*, V, 114.
10. *Réflexions sur le commerce des blés*, XI, 148.
11. Mercier de la Rivière, "L'Ordre naturel," in Daire (ed.), *op. cit.*, 547-548.
12. *Vie de M. Turgot*, V, 184-185.
13. *Lettre d'un laboureur de Picardie*, XI, 1-34 and *Réflexions sur le commerce des blés*, XI, 99-252.
14. *De l'influence de la Révolution d'Amérique sur l'Europe*, VIII, 34-35.
15. Weulersse, *op. cit.*, II, 668.
16. *Esquisse d'un Tableau historique*, VI, 179.
17. *Sur les préjugé qui suppose une contrariété d'intérêts entre Paris et les provinces*, X, 134.
18. *Que toutes les classes de la société n'ont qu'un même intérêt*, XII, 648.
19. Weulersse, *op. cit.*, I, 306.
20. Turgot, "Réflexions sur la formation et la distribution des richesses," *Œuvres* (Paris, 1914), 538.

21. *Notes sur Voltaire*, IV, 404.
22. *Tableau général de la science*, I, 565.
23. *Sur l'instruction publique*, VII, 395.
24. *Réflexions sur le commerce des blés*, XI, 170.
25. *Ibid.*, XI, 171.
26. *Esquisse*, VI, 40-41.
27. *Assemblées provinciales*, VIII, 459.
28. *Ibid.*, VIII, 458-459.
29. *Ibid.*, VIII, 460.
30. *Infra* chapter XI.
31. *Assemblées provinciales*, VIII, 477.
32. Quesnay, "Maximes générales," in Daire (ed.), *op. cit.*, 83.
33. The most important were *Des lois constitutionnelles sur l'administration des finances*, X, 105-117, and *Sur l'impôt progressif*, XII, 625-636.
34. *Mémoires sur la fixation de l'impôt*, XI, 460.
35. *Assemblées provinciales*, VIII, 295.
36. *Sur l'abolition des corvées*, XI, 190.
37. *Vie de M. Turgot*, V, 33.
38. *Déclaration des Droits*, IX, 203-204.
39. *Sur l'impôt personnel*, XI, 471-485.
40. *Sur l'impôt progressif*, XII, 625-636.
41. *Ibid.*, XII, 630.
42. Mercier de la Rivière, "L'Ordre naturel," in Daire (ed.), *op. cit.*, 615. The philosophes were strong believers in the natural right of property. Rousseau, in a famous passage in his *Discourse on Inequality*, asserted that the first man who had seized a piece of land and announced that it was his property was the founder of civil society. But once civil society was established, Rousseau believed that "the right of property is the most sacred of all the rights of citizens, and, in some respects, more important than liberty itself." C. E. Vaughn (ed.), *Political Writings of Rousseau* (Cambridge, 1915), I, 259.
43. J. Brissaud, *History of French Public Law*, trans. by J. W. Garner (Boston, 1915), 211-212, 549; I. Loutchisky, *L'Etat des classes agricoles en France à la veille de la Révolution* (Paris, 1911), ch. IV.
44. *De l'influence de la Révolution d'Amérique sur l'Europe*, VIII, 12.
45. Mercier de la Rivière, "L'Ordre naturel" in Daire (ed.), *op. cit.*, 616.
46. P. Sagnac, *La législation civile de la Révolution française* (Paris, 1898), 243.
47. *Vie de M. Turgot*, V, 178.
48. *Réflexions sur le commerce des blés*, XI, 168.
49. *Vie de M. Turgot*, V, 188.

CHAPTER EIGHT

50. *Réflexions sur le commerce des blés*, XI, 189.
51. *Dissertation philosophique et politique*, V, 362.
52. *Examen sur cette question: est-il utile de diviser une assemblée nationale en plusieurs chambres?* IX, 351.
53. *Assemblée provinciales*, VIII, 344.
54. Caillaud, *op. cit.*, 116.
55. Turgot, "Réflexions sur la formation et la distribution des richesses," *Œuvres* (Paris, 1914), II, 537.
56. *Réflexions sur le commerce des blés*, XI, 134.
57. *Assemblées provinciales*, VIII, 457.
58. See Introduction by E. R. A. Seligman to Adam Smith's, "Wealth of Nations," in *Everyman's* edition.
59. K. Marx, *Capital*, trans. by E. Untermann (Chicago, 1915), II, 415; *cf.* Weulersse, *op. cit.*, II, 703.
60. Jaurès, *Histoire socialiste de la Révolution française* (Paris, 1922), I, 134.

CHAPTER NINE: RELIGIOUS LIBERALISM

1. *Supra* chapter III.
2. Sainte-Beuve, "Condorcet" in *Causeries du Lundi*.
3. *Esquisse d'un Tableau historique*, VI, 30.
4. *Sur l'instruction publique*, VII, 289.
5. *Vie de M. Turgot*, V, 171.
6. *Notes sur Voltaire*, IV, 395.
7. F. Buisson (ed.), *Condorcet* (Paris, 1929), 37.
8. *Esquisse*, VI, 304.
9. *Dissertation philosophique et politique*, V, 367.
10. *Esquisse*, VI, 152-153.
11. *Notes sur Voltaire*, IV, 545.
12. *Esquisse*, VI, 121-124.
13. F. Buisson, *op. cit.*, 51.
14. Voltaire, Art. "Dieu," *Dictionnaire philosophique;* Diderot, Art. "Christianisme," in the *Encyclopédie* and "Des Ecoles Publiques," in M. Tourneux (ed.), *Diderot et Catherine II* (Paris, 1899).
15. A. Mathiez, *Contribution à l'histoire religieuse de la Révolution française* (Paris, 1907), ch. I.
16. *Infra* chapter XI.
17. *Infra* chapter X.
18. *Recueil de pièces sur l'état des Protestans en France*, V, 391-573.
19. *Sur la loi naturelle*, IV, 223.
20. *De l'influence de la Révolution d'Amérique sur l'Europe*, VIII, 37.
21. A. Aulard, *Christianity and the French Revolution*, trans. by Lady Frazer (Boston, 1927), 40.
22. *Vie de M. Turgot*, V, 144-145.

23. *Notes sur Voltaire*, IV, 537-539; *Réponse à l'adresse aux Provinces, ou Réflexions sur les écrits publiés contre l'Assemblée nationale*, IX, 496-497.
24. *Assemblées provinciales*, VIII, 443-444.
25. *Idées sur le despotisme*, IX, 169.
26. *Déclaration des Droits*, IX, 199.
27. *De l'influence de la Révolution d'Amérique sur l'Europe*, VIII, 37.
28. E. Joyau, *La Philosophie en France pendant la Révolution* (Paris, 1893), 76.
29. *Vie de M. Turgot*, V, 146; *Assemblées provinciales*, VIII, 649 ff.; *Ecrits pour les habitants du Jura*, IV, 252.
30. *Assemblées provinciales*, VIII, 442.
31. *Réflexions sur l'usufruit des bénéficiers*, X, 20.

CHAPTER TEN: FEMINISM

1. Article "Mariage" in the *Encyclopédie*.
2. See the uncomplimentary article on women ("Femme") in the *Encyclopédie*. Voltaire believed in the natural inequality of woman because of woman's physical inferiority; see article "Femme," *Dictionnaire philosophique*.
3. Rousseau, *Emile*, Book V; cf. Grimm, *Correspondance littéraire* (Paris, 1878), III, 238.
4. Diderot, "Sur les femmes," *Œuvres complètes* (Paris, 1875-1877), II, 251-262.
5. *Lettres d'un bourgeois de New-Haven*, IX, 1-93; *Sur l'admission des Femmes au droit de Cité*, X, 119-130.
6. *Sur l'admission des femmes*, X, 122.
7. *Ibid.*, X, 122.
8. *Sur l'instruction publique*, VII, 216-220.
9. *Sur l'admission des femmes*, X, 125.
10. *Esquisse d'un Tableau Historique*, VI, 264.
11. *Sur l'admission des femmes*, X, 128.
12. *Ibid.*, X, 129.
13. *Lettres d'un bourgeois de New-Haven*, IX, 17-18.
14. *Fragment*, VI, 632-633; *Sur l'admission des femmes*, X, 122-123.
15. *Sur l'instruction publique*, VII, 215-216.
16. *Lettres d'un bourgeois de New-Haven*, IX, 19.
17. *Esquisse*, VI, 523.
18. *Assemblées provinciales*, VIII, 465-466.
19. *Notes sur Voltaire*, IV, 564-565; *Sur le sens du mot révolutionnaire*, XII, 617.
20. *Réponse au Plaidoyer de M. d'Epresmenil*, VII, 43, 45.
21. *Esquisse*, VI, 257-258.

CHAPTER TEN 299

22. *Notes sur Voltaire*, IV, 361.
23. *Avertissement inséré par Condorcet dans l'édition complète des œuvres de Voltaire*, IV, 212-218.
24. *Ibid.*, IV, 218.
25. *Vie de Voltaire*, IV, 89.
26. *Esquisse*, VI, 264.
27. *Assemblées provinciales*, VIII, 469-470.
28. *Notes sur Voltaire*, IV, 561.

CHAPTER ELEVEN: POPULAR EDUCATION

1. Aulard, *Histoire politique de la Révolution française*, ch. I. On the subject of popular education in France: E. Allain, *L'Instruction primaire en France avant la Révolution* (Paris, 1881); A. A. Babeau, *Le Village sous l'Ancien Régime* (Paris, 1891); A. Duruy, *L'Instruction publique et la Révolution* (Paris, 1882); Article "Petites écoles," *Dictionnaire de pédagogie et d'instruction primaire*; H. Carré et al., *Le règne de Louis XVI* (Paris, 1910), 165; E. Levasseur, *La France industrielle en 1789* (Paris, 1865), 118; F. Vial, *Condorcet et l'éducation démocratique* (Paris, 1903); C. Hippeau, *L'Instruction publique en France pendant la Révolution* (Paris, 1883); G. Compayré, *Histoire critique des doctrines de l'éducation en France*, 2 vols. (Paris, 1885).
2. Compayré, *op. cit.*, II, 9-22.
3. This essay is translated into English in F. de la Fontainerie (ed.), *French Liberalism and Education in the Eighteenth Century* (New York, 1932), 27-169.
4. This essay of Turgot is translated in F. de la Fontainerie. *op. cit.*, 179-183.
5. M. Tourneux (ed.), *Diderot et Catherine II* (Paris, 1899), translated in F. de la Fontainerie, *op. cit.*, 199-310.
6. On Talleyrand's report see J. Jaurès, *Histoire socialiste de la Révolution française* (Paris, 1922-24), III, 431-452. The text is to be found in O. Gréard (ed.), *La législation de l'instruction primaire en France* (Paris, 1874), I. The constitution of 1791 provided for the creation of a system of public education "common to all citizens gratuitous as regards the parts of education indispensable for all men." F. M. Anderson, *Constitutions and Other Select Documents Illustrative of the History of France* (Minneapolis, 1908), 62.
7. *Sur l'instruction publique*, VII, 167-573, trans. in F. de la Fontainerie, *op. cit.*, 323-378.
8. E. Herriot, *Créer* (Paris, 1920), II, 123.
9. E. H. Reisner, *The Evolution of the Common School* (New York, 1930), 147.

10. *Sur l'instruction publique*, VII, 169. In his Declaration of Rights Condorcet included an article demanding universal education, *Projet de Déclaration des Droits*, XII, 421.
11. *Sur l'instruction publique*, VII, 449.
12. *Ibid.*, VII, 171.
13. *Ibid.*, VII, 179-180.
14. *Assemblées provinciales*, VIII, 477.
15. *Sur l'instruction publique*, VII, 174.
16. *Assemblées provinciales*, VIII, 458-460, 476-477; *Sur l'instruction publique*, VII, 192.
17. *Assemblées provinciales*, VIII, 474.
18. *Sur l'instruction publique*, VII, 217-220.
19. *Ibid.*, VII, 221-224.
20. *Ibid.*, VII, 223.
21. *Ibid.*, VII, 203-206; *Vie de M. Turgot*, V, 145.
22. See comment in Compayré, *op. cit.*, II, 277-278.
23. Cahen, *Condorcet*, 337-338.
24. *Dissertation philosophique et politique*, V, 363-365.
25. *Sur l'instruction publique*, VII, 211-213.
26. *Ibid.*, VII, 211-212.
27. *Ibid.*, VII, 215.
28. E. H. Reisner, *Nationalism and Education Since 1789* (New York, 1922), 23.
29. L. Liard, *L'Enseignement supérieur en France* (Paris, 1888), I, 159.
30. *Sur l'instruction publique*, VII, 278-279.
31. *Ibid.*, VII, 256.
32. *Esquisse*, VI, 223.
33. Compayré, *op. cit.*, II, 275.
34. *Sur l'instruction publique*, VII, 179.
35. *Ibid.*, VII, 552.
36. Jaurès, *op. cit.*, III, 434.
37. *Sur l'instruction publique*, VII, 325.
38. *Ibid.*, VII, 327.
39. *Ibid.*, VII, 341-344.
40. Cahen, *Condorcet*, 359-360; cf. Vial, *op. cit.*, 100.
41. *Sur l'instruction publique*, VII, 418.
42. *Ibid.*, VII, 351.
43. *Ibid.*, VII, 351.
44. *Vie de Voltaire*, IV, 97.
45. *Sur l'instruction publique*, VII, 420.
46. *Ibid.*, VII, 308-311, 512.
47. *Ibid.*, VII, 321; Vial, *op. cit.*, 51.
48. Brunetière, *Histoire de la littérature française classique*, III, 590.
49. Herriot, *op. cit.*, II, 121.

50. On the *Ecole Unique*, see *Les Compagnons, l'université nouvelle* (Paris, 1919); L. Brunschvicg, *Un ministère de l'éducation nationale* (Paris, 1922); P. Flottes, *La Révolution de l'Ecole Unique* (Paris, 1931); and I. L. Kandel, *Comparative Education* (Boston, 1933), 119-136.

CHAPTER TWELVE: THE REDISCOVERY OF AMERICA

1. On French admiration of the English: J. C. Collins, *Voltaire, Montesquieu and Rousseau in England* (London, 1908); J. Texte, *Jean-Jacques Rousseau and the Cosmopolitan Spirit in Literature*, trans. by J. W. Matthews (London, 1899), Book I; A. C. Hunter, *J. B. A. Suard, Un Introducteur de la littérature anglaise en France* (Paris, 1925); C. H. Lockitt, *The Relations of French and English Society (1763-1793)*, (London, 1920); F. C. Green, *Eighteenth-Century France* (New York, 1931), ch. III; G. Bonno, *La Constitution Britannique devant l'opinion française de Montesquieu à Bonaparte* (Paris, 1932); H. T. Buckle, *History of English Civilization*, I, ch. XII; F. Brunetière, *Etudes sur le XVIIIe siècle* (Paris, 1911), 274-281; R. Doumic, *Etudes sur la littérature française*, 5e série (Paris, 1906), 71-85; L. Strachey, *Landmarks in French Literature* (New York, 1923), ch. V; H. J. Laski, "Rise of Liberalism," *Encyclopaedia of the Social Sciences*, I, 103-124.
2. P. Gaxotte, *La Révolution française* (Paris, 1928), 66.
3. E. Clavière and J. P. Brissot, *De la France et des Etats-Unis* (London, 1787), and J. P. Brissot, *Nouveau Voyage dans les Etats-Unis* (Paris, 1791), 3 vols.
4. On the literary discovery of America by the French see G. Chinard, *L'Amérique et le rêve exotique dans la littérature française* (Paris, 1913); B. Fäy, *The Revolutionary Spirit in France and America*, trans. by R. Guthrie (New York, 1927) and *Bibliographie critique des ouvrages français relatifs aux Etats-Unis* (Paris, 1925); G. Atkinson, *The Extraordinary Voyage in French Literature from 1700 to 1720* (Paris, 1922); and F. Monaghan, *French Travellers in the United States, 1765-1832* (New York, 1933), an exhaustive bibliography.
5. On the idealization of the Pennsylvania Quakers see Edith Philips, *The Good Quaker in French Legend* (Philadelphia, 1932).
6. On the influence of this society on Franco-American affairs see D. J. Hill, "A Missing Chapter in Franco-American History," *American Historical Review*, July, 1916.
7. *Lettres d'un bourgeois de New-Haven*, IX, 1-93, and *Lettres d'un citoyen des Etats-Unis*, IX, 95-123.
8. *Eloge de Franklin*, III, 399.

9. *Discours sur les conventions nationales*, X, 214.
10. *Esquisse d'un Tableau historique*, VI, 199.
11. *Supra* chapter VI.
12. *Idées sur le despotisme*, IX, 168. For the Virginia Bill of Rights see B. P. Poore (ed.), *The Federal and State Constitutions* (Washington, 1878), II, 1908-1909.
13. *De l'influence de la Révolution d'Amérique sur l'Europe*, VIII, 11. Did the Declaration of Independence and the Bill of Rights of the states form a model for the French Declaration of the Rights of Man and of Citizens? On this subject there was, at one time, a heated controversy. G. Jellinek, *The Declaration of the Rights of Man and of Citizens*, trans. by M. Farrand (New York, 1901), stoutly maintained that the French Declaration was inspired by American models and not by the theories of Rousseau. His view was challenged by E. Boutmy, *Etudes politiques* (Paris, 1907), who evidently regarded it as a German attack on France. Boutmy asserted that the French Declaration was inspired by Rousseau, and that both the French and American documents were examples of eighteenth-century political thought. C. Becker, *The Declaration of Independence* (1922), emphasized the influence of Locke on Jefferson's ideas. For discussion of the influence of American ideas on the French Revolution see L. Rosenthal, *America and France* (New York, 1882); L. M. Gidney, *L'Influence des Etats-Unis d'Amérique sur Brissot, Condorcet et Mme. Roland* (Paris, 1930); and Ph. Sagnac, "Les origines de la Révolution française; l'influence américaine," *Revue des études napoléoniennes*, January, 1924.
14. On the subject of constitutional conventions see *Des conventions nationales*, X, 188-206, and *Discours sur les conventions nationales*, X, 207-222.
15. *Esquisse*, VI, 198.
16. H. Belloc, *The Contrast* (London, 1923), 150.
17. *Assemblées provinciales*, VIII, 258.
18. *Projet de constitution*, VIII, 69-113.
19. *Esquisse*, VI, 198.
20. *Lettres d'un Bourgeois de New-Haven*, IX, 84.
21. Woodrow Wilson, *Congressional Government* (Boston, 1925), 12-13, 284-285.
22. *Assemblées provinciales*, VIII, 223-224.
23. *Idées sur le despotisme*, IX, 151.
24. *Lettres d'un bourgeois de New-Haven*, IX, 69.
25. E. Dumont, *Souvenirs sur Mirabeau* (Brussels, 1832), 248.
26. *Eloge de Franklin*, III, 401.
27. This Pennsylvania constitution is to be found in B. P. Poore (ed.), *op. cit.*, II, 1540-1548.

28. *Ibid.*, II, 1548. However, a new constitution was adopted by Pennsylvania, in 1790, which repudiated the democratic features so much praised by Condorcet. The constitution of 1790 provided for a bicameral legislature and a governor; there was no provision for a Board of Censors. See Poore (ed.), *op. cit.*, II, 1549 ff.
29. *Supra* chapter VI.
30. Adams considered Condorcet as an impractical statesman and superficial philosopher, hence a dangerous man to guide the destinies of a nation. See C. F. Adams (ed.), *The Works of John Adams* (Boston, 1854), IX, 624.
31. *De l'influence de la Révolution d'Amérique sur l'Europe*, VIII, 1-113.
32. *Ibid.*, VIII, 37.
33. *Religion Catholique*, X, 99.
34. *De l'influence de la Révolution d'Amérique sur l'Europe*, VIII, 27-28.
35. *Ibid.*, VIII, 26-27.
36. *Aux amis de la liberté*, X, 181.
37. *De l'influence de la Révolution d'Amérique sur l'Europe*, VIII, 15.
38. *Ibid.*, VIII, 43-49.
39. *Ibid.*, VIII, 40-42.
40. *Ibid.*, VIII, 37.
41. *Contre l'esclavage des Noirs*, IX, 471.
42. *De l'influence de la Révolution d'Amérique sur l'Europe*, VIII, 12.
43. *Réflexions sur l'esclavage des Nègres*, VII, 138-139.
44. *L'état des Protestants en France*, V, 456-457.
45. *De l'influence de la Révolution d'Amérique sur l'Europe*, VIII, 29.

CHAPTER THIRTEEN: THE IDEA OF PROGRESS

1. On the history of the idea of progress consult: J. B. Bury, *The Idea of Progress*, Introduction by C. A. Beard (New York, 1932); J. Delvaille, *Essai sur l'histoire de l'idée de progrès jusqu'à la fin du XVIIIe siècle* (Paris, 1910); W. D. Wallis, *Culture and Progress* (New York, 1930); W. R. Inge, *The Idea of Progress* (Oxford, 1920); J. O. Hertzler, *Social Progress* (New York, 1928); H. Gillot, *La querelle des anciens et des modernes en France* (Paris, 1914); F. J. Teggart, *Theory of History* (New Haven, 1925); and F. Brunetière, *Etudes sur le XVIIIe siècle* (Paris, 1911) and *Etudes critiques*, 5e série (Paris, 1893).
2. Bury, *op. cit.*, 9.
3. *Ibid.*, 7-20.
4. *Ibid.*, 73-74.
5. Brunetière, *Etudes critiques*, 183-251.
6. Teggart, *op. cit.*, 89 ff.

7. C. Becker, *The Heavenly City of the Eighteenth-Century Philosophers* (New Haven, 1932), ch. III.
8. Brunetière, *Etudes critiques*, 183.
9. Bury, *op. cit.*, 98-126.
10. Brunetière, *Etudes critiques*, 183.
11. Bury, *op. cit.*, 135.
12. Turgot, "Tableau philosophique de progrès," *Œuvres* (Paris, 1913), I, 215.
13. R. Flint, *Historical Philosophy in France* (New York, 1894), 281-282.
14. J. B. Bury, *Selected Essays* (Cambridge, 1930), 27.
15. *Esquisse d'un Tableau Historique*, VI, 289-596.
16. Bury, *The Idea of Progress*, 215.
17. *Esquisse*, VI, 234.
18. *Ibid.*, VI, 233.
19. *Ibid.*, VI, 12.
20. *Ibid.*, VI, 13.
21. *Ibid.*, VI, 23.
22. *Assemblées provinciales*, VIII, 256.
23. *Vie de Voltaire*, IV, 95.
24. *Esquisse*, VI, 22.
25. *Ibid.*, VI, 236.
26. *Ibid.*, VI, 236.
27. *Ibid.*, VI, 298.
28. *Ibid.*, VI, 346.
29. *Notes sur Voltaire*, IV, 403-404.
30. *Esquisse*, VI, 30.
31. *Ibid.*, VI, 38.
32. *Ibid.*, VI, 35.
33. *Ibid.*, VI, 47. The opening up of Japan in the middle of the nineteenth century disclosed the existence of a feudal system in that country that was strikingly like that of medieval Europe. A recent historian of Russia maintains that the feudal system existed in Russia during the late Middle Ages, a view opposed to that of most historians of Russia. See M. M. Pokrovsky, *History of Russia*, translated and edited by J. D. Clarkson and M. R. M. Griffiths (New York, 1931), ch. II.
34. *Esquisse*, VI, 59.
35. *Ibid.*, VI, 66.
36. *Ibid.*, VI, 107.
37. *Ibid.*, VI, 107.
38. *Ibid.*, VI, 101-103.
39. *Ibid.*, VI, 109.
40. *Supra* chapter IX.
41. *Esquisse*, VI, 136.

CHAPTER THIRTEEN

42. *Ibid.*, VI, 134-135.
43. *Ibid.*, VI, 142.
44. Preserved Smith, *A History of Modern Culture* (New York, 1930), I, 7.
45. *Esquisse*, VI, 158.
46. *Ibid.*, VI, 153.
47. *Ibid.*, VI, 183.
48. *Eloge de l'Hôpital*, III, 565.
49. *Discours dans l'Académie française*, I, 390.
50. *Esquisse*, VI, 223-224.
51. *Ibid.*, VI, 178.
52. *Ibid.*, VI, 197.
53. This interpretation of the aims of the American Revolution was for a long time generally accepted. It is now challenged by historians, who assert that the American Revolution made great social and economic, as well as political, changes. See C. A. Beard and M. R. Beard, *The Rise of American Civilization*, I, chs. V-VII and J. F. Jameson, *The American Revolution Considered as a Social Movement* (Princeton, 1926).
54. Jaurès, *Histoire socialiste de la Révolution française* (Paris, 1924), VIII, 374.
55. *Esquisse*, VI, 201.
56. V. Branford, "The Founders of Sociology," *American Journal of Sociology*, X, 117.
57. *Esquisse*, VI, 237-241.
58. *Ibid.*, VI, 240, 244.
59. *Ibid.*, VI, 265.
60. *Ibid.*, VI, 244; cf. *Sur l'instruction publique*, VII, 170.
61. *Supra* chapter VII.
62. *Esquisse*, VI, 264; see also *supra* chapter X.
63. *Sur l'instruction publique*, VII, 169-170; see also *supra* chapter XI.
64. *Esquisse*, VI, 254.
65. *Ibid.*, VI, 628.
66. E. Halévy, *The Growth of Philosophic Radicalism*, trans. by M. Morris (London, 1928), 237.
67. *Esquisse*, VI, 255.
68. *Ibid.*, VI, 257-258. Malthus did not or professed not to understand Condorcet's solution of the problem of overpopulation by means of birth control. He asserted that Condorcet advocated either "promiscuous concubinage, which would prevent breeding, or of something else as unnatural. To remove the difficulty in this way will surely, in the opinion of most men, be to destroy that virtue and purity of manners, which the advocates of equality and of the perfectibility

of man profess to be the aim and object of their views." T. R. Malthus, *An Essay on the Principle of Population* (London, 1872), 266.
69. *Esquisse*, VI, 273. Condorcet's idea of prolonging human life appeared absurd to Malthus. "It may be fairly doubted," he wrote, "whether there has been really the smallest perceptible advance in the natural duration of human life since first we had any authentic history of man." Malthus, *op. cit.*, 267.
70. *Esquisse*, VI, 11.
71. B. Croce, *History*, trans. by D. Ainslee (London, 1921), 245.
72. *Sur l'instruction publique*, VII, 183.
73. Becker, *op. cit.*, ch. III.
74. *Esquisse*, VI, 22-23.
75. Delvaille, *Essai sur l'histoire de l'idée de progrès*, 670.
76. Halévy, *op. cit.*, 274-276.
77. Saint-Simon, "Correspondance avec M. de Redern," *Œuvres* (Paris, 1868), XV, 113-118.
78. For a discussion of Saint-Simon's views of Condorcet see Bury, *The Idea of Progress*, 282 ff.
79. A. Comte, *Cours de philosophie positive* (Paris, 1835-1852), IV, 252-263; cf., *Système de politique positive*, Appendice générale (Paris, 1854), 109 ff. In a recently published letter Comte wrote that he considered Condorcet far superior to Montesquieu, *Journal of Modern History*, June, 1929.
80. Croce, *op. cit.*, 244.
81. Saint-Beuve, "Condorcet" in *Causeries du lundi*.
82. E. Caro, "Le Progrès social," in *Revue des deux Mondes*, CVII, 757.
83. R. Flint, *op. cit.*, 329.
84. See interesting essay by Charles A. Beard dealing with this point of view, "Written History as an Act of Faith," *American Historical Review*, January, 1934.
85. *Sur l'instruction publique*, VII, 417.
86. Bury, *The Idea of Progress*, 334-335.

INDEX

Adams, John, 227, 283, 303
Agriculture, improvements in, 157; origin of, 246
Alengry, F., 83, 128
Amendments, constitutional, 127, 133, 225
America, influence of, on Condorcet, 88; and peace, 146; and constitutional government, 114, 134; and religious liberty, 185; as a Utopia, 216-218; and religious equality, 227; and antimilitarism, 228; and freedom of speech, 229; and free trade, 229; and slavery, 229-230; the future in, 231-232; and progress, 236; discovery of, 250
Anticlericalism, 178, 186
Antimilitarism, 143-147, 228
Antislavery, 148
Atheism, 29, 180
Aulard, A., 21, 32, 90, 91, 184, 197

Badeau, abbé, 158
Ballot, Charles, 9
Banking, coöperative, 154, 157
Beccaria, 142
Becker, Carl, 302
Bentham, 142
Bill of Rights, English, 221
Birth control, 193, 258
Bossuet, 235, 246
Bourgeois, buy lands of aristocrats, 15; buy titles, 16; hostility of, to church, 20; influence of, 21-22; and the philosophes, 25, 38; hostility of, to Old Régime, 111
Brissot, 79, 90, 99, 218
Brunetière, F., 212, 237, 238
Bury, J. B., 55, 240

Cahen, Léon, 107
Capitalism, rise of, 4; and land, 156; and the Physiocrats, 177
Capital punishment, 84, 98, 143
Caribbean islands, 228-229
Catholic church, triumphs over the Protestants, 18; attacks on the, 50; hostility of the philosophes to, 51-52; Condorcet's denunciation of, 86; and Protestantism, 251
Censorship, 40-44, 140
Chalotais, Réné de la, 197
Champion, E., 31
Chastellux, marquis de, 30, 217
Châtelet, marquise de, 45
Christianity, origin of, 248; *see* Religion
Civil rights, 5, 61, 100, 134, 275
Classics, Condorcet's hostility to the, 207, 251
Coal, 9
Coeducation, 202
Colonies, 255-256
Comte, 262, 263-264, 269
Condillac, 176
Condorcet, and censorship, 41, 42, 59, 60; early life of, 66-67; his interest in mathematics, 68-69; turns to the social sciences, 70; and the Suards, 71-72; takes office under Turgot, 73; elected to the Academy, 74; his marriage to Sophie de Grouchy, 75; his activity in reform movements, 79; his political views before 1789, 79-82; his activities during the Constituent Assembly, 84-90; becomes a republican, 89-90; elected to Legislative Assembly, 90; his Report on Education, 91; his attitude toward

307

INDEX

Louis XVI, 92-93; toward the Jacobins, 94; elected to the Convention, 95; drafts plan of constitution, 99-101; proscribed by the Convention, 104; his last days, 105-107; criticism of his Revolutionary career, 107-109
Condorcet, marquise de, 75, 189, 287
Constitutional law, 128
Constitution, Girondin, 99-102, 129-135; necessity of a, 114; amendments to, 127, 129; American, 219, 222, 223, 224-225; Pennsylvanian, 226
Convention, constitutional, 114, 133, 222
Corvée, 170
Cosmopolitanism, 145
Cotton, 9
Crèvecoeur, 217
Criminal code, reform of, 142-143
Croce, 260, 265

D'Alembert, 29, 35, 51, 67, 68, 74, 126
Danton, 79, 93, 94, 99
D'Argenson, 35
Declaration of Independence, American, 221, 302
Declaration of Rights, Condorcet's model, 84; his draft of a, 100, 129; Virginian, 221; American, 221
Democracy, attitude of the philosophes to, 60-61
Descartes, 24, 48-49, 115, 134, 237, 238, 260
De Tocqueville, 14, 280
D'Holbach, 29, 50, 58, 60
Diderot, 28, 36, 41, 44, 60, 63, 181, 187, 198
Divorce, 183, 192
Domestic system, 12
Du Pont de Nemours, 158

Ecole unique, 213-214
Education, a natural right, 129; a necessity in a machine civilization, 168, 201; secular, 183, 202-203; under the Old Régime, 196-197; pioneers of popular, 197-198; Condorcet's Report on, 91, 198 ff.; democracy in, 199-201; of women, 201-202; moral, 203; civic, 204, 209; and progress, 205; Condorcet's system of, 206 ff.; adult, 209-210; and equality, 257

Encyclopaedia, French, 29, 37, 51, 187, 206
England, influence of, on France, 216
Enlightened despotism, 17, 28, 36, 61-62, 111
Equality, economic, 152-154, 256-257
Esquisse d'un Tableau historique, 240 ff.
Evolution, 53-54

Family, attitude toward the, 187
Federalist, 219
Feminism, Condorcet's advocacy of, 189; *see* Woman suffrage
Feudalism, collapse of, 13-17
Flint, Robert, 266
Fontenelle, 237
Foreign trade, of France, 10
Franklin, Benjamin, 68, 79, 218, 219, 220, 226, 232
Freedom, American contributions to, 231-232
Freedom, religious, 183
Freedom of speech, 139-142; and America, 229; and Protestantism, 252
Free trade, 160-162

Gallicanism, 18
Girondins, 90, 95, 96, 101, 103
Gordon riots, 229
Gournay, 159
Grimm, baron von, 28, 30, 76
Guilds, 11; opposed by free enterprise, 11-12; by king, 12; disintegration of, 12-13

Halévy, Elie, 262
Helvétius, 29, 41, 68
Hérault-Séchelles, 102
Herriot, Edouard, 198, 213
History, teaching of, 210; and progress, 236-237, 241-243; and Condorcet, 261; contribution of *Esquisse* to the study of, 267-268
Holker, John, 9

Illegitimacy, 192-193
Illiteracy, in France, 26-27, 33, 196-197
Imperialism, abolition of, 256
Individualism, 113, 273
Industrial Revolution, in France, 9, 165
Inflation, Condorcet's attitude to, 86-87, 88

INDEX 309

Initiative, 132
Intelligentsia, origin of, 33

Jacobins, 96, 101, 102
Jansenism, 19, 126
Jaurès, Jean, 177, 254
Jefferson, Thomas, 219, 220, 232
Jesuits, 19
Judiciary, Condorcet's opposition to the, 124-125, 133

Kant, 144

Labor, rise of free, 11
La Girondine, see Constitution, Girondin
La Harpe, 72
Laissez faire, 4, 59, 159-161, 274
Land, property rights in, 14, 246
Laws, economic, 162
Lespinasse, Julie de, 68, 76-77
Liberalism, ideals of, 3; in France, 5; and natural rights, 46-47; and secularism, 52-53; and rationalism, 49-51; and the Natural Order, 53-55; and progress, 55-57, 277; and education, 57-59; and legislation, 58-59; and individualism, 59; and Condorcet, 138; and America, 221; and the Industrial Revolution, 273-274; criticism of, 273-275; contribution of, 275-276
Local government, 81, 131
Locke, John, 24, 57, 196, 252, 259
Louis XV, 18, 44
Louis XVI, 18, 61, 89, 92, 93, 97-99
Loutchisky, 280

Mably, abbé, 30, 60
Machinery, in France, 9; effects of, 167-168
Malesherbes, 43, 90
Malthus, 258, 262, 294, 305, 306
Man, origin of, 244
Marat, 94, 97, 100
Marriage, civil, 183
Marx, Karl, 177
Masonic order, 79, 218
Mathiez, A., 102
Mazzei, 218
Mercantilism, 73, 156, 160, 161, 163, 230
Mercier de la Rivière, 158
Mill, John Stuart, 262
Mirabeau, 158
Mohammedanism, 181, 249

Monasticism, Condorcet's views of, 185-186
Monroe Doctrine, 229
Montesquieu, 24, 29, 35, 36, 37, 41, 56, 61, 122, 123, 142, 261
Morals, natural basis of, 180; origin of, 244
Morellet, abbé, 30, 41, 76
Morelly, 30
Morley, John, 62, 63
Mornet, D., 35

Nationalism, 3, 130, 144, 205
Natural law, 53-55
Natural Order, 159, 198
Natural Rights, 46-47, 111-113, 173-174, 253
Necker, 73, 161
Negro slavery, *see* Slavery
Net Product, 164-165, 166
Newton, 53, 55, 252, 259

Old age pensions, 154, 257

Pacifism, 92, 144-147
Paine, Thomas, 76, 89, 95, 98, 99, 218, 219, 220, 232
Parlements, French, 16, 125-126
Parliament, English, Condorcet's views of the, 119, 122-123
Peasant proprietorship, 14-15
Pennsylvania, influence of, in France, 218, 226, 303
Perrault, Charles, 237
Philosophes, and the Intellectual Revolution, 24, 34-36; influence of the, 25; and the French Revolution, 31-32; as an intelligentsia, 32-33; and the bourgeois, 34, 38; methods of, 37-40; and religion, 20, 50-52; and democracy, 60; criticism of, 61-65
Physiocrats, 13, 36; and peace, 146; views of the, 150-177
Plebiscite, favored by Condorcet, 147
Pompadour, madame de, 45
Poverty, attitude of philosophes toward problem of, 151-152
Primitive life, 245
Printing, importance of, 250
Probability, theory of, 116-118
Progress, idea of, 55-57, 126; in ancient times, 234-235; in medieval times, 235; in early modern times, 236-237; contribution of Turgot to the, 239; contribution of Condorcet to the, 240, 265-266; history and

the, 241-242, 243; Darwinism and the, 269; Marxism and the, 270; liberalism and the, 277
Proportional Representation, 130
Property, under the Old Régime, 14; feudal, 171-173; bourgeois, 173; natural right of, 173-174; and the French Revolution, 174; Condorcet's attitude toward, 174-175
Protestantism, 18, 49, 51, 231, 252
Provincial assemblies, 81
Public interest, 54-55, 116-117
Public opinion, 28, 136-137
Puritanism, in France, 187; condemned by Condorcet, 194

Quakers, admiration of the, 218
Quesnay, 24, 118, 152, 158, 175

Rationalism, 49
Raynal, abbé, 30, 41, 217
Reason, worship of, 47 ff.; *versus* violence, 58
Referendum, 100, 132-133
Religion, freedom of, 4; attacks on, 35, 50, 178-179, 181-182; social utility of, 182-183; freedom of, in America, 227, 231; and primitive life, 245. *See also* Catholic church and Protestantism
Report on Education, Condorcet's, 198 ff.
Representative government, 80-81, 100, 114-120, 129-131
Republicanism, Condorcet's view of, 89, 95, 287
Revolution, American, Condorcet's interpretation of, 220; influence of, 220-221, 253-254; social interpretation of, 305
Revolution, French, and the philosophes, 31-32, 58; and property, 174; universality of, 254; repudiates tradition, 267; *see also* Chapter V
Revolution, intellectual, 23-24
Rights of Man, *see* Natural Rights
Robert, François, 101-102
Robespierre, 94, 97-98, 101
Robinson, James Harvey, 268
Roland, madame, 96
Rousseau, 33, 41, 43, 63, 144, 183, 187, 196, 212, 223, 244, 245, 246, 252, 253, 296

Roustan, M., 32
Royal manufacturers, 7-8, 11

Sainte-Beuve, 109, 179, 266, 271
Saint-Pierre, abbé, 30, 144, 197, 239
Saint-Simon, H., 262-263
Science, teaching of, 208
Scientific Revolution, 38, 39, 236, 251
Secularism, 52-53, 183
Separation of church and state, 184-185, 227
Separation of powers, 123, 132
Sex, attitude toward, 188, 193-194, 195
Shay's Rebellion, 229
Sieyès, abbé, 85, 99
Single tax, 168-169, 170-171
Slavery, opposition to, 79, 148, 149-150; Condorcet's plan of abolishing, 150; origin of, 245; revival of, 251; abolition of, 294
Smith, Adam, 76, 167, 175, 177, 244
Smith, Preserved, 251
Social laws, 54-56, 117, 119
Social legislation, advocated by Condorcet, 129, 154-155
Social sciences, origin of, 39; freedom of thought in, 141
Society of 1789, 85
Sociology, origin of, 264
Sorel, Albert, 32
Suard, 71-72
Staël, madame de, 45
Statistics, 117-119
Suffrage, 80, 85, 100, 115

Taine, 31
Talleyrand, 198
Taxation, under the Old Régime, 22, 168; Condorcet's views of, 170-171
Teachers, independence of, 211-212
Toleration, religious, 51; *see also* Freedom, religious
Turgot, 13, 22, 29, 61, 68, 70, 73, 138, 158, 164, 175, 176, 197, 239, 252, 271

Unigenitus, papal bull, 19
Universal laws, 119, 134; *see* Social laws
Utopias, 215

Value, theory of, 176
Van Robais, 8
Vernet, madame, 105, 106

Violence, revolutionary, opposition of philosophes to, 58; attitude of Condorcet to, 94, 137, 139
Virginia, 227
Voltaire, 24, 29, 35, 36, 37, 42, 44, 51, 60, 61, 63, 69, 70, 71, 74, 79, 137, 140, 157, 169, 178, 180, 182, 210, 215, 218, 222, 237, 242, 261

Wages, theory of, 150, 176
War, abolition of, 256; *see* Pacifism
Wilson, Woodrow, 224
Woman, abilities of, 191-192; education of, 192, 201-202; equality of, 257; *see* Chapter X
Woman suffrage, advocated by Condorcet, 80, 87, 100, 147, 189-191